Simplicity's®

Simply the Best
HOME DECORATING BOOK

Simplicity's

Simply the Best
HOME DECORATING BOOK

Illustrations by Martha Vaughan

Technical Art by Phoebe Gaughan

A FIRESIDE BOOK
Published by Simon & Schuster
New York London Toronto Sydney Tokyo Singapore

THE SIMPLICITY PATTERN COMPANY, INC.

FIRESIDE

Rockefeller Center
1230 Avenue of the Americas
New York, New York 10020

FIRESIDE and colophon are registered trademarks
of Simon & Schuster Inc.

DESIGNER: CHRISTINE SWIRNOFF

Library of Congress Cataloging-in-Publication Data

Simplicity's simply the best home decorating book /
    illustrations by Martha Vaughan;
    technical art by Phoebe Gaughan.
        p.   cm.
    Includes index.
    ISBN 0-671-76712-7
    1. House furnishings.   2. Interior decoration—
Amateurs' manuals.   3. Machine sewing.
I. Vaughan, Martha.   II. Simplicity Pattern Co.
III. Title: Simply the best home decorating book.
TT387.S55   1993
746.9—dc20   93-20374
                                    CIP

Manufactured in the United States of America

10   9   8   7   6   5   4

Acknowledgments

A successful book, like a beautiful room, begins with a vision. And when everyone involved has the expertise and the imagination to bring that vision to the printed page, the creative process is an exciting collaboration. This was the case as *Simplicity®'s Simply the Best Home Decorating Book* progressed from concept to finished book. Thus, we would like to gratefully acknowledge those individuals who contributed their extraordinary talents to this endeavor.

Judy Raymond, Simplicity's senior vice president, has enthusiastically supported this book every step of the way. Without her, there would simply be no book.

Janis Bullis, *Maureen Klein* and *Virginia Jansen*, contributing writers, brainstormed, researched, wrote and rewrote with steadfast enthusiasm. As a team, their knowledge in the field of home dec sewing is truly formidable.

Phoebe Gaughan spent many long days and late nights producing the clear, precise and accurate technical art. She is a rare find!

Martha Vaughan, who did the project illustrations throughout the book and the extraordinary color art in the center section, is an artistic wizard, whose talent and creativity continue to amaze.

Christine Swirnoff designed the book, skillfully blending the visual excitement of the subject matter with the sense of order and harmony that step-by-step sewing directions demand.

Donna Lang, an interior designer who is known for her special affinity for fabric, styled the entire color section and supervised every detail of the photography. We asked for beautiful rooms. What we got were breathtaking.

Judy Petersen is the sewing specialist whose skill with a needle is evident in the color photography.

Beth Greenfeld, copy editor, and *Didi Charney*, production editor, fine-tuned the text with good humor, good sense and good eyes.

Linda Berman organized the contents into a clear, easy-to-read index.

Harriet Ripinsky and *Linda Ripinsky*, of Ripinsky & Company, keepers of the deadlines, produced the book, encouraging and cajoling all who were involved, every step of the way.

While some parts of this book were developed from scratch, others drew on the patterns and projects produced by Simplicity's staff. Special recognition must be given to *Abbie Small* and her staff in *Simplicity's Craft and Home Dec Department*. In addition, Simplicity's *Alicia Von Rhein* helped in many ways that may seem small to her, but meant a great deal to the rest of us.

Finally, special credit goes to *Marlene Connor* of the Connor Literary Agency, who acted as agent for this book.

Anne Marie Soto
Editor, senior copywriter
and project coordinator

Contents

*A sixteen-page color section
follows page 120.*

Introduction

Introduction

It is no accident that we talk about *home* decorating, not *house* decorating. After all, a house is just a house. But when you give it the stamp of your personality, it becomes a home.

Few of us embark on our decorating journey with completely empty interiors. Hand-me-downs, family heirlooms, personal mementos, thoughtful purchases and items bought on a whim fill our rooms. Even if we could afford to throw it all out and start anew, how many among us would really want to do that?

Whether the restraining hand is economics or sentiment, using what we have is the reality that most of us must deal with in our desire to achieve beautiful, as well as functional, rooms.

A LOVE AFFAIR WITH FABRIC

Fabric and color go hand in hand. Color is the easiest and most economical way to change the personality of a room—and fabric is the most versatile and inspiring source of color we know. This book focuses on the many ways you can use fabric to realize your decorating goals.

Fabric can be used to decorate, to insulate, to disguise, to enhance. It is the essential decorative element for throw pillows, bedcoverings, table linens and most window treatments. On ceilings and walls, it's a wonderful substitute for paint and wallpaper. And as slipcovers and table skirts, it's the perfect camouflage for worn furniture or pieces that are incompatible with your revised decor.

A LOVE AFFAIR WITH SEWING

We at Simplicity have watched with delight as sewing for the home has steadily increased in popularity. The reasons are many:

● As modern technology brings the outside world inside, we are spending more time at home. Videotape players, camcorders, fax machines, home computers, wide-screen televisions and cable access have made staying home more attractive than ever before.

● The consumer's passion for fashion has spilled over into the home arena. (Does anyone remember when sheets came in only one color—white?) As our taste becomes increasingly sophisticated, we are learning to appreciate the beauty of a custom-coordinated decor.

● Appreciating the aesthetics of a custom-coordinated decor is one thing; being able to afford it is quite another. The price of paying someone else to create exactly what you desire is a high one. If you need proof, check out the cost of custom slipcovers or made-to-order window treatments in your area. It makes good dollar sense to sew them yourself.

• Minimal sewing skills are all that are required for most home dec projects. This means that both novice sewers and seasoned pros can enjoy the satisfaction of creating a single project or of decorating an entire room.

OUR PHILOSOPHY

This book is designed to be your best source for home decorating.

• The projects contained in this book were carefully selected for their versatility. Many are decorating classics that can be interpreted in countless ways, just by adding a trim or changing a fabric. Beautiful examples abound in the illustrations throughout the book, as well on the pages of the center color section. All in all, you'll find more than two hundred ideas to get your creative juices flowing.

• If all the ideas on these pages aren't enough inspiration for you,

we've designed the book to take care of that, too. You'll be able to duplicate, or closely approximate, many of the ideas you may find on the pages of your favorite decorating magazines. To accomplish this, simply turn to the appropriate chapter for the basic project directions. Then consult Chapter 4, THE SEWING BASICS, for information on the techniques that make the project special.

• Finally, although we've included projects that meet our criteria for being simply the best, we realize that a book of this size can't include everything. We hope that you will become such a devotee of sewing for the home that you will regularly check the pages of the *Simplicity*® *Pattern Catalog* for more ideas. Although Simplicity's pattern instructions are as complete as humanly possible, we can't anticipate every decorating situation. Use this book as your sewing reference to expand on, or offer an alternative to, the techniques in any pattern's instructions.

HOW TO USE THIS BOOK

Although it is every author's dream that the reader start at the beginning and read straight through to the end, we know that a book like this invites chapter hopping. So we've organized it in a sequence that's logical for the methodical reader, but flexible for the information-scanner.

If you're unsure about how to begin your decorating plan, start with Chapter 2, DECORATING THEORY. Here's where you'll find out how to blend all of the elements of a decorating scheme into a harmonious whole.

A great print and/or a smashing color is not the only criterion for selecting fabric. Other factors, such as durability, washability and stain repellency, may come into play. Chapter 3, CHOOSING FABRICS, offers guidelines for making the best possible fabric choices for your needs. Information is also included concerning many of the properties

and special finishes that are important to home dec fabrics. A special fabric glossary is included to help you identify your fabric choices.

If you're new to the world of sewing, Chapter 4, THE SEWING BASICS, will quickly become your sewing bible. However, even if you have some sewing experience under your belt, you'll find the chapter full of new information that will make your sewing easier. Here's where you'll learn the basics of cutting and sewing, as well as how to efficiently determine how much fabric you will need. The "Special Touches" section focuses on a broad range of embellishment techniques, including appliqués, bindings, edgings, machine embroidery, machine quilting, piping, pleats and ruffles. These embellishments are adaptable to almost any project in the book.

Chapter 5, WONDERFUL WALLS AND CEILINGS, introduces the idea of fabric as a substitute for paint and wallpaper—a real confidence-builder that requires minimal sewing skills. Three different techniques for applying fabric are presented. Whichever one you choose, the results will be stunning!

Every home has windows . . . and everyone ponders what to do with them. Chapter 6, WINDOWS: A DIFFERENT VIEW, covers the basic how-tos of curtains, drapes, tiebacks, valances, Roman shades, balloon shades, and swags and jabots. We've combined traditional home sewing methods with custom workroom techniques so you can create simply the best window treatments.

Whether fantasy or practicality dominates your dreams of the perfect bedcovering, Chapter 7, SLEEPING BEAUTY, will help make your slumber time wishes a reality. The bedspreads, comforters, duvet covers and dust ruffles can be custom-fit to any size bed, including cribs, daybeds and studio couches.

Pillows are great first projects, thoughtful hostess gifts and wonderful accents for your decor. Throw pillows, bed pillows and floor pillows are yours to sew in abundance in Chapter 8, PILLOW PIZZAZZ.

In the decorating world, as everywhere else, things go in cycles. Happily, slipcovers are enjoying a revival as the darlings of even the most chic decorators. Chapter 9, SITTING PRETTY, presents you with step-by-step directions for both traditional slipcovers and supereasy wrap-and-tie covers.

Unless you sew, surprisingly large portions of your decorating budget can go for those "little" things that provide the finishing touches to a room. Put an end to this decorating dollar drainage with Chapter 10, DECORATIVE ACCESSORIES. Grace your tables, your walls, your light fixtures with beautiful, cost-effective accessories made from fabric.

Not everything you create for the home must be done at the sewing machine. Chapter 11, TIMESAVERS, shows you how to work decorating magic with scissors, an iron, a staple gun, even some glue.

The color section following page 120 is the culmination of all the sewing skills and decorating secrets contained in this book. Start with a warm welcome at the front door. Travel through the house, room by room, experiencing the wonderful effects you can achieve with fabric. Study the accompanying sketches.

These have been designed to help you visualize how fabric can change the look of a room, even though the architectural features and the furniture placement remain the same. For information regarding the individual projects in these room settings, consult the glossary at the back of the book.

Our GLOSSARY contains furniture templates drawn to $1/4''$ (6mm) scale. Use them to develop your own floor plan, as described in Chapter 2.

As a how-to manual, an encyclopedia of home dec sewing techniques and a constant source of inspiration, it is our hope that *Simplicity®'s Simply the Best Home Decorating Book* will help you transform your house into the home of your dreams.

Simplicity

HOUSE TOUR

HOME

CAT

Decorating Theory

Decorating Theory

What is it that makes one room "work," while another looks as if it was just thrown together? Why do some rooms make you feel welcomed and comfortable, while others make you wish you were someplace else?

Successful decorating is the artful blending of colors, patterns and textures to create a pleasing, harmonious effect. If you are one of those people who have an instinctive knack for decorating, consider yourself lucky. But if you aren't, there's no cause for concern. The world around you is full of ideas that can be translated into successful decorating schemes. All you need to know is where—and how—to look.

❀

GO IDEA SHOPPING

Before you purchase one piece of fabric or decide on even the simplest of window treatments, go idea shopping.

● Start with the shelter and home improvement magazines. Develop a clipping file of room settings that please you. As you clip and save, circle the parts of the photos that you find most appealing.

● Take a trip to one or more furniture stores that specialize in room settings. Try to keep an open mind.

Remember that your mission right now is to find out what is available and to gather ideas, not to buy.

● Take advantage of any show houses or house tours in your area. Remember that show houses are just that—for show. So while you might not want to duplicate exactly many of the rooms, you will certainly find a wealth of ideas. Pay particular attention to the way the rooms are arranged and accessorized. House tours, especially ones of homes that are actually lived in, will give you another perspective. Since picture taking is almost always prohibited, tuck a pencil and sketch pad into your pocket. Then, when you stop

for coffee or go back to your car, you can jot down the ideas, themes and color schemes that caught your eye.

As you "shop," you'll discover that there are some constants that usually appeal to you. You also may find that certain preferences, such as color, the amount of light or the overall style of the decor, are affected by the function of the room. For example, you may prefer kitchens that are bathed in light but bedrooms that are shaded and cozy, bathrooms with very contemporary fixtures but living rooms in a more traditional mode, vibrant color in the family room but restful neutrals in the bedroom.

Once you've done your research, you're ready to apply your discoveries to your personal surroundings.

❀

MAKE A PLAN

Your decorating plan can be as simple as new window treatments and throw pillows, or as extensive as a complete room (or home!) redo.

If you were to employ a professional interior designer, he or she would approach your project very methodically. Rooms would be measured, architectural features noted, each room's function and traffic pattern analyzed—all this before any discussion would take place regarding style, color or texture.

If you're planning a new room— or if a current room could use some rethinking—do as the pros do: Create a maquette.

Begin by carefully measuring the room. Using a metal tape measure (because it is more exact), measure the floor. Transfer these exact measurements to a sheet of $^1/_4''$ (6mm) graph paper. Each $^1/_4''$ (6mm) square will equal 1 foot (meter) of your room size.

Once you have laid out the floor plan, measure each wall. Include all the architectural features, such as doors, windows, even electrical outlets and switches. Transfer these measurements to graph paper. By drawing the corresponding walls, you will be able to get the best overall view of the room.

Next, analyze the room from several perspectives:

1. What do my family and I want to be able to do in this room? Today's rooms accommodate a multitude of functions, such as eating, sleeping, watching television, sewing, entertaining, reading and so on.

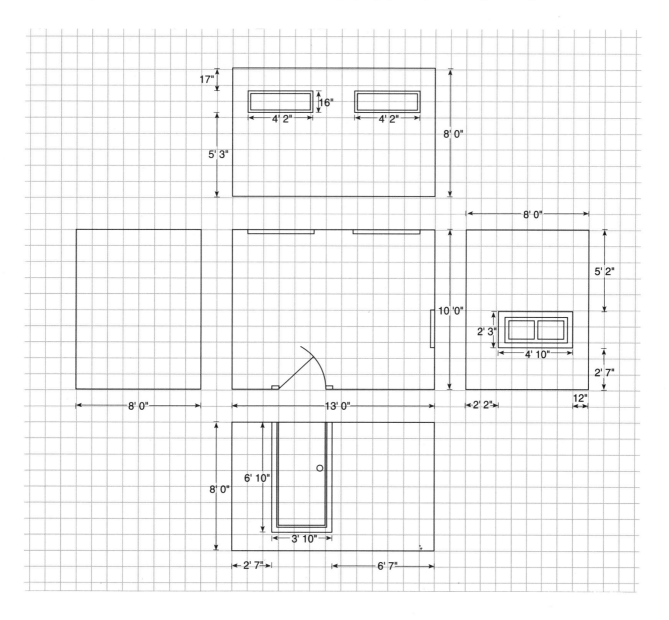

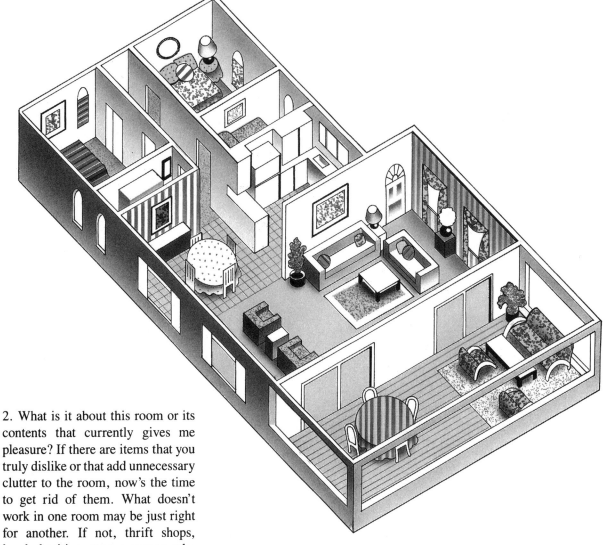

2. What is it about this room or its contents that currently gives me pleasure? If there are items that you truly dislike or that add unnecessary clutter to the room, now's the time to get rid of them. What doesn't work in one room may be just right for another. If not, thrift shops, local charities, even a garage sale, are wonderful ways to turn your discards into someone else's treasures.

3. Does the room have a focal point, such as a beautiful view or a fireplace? If not, it will be up to you to create one. It could be as simple as an eye-catching painting, a special furniture grouping or a collection of cherished objects.

Using the templates in the GLOSSARY at the back of this book, trace the shapes that represent the furniture you are keeping in the room.

TIP

If you don't know where to start, or if you're suffering from a crisis of confidence, a bit of professional advice may be in order. Consider engaging the services of a professional interior designer, one who is skilled in both space planning and decor. Choose one who, for a set fee or an hourly rate, will provide you with a plan of action that you can implement on your own. Ask friends for a recommendation or contact the local chapter of a professional design organization, such as the American Society of Interior Designers (ASID). Many of the latter operate a free referral service for consumers. To find a chapter near you, check the phone book or write to the national headquarters of the American Society of Interior Designers, 608 Massachusetts Avenue, NE, Washington, DC 20002.

Using your floor plan, experiment with different furniture arrangements. A bit of glue stuck on the back of each shape will make it easy to rearrange the "furniture."

Because you have drawn the corresponding walls, you also will be able to take into account the heights of furniture, walls, architectural details, etc. This will help you create balance and harmony in the room. A room will not balance if all the height or all the color is at one side.

Next, consider the adjacent rooms. In a well-decorated home, there is a sense of continuity from room to room. Try visualizing your living space from up above, mentally removing the roof. From this bird's-eye view, the total effect should be harmonious.

This doesn't mean that all the rooms have to repeat the same color scheme. Pulling a dominant color from one room to another, then adding a new accent color, is one way to achieve the desired effect. Another way is to use colors of the same intensity throughout the house. For example, jewel tones might predominate, or pastels or grayed "colonial" colors. If one furniture style predominates throughout the house (e.g., Queen Anne, Art Deco, Victorian), then the furniture can provide the necessary continuity.

CHOOSE A COLOR SCHEME

When it comes to selecting a color scheme, many decorating books recommend a thorough understanding of the principles of color theory and a familiarity with the color wheel. However, we think there are easier ways to come up with a satisfactory plan.

The information you gathered as you "idea-shopped" will help you get started on choosing a color scheme. In fact, it may furnish you with all the color direction you need. If not, there are other avenues of inspiration.

One that's close at hand is your wardrobe. What colors do you wear most frequently . . . and what outfits reap the most compliments when you wear them? Colors that make you happy when you wear them will also be a pleasure to live with.

Mother Nature is a constant source of ideas. From the brilliant macaw to the humble martin, she clothes her feathered creatures in endless color combinations. Whether your taste leans toward the subtle or the vivid, or somewhere in between, there's inspiration to be found here.

In addition, each of the four seasons has a distinct color palette, as evidenced by the flowers and foliage, the tones of the earth and sky. Pick a season, then work with its colors as nature presents them. Spring is full of light, airy tones; summer has rich, ripe, full-bodied colors; fall has warm, golden hues; and in winter, whites and browns predominate.

Art objects, from a favorite painting to a piece of porcelain to a hand-woven basket, can also start the decorating ball rolling.

Last, but not least, there's fabric. Falling in love with a beautiful print, a gorgeous stripe or a stunning plaid is perhaps the easiest way to achieve a successful color scheme. Once the fabric is discovered, a simple—but foolproof—

path is to use the print's background color on the walls and the print itself for major areas, such as window treatments, slipcovers or bedcoverings. The accent colors in the print become the accent colors in the room, enriching smaller items, such as pillows, cushions, lamps, occasional chairs, wall hangings and area rugs.

PUT IT ALL TOGETHER

Once you've zeroed in on a color scheme, how do you translate it into a gorgeous room?

Develop a Swatch Packet

Begin by taking a photo of every angle of the room. Be sure you get good shots of any of the elements that you will not be changing. This could include flooring, wall treatments and upholstered pieces. Staple these photos to one side of a manila folder. If swatches are available, attach them next to the appropriate photos. If none are available, choose paint chips that duplicate the colors. Your maquette, with floor plan and wall elevations, should also go in this folder.

This portable packet, containing vital information, can substitute for the room itself as you shop for fabric and trim. As you progress, making decisions about individual style elements, add the appropriate information regarding measurements and yardage requirements.

Even if you can't afford to redecorate your whole house at one time, creating a swatch packet for every room will help you organize a total color scheme and assess each room as a part of the overall picture.

Borrow Secrets from the Pros

Although there are always fabulous exceptions to any decorating rule, it helps to have a few designer-tested guidelines to follow.

According to Barbara Ostrom, ASID, a professional interior designer whose work has graced the pages of some of the leading decorating magazines, there are five elements that make a good room: a solid, a texture, a stripe, a plaid and a print. As you decide on wall coverings, window treatments, slipcovers, throw pillows and the like, keep these five elements in mind. Depending on your color scheme, they can provide drama and contrast, or the subtlety of tone on tone. Whether your decor features one color or a combination of colors, these elements are what make the difference between a room that's warm and interesting and one that's cold and boring.

The solid could be a plain fabric, a painted wall or an expanse of wall-to-wall carpet. The texture might be a stucco wall, velvet drapes, tweed cushions, canvas upholstery, a handwoven lap robe or a wall hanging. Fabric can provide the print, as can a visual element, such as a painting or a wall of books. The stripe and the plaid are there to impart linearity and a sense of order.

To avoid competition between the stripe, the plaid and the print, and to make the room more interesting, vary their scale. One large motif should be balanced by two small or one medium and one small motif.

An all-white room might look wonderful in a magazine, but it may be extremely difficult to live in. As a result, most people end up adding color. To make it warm, a white room must include many shades of white.

To add snap to any color scheme, introduce some black and some white.

Finally, it's risky to use a color just once in a room. Even a little repetition can provide a pleasing balance. Sometimes a bit of piping, bands of ribbon trim, a throw pillow or two, or even a flower arrangement will do the trick.

To explore more ways to add color to many of your decorating projects, see "Special Touches" in Chapter 4, THE SEWING BASICS.

TIP

Although brown, gray, black and white are the obvious neutrals, green is one of nature's neutrals. If your color scheme needs "something" to pull it together, consider a bit of green. If you aren't convinced, the next time you get a bouquet of flowers, take out the greenery and see how the arrangement loses its punch.

SOME THOUGHTS ON COLOR

- Green denotes friendliness. It also can be used as a neutral to make other colors click.

- Red is the color of passion and hunger, which accounts for its popularity in kitchens, dining rooms and bedrooms.

- Brown is a homey, earthy color. Think deep warmth, a return to the cave. For a fresh look, offset it with peaches, oranges and white.

- Light blue will open up a room. A crisp light blue looks great with white, yellow and red. Dark blue adds drama to a small, uninteresting room.

- Purple is a regal color.

- Lavender is particularly attractive with lots of white and green.

- Yellow is a morning color. Think sunshine!

CHAPTER **3**

Choosing
Fabrics

Choosing Fabrics

Fabric combines three of the elements necessary for a successful decorating scheme—color, texture and pattern. And it has almost limitless applications, from window treatments to wall coverings, from slipcovers to throw pillows. A room without fabric is like a cake without flour—while it's possible to get good results, the outcome is usually flat and uninteresting!

Successful fabric choices are the ones that reflect the personality of the room and the life-style of its occupants. Good looks alone may not be enough. Practical considerations, such as durability, washability and stain repellency, assume varying degrees of importance, depending on where you plan to use the fabric and how much traffic it will have to endure.

A basic understanding of how fabric is made will help you select a fabric that suits your needs.

FIBERS AND YARNS

Fabric is made from either natural or synthetic fibers that have been spun or twisted into yarns. These yarns may use only one type of fiber or a combination of fibers. The quality of the yarn will vary depending on the tightness of the twist, the length of the fiber and the number of strands used. Consequently, the quality of the fabric will depend on the quality of the yarn or the combination of yarns used in production. Natural fibers, such as cotton, linen, silk and wool, come from animals or plants. Synthetic fibers, such as acrylic, polyester and nylon, are manufactured (man-made).

WEAVING PATTERNS

Although knitted fabrics, or even some nonwoven fabrics such as synthetic suede, may be part of the decorating scene, woven fabrics predominate.

Woven fabrics consist of a series of interlaced *warp* and filling yarns. Warp refers to the series of yarns that extends lengthwise on a loom. During the weaving process, these yarns are crossed by the *woof*, also called *weft*, or *filling*, *yarns*. Different effects can be created by changing the weaving pattern and/or the number of sets of warp or filling yarns. Although the possibilities are almost endless, most of the fabrics you choose will fall into one of five basic weaving patterns.

PLAIN WEAVE

● A *plain weave,* formed by yarns that are interlaced in an alternating pattern, is the simplest version. Most of these fabrics are flat, with a smooth surface.

RIBBED WEAVE

● A *ribbed weave* is a variation of the plain weave. A heavier yarn is interlaced in one direction over another yarn of lesser weight.

BASKET WEAVE

● A *basket weave* is another variation of the plain weave. Two or more yarns are interlaced as if they were one.

TWILL WEAVE

● A *twill weave* gives the appearance of diagonal lines on the surface of the fabric. The filling yarns pass over one and under two or more of the warp yarns. This type of weave has many variations, based on the number of yarns used per weaving pattern.

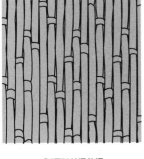

SATIN WEAVE

● A *satin weave* generally creates a smooth fabric with a lustrous surface. The weave requires at least five yarns, in a four-over, one-under pattern that produces floats on the surface of the fabric.

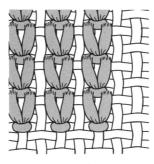

PILE WEAVE

● A *pile weave* produces a velvety surface that gives depth to the fabric. An extra set of filling yarns forms raised loops, which are later cut or sheared. Patterns can be created by shirring some loops and leaving others uncut.

JACQUARD WEAVE

● A *Jacquard weave* is a patterned design that is produced on a special "Jacquard-equipped" loom. Combinations of plain, twill and satin weaves are used to create the design on a plain- or satin-weave background.

PROPERTIES AND SPECIAL FINISHES

A fabric's quality, durability and performance features are determined by three factors—the basic fiber content, the number of yarns used in the manufacturing process and the finishing process. New synthetic fibers and blends, as well as new processing and finishing techniques, are constantly being introduced—and old, familiar ones improved. Fortunately, all fabrics are now labeled with fiber content, care instructions and special finishes. Before you make your final decision, carefully read these labels, as well as any information printed along the edge of the fabric itself. This is where you find the answers to such important questions as:

● How can the fabric be cleaned?

● Will it shrink?

● Is it crease-resistant?

● What types of stains will it resist?

● Is it flameproof?

Because fabric plays such an important role in your home, these questions should be answered to *your* satisfaction.

Fabrics destined for home decorating use are subject to greater environmental stresses than apparel fabrics are. Sunlight, heat, smog, gases and oils all take their toll. Special finishes can do more than add body and improve a fabric's appearance. They also can increase its durability and make the fabric more resistant to the destructive elements of nature.

PROPERTIES OF FIBERS COMMONLY USED IN HOME DECORATING FABRICS

FIBER	USES	ADVANTAGES	DISADVANTAGES	CARE
Acetate	Taffeta, satin, brocade, faille and silk-like fabrics.	Silk-like luster; drapes well; dries quickly; stable if blended; colorfast; soft and pliable; resists mildew and moths; relatively inexpensive.	Fades; relatively weak; subject to static cling, wrinkles and abrasion.	Dry-clean or gently machine-wash; tumble-dry; iron at low temperature.
Acrylic	Pile fabrics, fleece, wool-like fabrics and fake fur.	Soft, warm and lightweight; stable; durable; colorfast; resists mildew, moths, oily stains and wrinkles.	Sensitive to heat; pills and is subject to static cling.	Machine-wash; tumble-dry; needs no ironing.
Cotton	Batiste, broadcloth, calico, chintz, corduroy, denim, canvas, seersucker, velveteen and gauze, to name just a few.	Absorbent; cool; strong; resists static cling, moths and abrasion.	Wrinkles; subject to shrinkage; can be damaged by mildew and sunlight; soils easily.	Machine-wash; tumble-dry; iron while damp; can be bleached.
Linen	Chambray, lawn, damask and many fabrics with a nubby texture.	Absorbent; cool; strong; resists static cling, moths and stains.	Subject to wrinkles, shrinkage and mildew; yellows with age.	Dry-clean to retain crispness or wash to soften; iron while damp.
Nylon	Velvet, plissé, wet-look ciré and some sheers.	Strong; warm; lightweight; resists wrinkles, mildew, moths, oils and abrasion; supple; lustrous; accepts dyes.	Subject to static cling; pills; holds body heat; fades in sunlight.	Hand- or machine-wash; tumble-dry; iron at low temperature.
Olefin	Upholstery fabrics.	Strong; durable; resists soil, abrasions, mildew, moths and wrinkles.	Subject to moderate fading; low melting point; shrinks.	Machine-wash and -dry; iron with a cool iron, using a press cloth.

CHOOSING FABRICS

PROPERTIES OF FIBERS COMMONLY USED IN HOME DECORATING FABRICS

FIBER	USES	ADVANTAGES	DISADVANTAGES	CARE
Polyester	Alone or in blends for cotton-, silk- and wool-like fabrics, including batiste, taffeta, faille, percale.	Strong; warm; resists moths, mildew, pollution, abrasion and wrinkles; sunfast.	Subject to static cling; pills; stains; attracts lint.	Machine-wash; tumble-dry; little or no ironing.
Rayon	Rayon, faille, challis, linen-like fabrics.	Absorbent; soft; drapes well; resists moths.	Relatively fragile; subject to wrinkles, shrinkage, abrasion and mildew; will sun-rot.	Dry-clean or gently machine-wash; iron at moderate temperature; can be bleached.
Silk	Chiffon, organza, linen, broadcloth, taffeta, etc.	Warm; absorbent; lustrous; drapes beautifully; stable; durable; resists abrasion and moths.	Subject to damage from sunlight, perspiration and mildew; attracts static cling. NOTE: Lightly woven silk wrinkles easily; upholstery-weight silk is wrinkle-resistant.	Dry-clean. Silk also can be hand-washed but must be ironed while still damp, on the wrong side at low temperature.
Triacetate	Velour, velvet suede types, novelty wovens.	Drapes well; good pleat and crease retention; easy care; stable; sunfast; resists wrinkles and the effects of pollution.	Poor durability and elasticity.	Machine-wash and -dry; no ironing needed.
Wool	Flannel, tweed, bouclé, gabardine, challis.	Absorbent; warm; resists wrinkles; good insulation; stable; durable.	Subject to shrinkage, moths, sun rot, fading.	Dry-clean but can be machine-washed; use steam iron with press cloth on the right side.

* NOTE: Special finishes can be applied to counteract the disadvantages of a fiber or to improve its performance. Be sure to check the label.

Although no fabric will last forever, there are some factors that contribute to a fabric's longevity.

● Natural colors will retain their original appearance longer than those that have been dyed or treated. Fabrics made up of yarns or fibers that have been dyed prior to construction—motifs that are woven in, rather than printed on, for example—are a better choice for colorfastness (unless, of course, the printed-on fabric has been treated with a colorfast finish).

● The quality of the dye will also affect colorfastness. Smooth, dark-colored fabrics generally fade faster than textures do. Solids tend to lose their life faster than tweeds do. Patterned fabrics usually maintain their fresh appearance over an extended period of time.

Colors can vary from one dye lot to another; even the slightest variation may be noticeable on the finished project. If possible, purchase the yardage required for your total decorating project—plus an additional ¹⁄₂ yard (.5m) for testing—from the same bolt. If you must buy from different bolts, purchase enough from one bolt to complete each project. For example, if you are making curtains and a bedspread, have the fabric for the bedspread cut from one bolt and the fabric for the curtains cut from another bolt.

Here are a few of the terms and finishes you will encounter in your search for the perfect fabric:

Bonding is the process used to fuse two fabrics together to make a stronger cloth.

Carded means that the fibers are combed to remove dirt, impurities and some of the short fibers.

Ciré refers to an application of wax, heat and pressure that creates a shiny, patent-leather finish. It is particularly suited to outdoor furnishings.

Colorfast is a term used to describe a fabric that will retain its original hue without running or fading.

Combed means that the fibers are cleaned again, after carding, to remove even more impurities and short fibers, producing a finer fiber.

Crease-resistant (*permanent press*) means the fabric requires little or no ironing. Cottons treated with a permanent-press finish retain the look and feel of the natural fiber, without the wrinkling. However, when you sew a permanent-press cotton, it will handle like a synthetic. You won't be able to use your iron to steam out any puckers. Instead, you must carefully hold the fabric taut—one hand in front and one hand behind the presser foot—as you machine-stitch.

Drip-dry, or *wash-and-wear*, describes fabrics that require little or no ironing. Many of these fabrics can be hung immediately after washing. Adjust them to hang correctly and they will gently dry to their original shape. A few of these fabrics will require a light touch-up with the iron.

Laminated fabrics are composed of layers of firmly bonded material. Shades may be custom-laminated for you, or you may purchase special bonding material to laminate them yourself. (See "Roller Shade" in Chapter 11, TIMESAVERS.)

Mercerized means that a finish has been applied to the cotton yarns, or to the cotton or cotton-blend fabric, which adds luster and improves the fabric's affinity for dyes.

Mildew-resistant denotes a fabric treated to hinder mold growth.

Preshrunk (*shrink-resistant*) means the fabric has been treated to keep residual shrinkage to a minimum.

A *soil-release* finish is treated to absorb water better, thus making it easier to remove soil and stains during washing. This finish is a real plus if the fabric is intended for tablecloths, napkins or similar soil- and stain-attracting situations.

Soil-resistant finishes, such as *Scotchgard*®, *Zepel*® and *Teflon*®, temporarily hold the soil or spill on the surface of the fabric so that it can be cleaned. However, stains that are left untreated will be difficult to remove later on because, over time, they will penetrate through minute cracks in the finish to the fabric underneath. In addition, some of these finishes must be reapplied after the fabric is cleaned.

Waterproof fabric is treated so no moisture or air can penetrate it. This type of fabric is generally coated with rubber, resin or plastic.

Water-repellent/-resistant means that the fabric will resist the absorption of liquids. This is a particularly useful finish if the fabric will be exposed to high humidities or condensation.

FABRIC GLOSSARY

Listed in the following glossary are some of the fabrics that are particularly suitable for home decorating.

Use this glossary to help identify the fabrics that suit your needs. Then, when you go fabric shopping, it will be easier to describe the types of fabrics you are looking for. Once you are in the store, the salesperson will be able to direct you to the fabrics of your choice, as well as to others with similar qualities.

FABRIC	DESCRIPTION
Antique satin	A widely used term for drapery and upholstery fabrics with a satin weave. It is available in many textures, fibers and weights.
Austrian shade cloth	A cloth woven in wide stripes with a crinkled effect, frequently used for window shades.
Bark cloth	A plain, firmly woven cotton with an irregular texture, available in both solids and prints. It is designed to resemble true bark cloth, a fabric made from the inner bark of certain trees from the South Pacific.
Batiste	A fine, delicate, soft, sheer fabric woven of high-count combed cotton or polyester. It can be found in many soft colors, screen printed or embroidered.
Bedford cord	A long-wearing, durable, worsted fabric with vertical ribs, made of cotton, rayon or blends.
Bouclé	A plain- or twill-weave fabric with looped yarns that create a textured, nubby surface.
Broadcloth	A fine, tightly woven fabric in a plain or twill weave with a slight horizontal rib.
Brocade	A fabric characterized by raised designs on a flat surface, woven in cotton, silk, wool or synthetic-fiber combinations on a Jacquard loom. It can be medium- to heavyweight, in tones of one color, in florals or in traditional patterns.
Brocatelle	A heavy brocade with a more elaborate raised pattern on the right side.
Burlap	A better grade of plain-weave jute, bleached or dyed, generally with a coarse, interesting texture produced by a loose basket weave.
Calico	Any variety of plain-weave cotton fabric printed with small motifs.

CALICO

CHOOSING FABRICS

FABRIC	DESCRIPTION
Canvas	A firm, plain, medium- to heavyweight woven cotton, available in a variety of colors, stripes and prints.
Casement cloth	A general term for fabrics in a variety of weaves and textures, usually semisheer, translucent or opaque, commonly used for casual draperies.
Challis	A lightweight, soft, firmly woven fabric, usually wool, cotton or a synthetic, especially rayon. It can be a solid color, or traditionally printed as a vivid floral on a dark ground or with a paisley pattern.
Chambray	A light- to medium-weight, plainly woven cotton or linen with a colored warp and white filling yarns. This gives the fabric a frosted look.
Chintz	A lustrous, plain, closely woven cotton fabric available in a variety of colors and prints. A glazed finish (usually permanent) provides the surface shine and the crisp hand. Chintz can be smooth, embossed or quilted.
Corduroy	A cotton or synthetic fabric with lengthwise wales of cut pile, which create pronounced vertical lines, or wales. It is durable, casual and available in a wide variety of colors and prints.
Cotton satin	A warp-face weave, highly mercerized to give luster. It is superior to sateen and is available in solids and prints.
Crash	A coarsely woven cloth of cotton, linen or blends, usually made from uneven or irregular yarns, often hand-blocked or printed, and used for curtains.
Damask	A cloth of various fibers characterized by a flat and reversible woven Jacquard design combining plain and satin weaves, generally in one color. In its lightweight versions, it is particularly popular for table linens.
Denim	A heavy, durable cotton twill weave with a colored warp and white filling. Also available in plaids and stripes.
Dimity	A delicate, sheer fabric, generally woven of combed or carded cotton in a fine stripe or checkered pattern.

DAMASK

FABRIC	DESCRIPTION
Dotted swiss	A sheer, crisp cotton with dots that are machine-embroidered or woven into the ground, or chemically applied to the surface.
Drill	A strong, durable, closely woven cotton twill similar to denim.
Duck	A durable, closely woven, plain or ribbed cotton fabric. It is similar to canvas but lighter in weight.
Faille	A somewhat shiny, closely woven fabric of silk, cotton or synthetics, characterized by flat, crosswise ribs. It can have a stiff or a soft finish.
Filet lace	Originally a net, knotted by hand. Today, machinery has made it possible to imitate the plain net background with geometric designs darned into it. The lace is generally soft and filmy, but can also be coarsely woven.
Gabardine	A twill-weave, worsted fabric made from wool, cotton, rayon or nylon yarns, alone or blended, with obvious diagonal ribs.

FAILLE

GINGHAM

Gauze	A thin, sheer fabric with a loose, extremely open weave. Think gauze bandages and you've got the picture!
Gingham	A yarn-dyed, plain-weave cotton or synthetic fabric. Checked gingham is the most common version, but it can also be plaid, striped or plain.
Homespun	A loosely woven, irregular, coarsely textured fabric, originally made from yarn spun by early American homemakers. Today, it is machine-woven of mixed yarns and has a sturdy, informal character that resembles hand weaving.
India print	A hand-blocked cotton print with native designs, usually Indian or Persian.

CHOOSING FABRICS

FABRIC	DESCRIPTION
Jaspé	A plain-weave fabric with a series of warp, or lengthwise, irregular stripes, created by varying shades of yarn in the same color family.
Lace	An openwork geometric or floral design with or without a net background.

LACE

Lawn	A fine, sheer fabric, originally made from linen. Today, it is commonly made from cotton or cotton and synthetic blends. It is similar to, but somewhat stiffer than, batiste.
Marquisette	A sheer, meshed, open-weave fabric, commonly used for curtains and drapes, which can be woven so it is fine and soft or coarse and crisp.
Matelassé	A heavy upholstery-weight fabric that is woven with two sets of warp and woof yarns on a Jacquard loom. The result is a quilted, or puckered, texture. It is sometimes called "double cloth."
Moiré	A plain, ribbed weave of silk, cotton or rayon with a watermark pattern produced with engraved rollers, heat and pressure.
Monk's cloth	A heavy, coarse, loosely woven basket-weave cotton, or cotton blended with jute, hemp or flax. Commonly used for drapes and upholstery, it can be a natural color or have dyed or woven stripes.

MOIRÉ

CHOOSING FABRICS

FABRIC	DESCRIPTION
Muslin	A soft, plainly woven cotton similar to, but coarser than, percale. It is available in light- or heavyweight weaves, bleached or unbleached, and as a base for printed and dyed fabrics.
Net	Machine-made mesh fabric. The yarns are knotted, twisted or woven together at regular intervals.
Ninon	A plain, smooth, sheer drapery or curtain fabric usually made of acetate or polyester.
Organdy	A finely woven, transparent fabric made from combed cotton or nylon with a crisp finish. Available in pale colors, it can be plain, printed or embroidered.
Osnaburg	A plainly woven cotton fabric with small flecks of cotton stalks remaining within the weave. Its appearance is similar to a coarse muslin.
Percale	A medium-weight, plainly woven cotton or cotton and polyester blend with a finer texture than muslin.
Pima cotton	A cotton fabric with exceptional strength and firmness. Its long, staple fibers were developed in southwestern United States by the selection and breeding of Egyptian and Peruvian cottons.
Piqué	A fabric with raised, lengthwise cords that create a three-dimensional, geometric effect, usually in cotton or a cotton blend.
Plissé	Usually made from cotton, rayon or nylon, this fabric is chemically treated to produce an allover puckered surface with a blistered effect.
Point d'esprit	A lace woven with small oval dots or squares on a mesh net ground.

NINON

POINT D'ESPRIT

CHOOSING FABRICS

FABRIC	DESCRIPTION
Pongee	A modern imitation of a fabric that was originally woven by hand from wild silk, using irregular yarns. Today, it is made from man-made fibers, generally in the color ecru.
Poplin	A coarse broadcloth with a pronounced horizontal rib.
Sailcloth	A fabric similar to canvas and duck, it is a heavy, plainly woven cotton available in colors, stripes or prints.
Sateen	A satin-weave fabric in mercerized cotton. It has a lustrous surface and a dull back.
Satin	A fabric made in an irregular twill weave with a long float that produces a highly lustrous surface. It is available in a variety of weights and fibers, generally with a cotton back.
Seersucker	A plainly woven fabric that can be recognized easily by its alternating plain and puckered stripes.
Shantung	A plain weave with irregular "nubs and slubs" made of silk, cotton or other fibers. It is similar to pongee in texture and appearance.
Sheeting	A plain-weave fabric, usually in cotton or cotton and polyester blends. The quality of the fabric is indicated by its thread count (the number of threads per inch, or per 2.5 centimeters). Percale, a finely woven sheeting, has a 180 thread count, while the coarser muslin sheeting has a thread count of between 128 and 140.
Strié	Another name for jaspé.

SATEEN

STRIÉ

Suede cloth	A fabric woven from cotton, rayon, wool or nylon and finished to give it a napped surface that resembles suede.

FABRIC	DESCRIPTION
Taffeta	A crisp, tightly woven fabric with a fine, crosswise rib. Originally made from silk, today's taffeta is also made from cotton, acetate, rayon or polyester. You may also recognize it by its rustling sound!
Tapestry	Originally a hand-woven, reversible textile characterized by pictorial scenes. Today's machine-made reproductions, fashioned on Jacquard looms, are heavyweight fabrics best suited for upholstery, cushions and throw pillows.

TAPESTRY   TICKING

Ticking	A closely woven satin or twill weave commonly in linen or cotton. Striped ticking—narrow colored stripes on a white or cream background—is the most popular motif.
Toile de Jouy	Scenes of rural French country life and people from the eighteenth and nineteenth centuries, printed in one color (usually navy, cranberry or black) on a white background.
Tweed	Originally made in Scotland from hand-spun woolen yarns and woven on hand looms. Today, it is a plain-weave, irregularly textured fabric of many colored yarns, dyed before weaving. It also can be fashioned from a twill or herringbone weave or have a distinct checked pattern, such as houndstooth. In home decorating, this heavyweight fabric is best suited for upholstery and cushions.
Velvet	A broad term that applies to a warp-pile fabric with a soft, sturdy face created from dense loops that may or may not be cut. It is a luxurious fabric, originally made from silk, but now made from a wide variety of fibers. Velvet can be woven singly or as two fabrics, woven face-to-face and then cut apart.

FABRIC	DESCRIPTION
Velveteen	A plain-weave cotton or cotton-blend fabric that resembles velvet. It has a closely sheared weft pile and is always woven singly.
Voile	A plain-weave, semisheer fabric made from tightly twisted yarns. It is available in a variety of textures and colors, sometimes with novelty effects.

VELVETEEN

FABRICS: A DECORATING PROFILE

FOR FORMAL SETTINGS	FOR INFORMAL SETTINGS	FOR CASUAL SETTINGS	
Antique satin	Bouclé	Bark cloth	Gingham
Brocade	Chintz	Bedford cord	Homespun
Chambray	Cotton sateen	Broadcloth	Monk's cloth
Damask	India print	Burlap	Muslin
Faille	Linen	Calico	Osnaburg
Lace	Pongee	Canvas	Oxford cloth
Matelassé	Seersucker	Casement cloth	Pima cotton
Moiré	Sheeting	Corduroy	Poplin
Shantung	Toile de Jouy	Crash	Sailcloth
Silk		Denim	Suede cloth
Strié		Drill	Ticking
Velvet		Duck	Tweed
Velveteen		Gabardine	

For a listing of fabrics commonly used for sheer curtains and drapes,
see Chapter 6, WINDOWS: A DIFFERENT VIEW.

❀   ❀   ❀

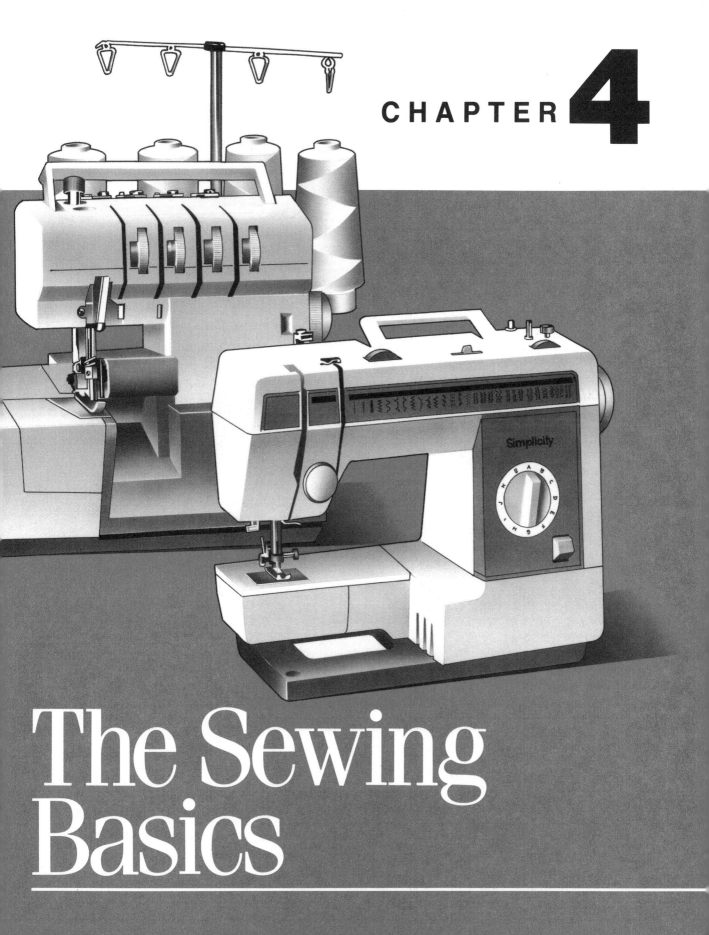

CHAPTER 4

The Sewing Basics

The Sewing Basics

The techniques you need to know to create home decorating items worthy of the finest custom workrooms are blissfully easy to master. While curtains, tablecloths and dust ruffles may look very different, the "how-tos" for putting them together are remarkably similar.

SEW IT

One of the nicest things about sewing for the home is that just about any sewing machine will do. If you're a novice sewer, or one who's brushing up on your skills, don't make the mistake of equating the fanciest machine with the best results. While state-of-the-art, computerized machines are certainly more exciting to use, even a garage-sale-variety, straight-stitch machine—provided it's in good working order—can be the workhorse of your personal workroom.

SERGE IT

If you own, or have access to, an overlock machine, home dec sewing is the perfect place to use it to full advantage. This machine, also called a serger, simultaneously stitches, trims and overcasts a seam. That's three operations in one—and at twice the speed of the fastest conventional home sewing machine. Talk about saving time!

Another advantage of the overlock is its ability to create a narrow, rolled hem. This edge finish, which consists of small, tight stitches and no visible hem allowance, is the same one you find on commercially made napkins and tablecloths. It is also used for details such as self-ruffles where a fine, narrow finish is particularly desirable.

While some items can be created solely on the overlock, others are the result of the marriage of overlock and conventional techniques. The techniques in this chapter include both the overlock and the conventional methods.

FUSE IT

With today's exciting technology, you can hem a tablecloth, make curtains or even cover a lampshade without sewing a stitch. Products such as iron-on drapery tapes and fusible web replace techniques at the

TIP

To keep your conventional sewing machine and your overlock running smooth and trouble-free, follow these simple rules:

- **Read the manuals.**
- **Change the needle(s) with every new project.**
- **Keep the machines clean.**
- **Keep the machines well oiled, in accordance with each manufacturer's instructions.**

sewing machine with techniques at the ironing board. While we don't pretend you can make *everything* without a sewing machine, these products are fun to use and can be great confidence boosters. Some basic techniques, such as fusing hems and appliqués, are included in this chapter. For additional timesaving ideas, incorporating both gluing and fusing techniques, see Chapter 11, TIMESAVERS.

EQUIPMENT ESSENTIALS

Don't worry about an elaborate inventory of equipment. Home dec sewing is essentially quite simple, and your basic equipment should reflect that.

Measuring Tools

Since home dec sewing is almost more about measuring than about sewing, these tools are the foundation for the items you create.

● *Tape measure.* A flexible 60″ (153cm) synthetic or fiberglass tape measure is a handy, all-purpose measuring tool.

● *Retractable metal tape measure.* This type of tape measure is flexible enough for curves, but rigid enough and long enough (8′–12′, or 2.5m–3.7m) for measuring larger areas, such as windows.

● L-*square* or *carpenter's square* (or a T-*square plus right-angle triangle*). Choose any one, in metal or plastic. You'll need it for drawing right angles, such as those found at the corners of pillows, window

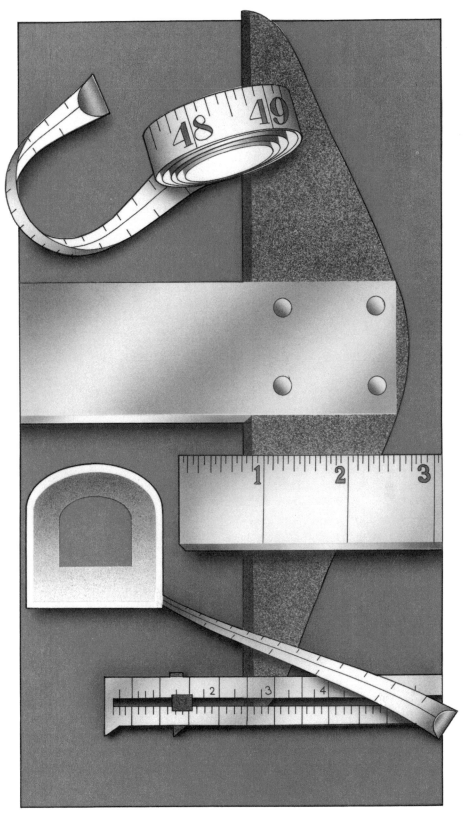

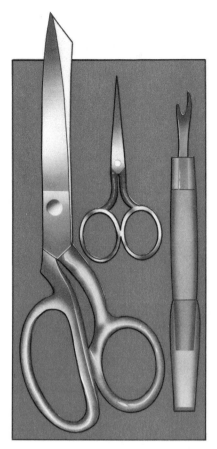

CUTTING TOOLS (L. TO R.):
SHEARS, SCISSORS, SEAM RIPPER

shades, tablecloths and napkins, and to help establish the crosswise grain and the bias grain on your fabric.

● *Yardstick.* This 36″ (1m) wooden ruler is particularly handy for measuring and marking your fabric.

● *Seam gauge.* This small metal ruler with sliding marker is great for marking or for checking smaller measurements during construction. As a substitute, use a short (6″, or 15cm) plastic ruler.

Marking Tools

Anything that will make a pale but visible mark on the fabric, but will not be noticeable on the finished project, will do. This includes *tailor's chalk*, a *sliver of soap*, a *fabric marking pen* or a *soft lead pencil*. Test your choice on both the right and wrong sides of the fabric to determine if it is suitable.

Cutting Tools

● *Shears.* Sturdy, bent-handle dressmaker's shears are capable of cutting through both light- and heavyweight fabrics. Because the handles are bent up, the fabric will lie flat as you cut—easier to be accurate and easier on the hands!

● *Scissors.* A small pair of sewing scissors or embroidery scissors for detail work.

● *Seam ripper.* "As you sew, so shall you rip." *Everybody* makes mistakes, and this little tool, used carefully, makes it easy to remove stitches without harming the fabric.

Stitching Tools

Pins. Because you're handling large quantities of often heavy fabric, dressmaker's pins tend to get lost in the folds and fullness of the fabric. Instead, choose pins with glass or plastic heads that will be easy to see and easy to remove. Plus, glass heads won't melt if they come into contact with a hot iron.

Thread. Pick the thread that matches the job.

● *All-purpose thread* in 100 percent polyester or cotton-covered polyester will be suitable for most of your needs. Finer versions of these threads, available on 1,000–6,000 yard (meter) cones, have been developed especially for use on the overlock. At least one manufacturer is also offering a strong, slightly heavier-weight thread on cones, which is specially designed for home dec sewing on the overlock.

● *Upholstery thread*, in 100 percent nylon or polyester, is an extra-strong thread for sewing on heavyweight fabrics. Because it is treated to resist chemicals, rot and mildew, it's an excellent choice for outdoor items.

● *Woolly nylon thread* is a texturized overlock thread that is both soft and strong. In home dec sewing, it is used primarily for serger rolled hems. Prize attributes are its ability to stretch and recover, its beautiful sheen and the resulting smooth, filled-in appearance.

● *Button, carpet and craft thread* is a strong, heavy, cotton-covered polyester thread designed specifically for hand sewing. Use it for tasks such as attaching buttons to cushions, pillows and upholstered furniture or for assembling a braided rug by hand.

Needles. Check your sewing machine manual to see what brands/

Sometimes, a project is easier with special pins:

● Quilting pins are extra long, making them a great choice for bulky or heavy fabrics.

● T-pins are also useful when working with very heavy fabrics and for anchoring fabric to a padded surface.

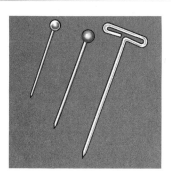

types are recommended, then keep an assortment of sizes on hand. Use the recommendations on the needle package as a guide to matching needle size to fabric. If you've made the wrong choice, you'll find out quickly. If the needle breaks (and you didn't sew over a pin), it's too small. If the seam draws up, or if your machine skips stitches, the needle is too large. Always, *always* change to a new needle at the start of a new project. While you may not be able to spot a worn or bent needle, your machine will know it fast enough. All too often, we blame the thread or the sewing machine for our difficulties, when the real culprit is the needle. Problems such as skipped stitches, puckered seams, poor tension and thread breakage may all be the result of a damaged needle.

Pressing Tools

Iron. Pressing is an integral part of sewing. A standard household steam iron, in good working order, will serve your needs.

Press cloths. Used between your iron and your decorating fabric,

these help prevent scorch and shine. Commercial versions, some with special finishes, available in the notions area of the fabric store, are a pleasant luxury. However, a piece of muslin or batiste, an old diaper or a man's handkerchief will work just fine.

Extras

Here is a list of tools and notions that are so nice to have that you'll quickly regard them as home decorating essentials.

Seam sealant. This colorless liquid comes in a squeeze bottle for handy application. Use it in small, detail areas that might fray, such as the cut ends of ribbon, or to add extra security to thread knots and cording knots.

Cutting board. This heavy-duty cardboard surface usually opens up to 36″ × 68″ (91.5cm × 173cm) and accordion-folds for easy storage. It's marked with a 1″ (2.5cm) grid, as well as special markings to aid you in cutting circles, scallops and bias strips. A variation on the cutting board, called the Spaceboard™, is a

single-fold board that opens to a 33″ × 51″ (84cm × 130cm) work surface. Constructed of heat-resistant materials in double-layer table pad quality, this board provides a large surface for pressing, as well as for measuring, cutting and pinning.

Magnetic pin cushion. Say good-bye to pins and needles all over the floor. A useful magnet, embedded in a small, thick plastic dish, provides a nice home for your pins and makes it easy to "sweep" up spills.

Fabric marking pens. These pens contain a disappearing ink that makes it possible to mark on either the right or the wrong side of the fabric. One type contains a blue water-soluble ink that disappears when the marks are treated with water. The other type contains an air-soluble purple ink that evaporates in less than forty-eight hours. To be super safe, use the purple ink only when you plan to sew immediately after marking. And, no matter which type you choose, test first on a scrap of fabric to make sure the ink

To get maximum satisfaction from your sewing machine, it is absolutely essential to read, and follow, the manual. If you've misplaced yours, write to the manufacturer for a new one. To be sure you get the right one, include the model number of your machine. On a free-arm machine, the number is usually stamped on a small metal plate secured to the back of the machine; on a flatbed machine, it's located on the front.

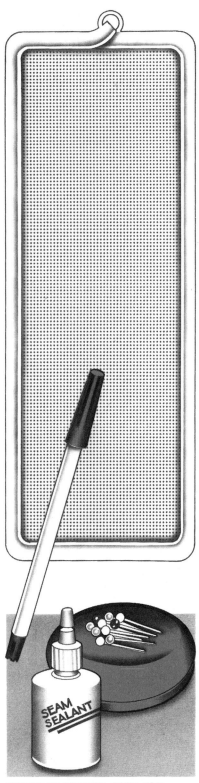

EXTRAS (CLOCKWISE, FROM TOP):
NEEDLE BOARD, MAGNETIC PIN CUSHION,
SEAM SEALANT, FABRIC MARKING PEN

totally disappears, with no water spots or faint residue.

Needle board. If you're making lots of throw pillows, seat covers and the like from velvets, velveteens and corduroys, a needle board is a good investment. When the fabric is placed facedown on the board during pressing, its short, dense needles keep the fabric's raised surface (the "pile") from being flattened by the weight of the iron. If you are only making an occasional project from these fabrics, a fluffy terry cloth towel or a scrap of self-fabric will provide the necessary cushioned surface.

FABRIC BASICS

Decorator fabrics come in several different widths. A few are 45″/48″ (115cm/122cm), but most are either 54″ (138cm) or 60″ (153cm) wide. Newer are the 90″ (229cm) and 120″ (305cm) wide goods. For larger projects, such as coverlets, curtains and dust ruffles, the wider fabrics are particularly easy to work with because less piecing is required.

Before you get set to cut and sew, there are some things you should know about your fabric.

How Much Fabric?

Factors such as the dimensions of your windows and walls, the height of your bed, the width of your table—even the distance between the design repeat on your chosen

fabric—are all variables. Only you will be able to determine, with assurance, how much fabric a project requires. If you learn a few simple terms and then follow our step-by-step directions, it's easy to do!

Usable Width

If the perfect fabric is too narrow for your needs, you'll have to piece several panels together to achieve the required width. Most bedspreads and comforters, as well as many tablecloths and window treatments, require piecing.

Usable fabric width refers to how much of the fabric's width you will be able to utilize for your project. It may or may not be the same as the fabric's actual width.

Selvage refers to the finished lengthwise edges of the fabric. These edges are a bit stiffer and firmer than the cut (crosswise) edge of the fabric. They also will not ravel. On home dec fabrics with a printed design, rather than one that is knitted or woven into the fabric, the motif usually does not extend into the selvage area. Instead, the name of the manufacturer and information on any special finishes may be printed along this edge.

If the selvages are tightly woven, using them as seam allowances can distort your project. Most of the time, it's best to cut them off. There are times, however, when the selvages can be incorporated into your project.

● When you need to conserve fabric, the straight seams common to many home decorating projects make it possible to utilize the selvages as seam allowances. However, since the selvage area is not always ¹/₂″ (1.3cm) wide—and both the right and left selvages may be different widths—you'll need to check and adjust the width of your seam allowances accordingly.

● Printed decorator fabrics are usually engineered so that the motif can be matched by joining two widths just inside the selvage. If the selvage is trimmed away, you must find an-

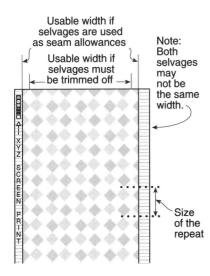

Usable width if selvages are used as seam allowances

Usable width if selvages must be trimmed off

Note: Both selvages may not be the same width.

Size of the repeat

other vertical matching point, which may narrow considerably the usable width of your fabric. To solve this problem, make small (¹/₄″, or 6mm) clips in the selvage area, every 3″–4″ (7.5cm–10cm), so that the

fabric lies flat. If the clips need to be closer together, the result will be a very weak seam allowance. In that case, it is better to trim off the selvages and, if necessary, purchase extra yardage.

Trimming the selvages will reduce the usable width of your fabric. After trimming, where piecing is required, even more of the width will be taken up by the piecing seams. To determine the usable width of the fabric, measure its inner width, between the selvages. Subtract 1″ (2.5cm) for the piecing seam.

If the selvages can be incorporated into your project—or if you are using sheets or dressmaking fabric that does not have a printed selvage—then the actual fabric width and the usable fabric width are the same.

Figuring Fabric: Step by Step

To utilize these formulas, you need to know three things about your project:

● *Cutting width of your project* (including seam and/or hem allowances).

● *Cutting length of your project* (including seam, hem and/or casing allowances). Chapters 5–11 cover a range of wonderful decorating ideas that you can apply all through the house. Each individual project or technique includes the information you need for determining the cutting width and cutting length.

● *Usable width of your fabric.* Can you use the selvages, or must you trim them off? Determine as described above.

Now you're ready for the two simple steps:

Step 1: How Many Panels? To determine the number of lengths, or panels, of fabric you need, divide the cutting width of your project by the usable width of your fabric. The answer, rounded up to the nearest whole number, is how many panels you need.

Step 2: How Many Yards? To determine the amount of fabric you need to purchase, multiply the number of panels by the cutting length of the project. To convert inches to yards (centimeters to meters), divide by 36″ (91.5cm).

● As a margin for error, add a few extra inches (centimeters) and round up to the next eighth of a yard (tenth of a meter) when making your purchase.

● To allow for matching a repeating motif, you'll also need extra fabric. Measure the distance between repeats. Multiply this distance (i.e., the size of the repeat) by the number of panels. That's how much extra to buy. For example, if your bedspread requires three panels of fabric, and the floral pattern has a 6″ (15cm) repeat, then you'll need to buy an extra 18″ (45.5cm) of fabric.

TIP

On printed fabric, arrow markings on the selvages indicate which end is up. Before trimming them away, lightly mark directional arrows every few feet (meters) on the back of the fabric.

A Good Press

Before measuring and cutting, fabric should be pressed smooth and flat to remove any wrinkles or folds. This step will also give you a good chance to take another "up close" look at your fabric. If you have purchased fabric labeled "seconds," double-check to make sure you've located all the flaws. And if you have identified your print as a random design, check one more time to be *absolutely sure* it doesn't require matching. Better to find out now, when you are still able to buy more fabric or consider an alternative use for it!

Getting It Straight

One of the recurring myths of sewing is that *every* fabric should be straightened so that it is perfectly on grain (i.e., with lengthwise and crosswise threads exactly parallel to one another). If the project is cut on grain, the theory goes, the finished item will maintain its straight lines and geometric shape. In reality, most decorator fabrics have a permanent finish that locks the threads in place. If the threads have been pulled off grain during the manufacturing process, no amount of fussing on your part will alter this fact.

The trick is to create the illusion of an on-grain piece of goods, no matter what the reality, by "squaring" the fabric.

● Align one leg of the carpenter's square with one selvage edge. Working along the other leg of the square, mark across the fabric.

● The selvage is your reference point for measuring and marking lengthwise lines; the marked line is your reference point for measuring and marking horizontal lines.

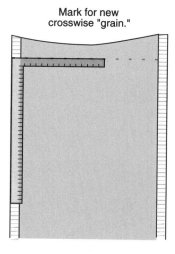

Mark for new crosswise "grain."

TIPS

Carefully check the size of your repeat. Screen prints can easily have a repeat as large as 27" (68.5cm).

If you have a motif that must be matched, glue stick, fusible thread or double-faced basting tape can help you get perfect results. Check out "Basting Techniques" on page 34 for the how-tos.

Forget what you may have learned in fashion sewing about *always* preshrinking your fabric. When it comes to home dec fabrics, that rule is meant to be broken. Many of these fabrics are treated with special finishes that help resist soil, retain luster and protect their beauty. Washing may destroy these finishes and alter the character of your fabric.

Of course, if you have chosen to use a dressmaking fabric, such as eyelet, calico, gingham or muslin, particularly for items that will be washed frequently, such as kitchen curtains or throw pillows, then prewash it, following the manufacturer's care code. If in doubt, use cold water and nondetergent soap.

Sooner or later, things do get dirty. When that happens, dry cleaning is generally the preferred method. However, even dry cleaning can shorten the life of a fabric. If the item is the victim of dust and surface dirt, rather than real soil, vacuum it thoroughly . . . or, if possible, give it a tumble in the clothes dryer, accompanied by several sheets of fabric softener. These will absorb the surface grime.

If the design has a crosswise element, such as a plaid, a horizontal stripe or a motif that is repeated across the width of the fabric, check the marked line to be sure it runs exactly parallel to the crosswise element. If it does not, reverse the process to square up your fabric.

● Draw a horizontal line across the fabric, exactly parallel to the crosswise element.

● Align one leg of the carpenter's square with the marked line so that the other leg is close to the selvage. Mark the lengthwise line.

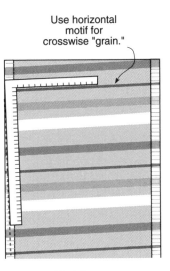

Use horizontal motif for crosswise "grain."

Mark for new lethwise "grain."

TERMS TO KNOW

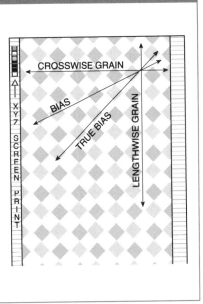

Straight, or lengthwise, grain refers to the fabric threads that are parallel to the selvages.

Crosswise grain refers to the threads that run across the fabric between the two selvages, perpendicular to the lengthwise threads.

Bias is any diagonal direction. *True bias* is the diagonal edge formed when the fabric is folded so the lengthwise and crosswise grains match. Fabric has the greatest amount of stretch along the true bias. For more information, see *custom-made binding* on page 48.

Trim the fabric along the marked lines. Use the cut edges of the fabric as reference points for measuring and marking.

The Cutting Surface

Whether you are using a commercial pattern, or creating one of the projects featured in this book, sewing for the home seldom involves actual pattern pieces. Instead, the required shapes are plotted out directly on the fabric.

● Work on a large, flat surface. If you don't have a table that's big enough, consider the floor, the bed (with a cutting board as protection) or even a Ping-Pong table.

● Support the excess fabric by keeping it at, or above, the level of the cutting surface. Use a chair, a stool, the ironing board. The point is to prevent the fabric from being pulled or distorted by its own weight.

● Begin measuring and marking from the squared-up edges of the fabric.

● Some fabrics will change the way they look depending on which way you hold them. For example, shiny fabrics such as satins and damasks, and pile fabrics, such as velvet, velveteen and corduroy, change color slightly depending on which end is up. Other fabrics may have a printed or woven motif that looks different depending on which way the fabric is held. The difference can be very obvious—such as flowers that "grow" in one direction—or so subtle that you may not notice it until the project is finished. To be on the safe side, measure and mark all sections so they run in the same direction. Then lightly mark on the back of each shape with an arrow to indicate "this end up."

TIPS

If you are planning on doing a great deal of sewing for your home, do as the pros do. Make your own portable cutting surface. Purchase a 4' × 8' (1.3m × 2.5m) piece of ³/₄" (2cm) wide plywood. Pad the surface with a flannel blanket or a layer of cotton batting. Cover it tightly with a sheet or piece of muslin stapled to the underside. Not only do you have a large cutting surface, you also have a right-angle corner for squaring up your fabric. Plus, you can use pushpins to secure the fabric to the surface while you measure, mark and cut.

To mark "this end up" on lightweight or sheer fabrics, use a fabric marking pen or stick masking tape on the wrong side of the fabric. Draw the arrow on the tape.

SEWING FUNDAMENTALS

Basting Techniques

Basting refers to any of several methods that can be used to temporarily hold layers of fabric in place until they're permanently secured.

Pin basting is the most common method. Place pins perpendicular to the seamline. On smaller projects or shaped edges, place pins 1″–3″ (2.5cm–7.5cm) apart. On long, straight seams, pins can be 4″–8″ (10cm–20.5cm) apart. Insert the pins so you take small bites of fabric right at the seamline. Position the heads so the pins can be removed efficiently as you stitch: to the right, if you're right-handed; to the left, if you're left-handed.

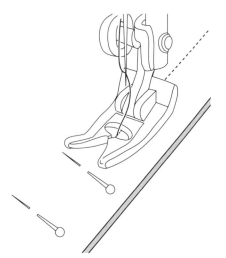

If your machine has a hinged presser foot, it *is* possible to sew right over the pins but *only* if your manual describes this feature. Otherwise, don't experiment. The sad result will be a damaged sewing ma-chine needle that can cause all sorts of stitching problems.

Paper clips are a quick substitute for pins on bulky, hard-to-pin fabrics, such as fake fur, or where pins would leave permanent holes, such as leather and vinyl. Never, never try to stitch over a paper clip!

Machine basting is most often used to temporarily assemble a project to check the size or shape.

● Pin-baste the fabric layers to-gether, matching the markings.

● Loosen the needle thread tension, adjust the stitch setting to the long-est length and stitch. Don't bother to secure the stitching at the ends of the seams.

To easily remove the basting, clip the needle thread every 1″ (2.5cm) or so, then pull out the bobbin thread.

Hand basting is a very secure method of basting. It is frequently used in detail areas where pin bast-ing would not be accurate enough or secure enough and where machine basting would be difficult to do. It can also be used on sheer or very slippery fabrics.

For the firmest holding power, weave the needle in and out of the fabric so that the stitches and the spaces between them are all the same size—approximately ¼″ (6mm) long. For areas that don't need to be as secure, make the stitches ¼″ (6mm) long and the spaces between them ½″–¾″ (1.3cm–2cm) long.

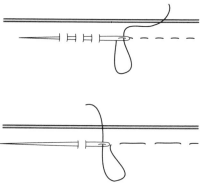

Double-faced basting tape is a valu-able aid when you need to be sure that stripes or plaids match at the seamline, or for positioning detail areas such as zippers. Do not stitch through the tape, as it will gum up your needle.

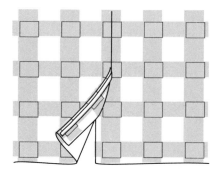

Glue stick, shown on the next page, can be used instead of basting tape. Unlike basting tape, you can stitch right through the glue without harming your needle. Just be sure you've allowed a few minutes for the glue to dry thoroughly.

Fuse basting is a fast way to hold fabric layers in place for hand finishing or to secure trims for permanent stitching. Use fusible web, sandwiched between the two layers. Easiest to use are the paper-backed fusible webs, which can be cut into any shape or width. Apply, web side

Apply fusible web to one surface.

down, to one surface. Let cool, peel the paper backing away and then fuse the two layers together, holding the iron in place for only a few seconds. Follow the manufacturer's recommendations for heat and steam. For more information about fusible and iron-on products, see Chapter 11, TIMESAVERS.

Fusible thread is particularly useful for details such as zippers or trims, where exact positioning is required, or for perfectly matching a fabric's motifs. This thread has an extra component that melts under the heat of the iron. It comes on a cone—

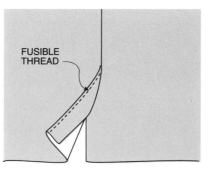

FUSIBLE THREAD

ready to use in one of the overlock's loopers. For a conventional machine, use it in the top or wind it by hand onto the bobbin. (Experiment to see which way your machine likes best!) Some ideas:

● *For trim placement*, zigzag along the trim placement line, then fuse-baste the trim in place.

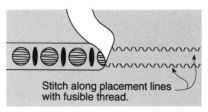

Stitch along placement lines with fusible thread.

● *For matched seams*, use fusible thread in the bobbin. With the right side of the fabric facedown, stitch within the seam allowance, just next to the seamline. Place the two panels right side up on a padded table or ironing board. Lap the panel with the fusible thread over the other panel. Working a short distance at a time, fold the overlapping

panel under so that the fusible thread is just inside the seamline. Match the motif on the overlap to the motif on the underlap and press in place with a warm iron. Continue down the length of the seam. Change the bobbin back to regular thread. With creased side up, stitch or serge the seam. If necessary, trim the seam allowances to ½" (1.3cm). Press the seam allowances to one side.

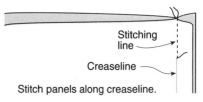

Stitching line

Creaseline

Stitch panels along creaseline.

Seams and Seam Finishes

The Plain Seam

The *plain seam* is the most commonly used seam.

● With right sides together, stitch along the seamline. For most of the projects in this book, that's usually ½" (1.3cm) from the cut edge. Use twelve to fourteen stitches per inch (per two and a half centimeters).

● Press the seam flat. Then press the seam open, unless the instructions tell you to press it to one side.

If your fabric ravels easily, or the project will be washed frequently, the plain seam should be finished. Zigzag, machine-overcast, or serge (using the 2-thread or 3-thread overlock stitch) as close as possible to each raw edge. If you are working on a large project, such as a bedspread or a dust ruffle, it is generally easier to finish the raw edges before the seams are stitched.

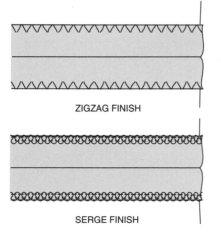

ZIGZAG FINISH

SERGE FINISH

A corner requires some special treatment.

• To strengthen the seam, shorten the stitch length for about 1″ (2.5cm) on either side of the corner. This will help keep the corner from fraying after it is trimmed.

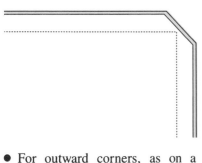

• For outward corners, as on a square pillow, trim the seam allowances diagonally at the corner before turning the project right side out.

• For a perfect corner, use chalk or a fabric marking pen to mark the intersection of the two seamlines.

Stitch down one seamline, stopping within a few stitches of the mark. Then use the hand wheel to form the next few stitches until the needle is exactly at the mark. With the needle still in the fabric, raise the presser foot. Pivot the fabric to bring it into the correct position for stitching along the seamline on the second side of the corner. Lower the presser foot and continue stitching.

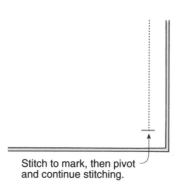

Stitch to mark, then pivot and continue stitching.

Curves, too, need some help from your scissors to make the seams lie flat.

• On inside, or concave, curves, take little snips in the seam allowance, just to, but not through, the stitching.

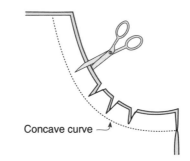

Concave curve

• On outward, or convex, curves, cut wedge-shaped notches from the seam allowance. This eliminates fullness when the seam is pressed open or the project is turned right side out.

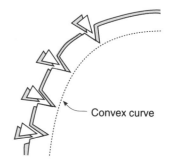

Convex curve

The Overlock Seam

The *overlock seam* is a superfast way to assemble your projects and finish the seams at the same time. Serge, using a 3-thread or 4-thread overlock stitch.

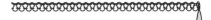

Specialty Seams

There are some special-purpose seams that incorporate the seam finish into the construction technique. Because they are not flexible enough for curves and corners, they are not as commonly used as the plain or overlock seam.

The *French seam*, shown on the next page, is a good choice for sheers and lightweight fabrics, particularly if you don't own an overlock machine. It encases and protects the raw edges of the fabric.

• With wrong sides together, stitch a ¼″ (6mm) seam.

• Trim the seam allowances to a scant ⅛″ (3mm), then press them open.

• Fold the fabric right sides together along the stitching line; press.

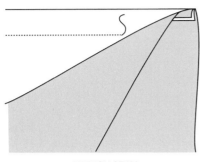

FRENCH SEAM

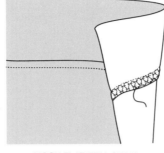

MOCK FLAT-FELL SEAM

Gathers

Gathering is a way to draw up fullness. It can be done on the conventional machine or on the overlock.

No matter which technique you choose, divide and mark the straight edge and the edge to be gathered into quarters, eighths or sixteenths, depending on the length of the sections.

Straight Stitch Gathering

Because it can be used to draw up fullness along the edge of the fabric or between two finished edges, as on an applied ruffle (see "Ruffles" on page 55), this is the most versatile gathering technique.

● Stitch ¼″ (6mm) from the fold. Press the seam allowances flat, then to one side.

The *flat-fell seam* is functional, sturdy and subtly decorative. It is a good possibility for the piecing seams on a tailored bedspread or tablecloth.

● With wrong sides together, stitch a plain seam and press the seam allowances to one side.

● Trim the underneath seam allowance to a scant ⅛″ (3mm). Turn under ¼″ (6mm) on the top seam allowance. Use pins or glue stick to baste it in place.

● Edgestitch close to the fold.

● With right sides together, serge the seam. Press the seam allowances to one side.

● On the right side of the fabric, topstitch through all layers, ¼″ (6mm) from the seamline.

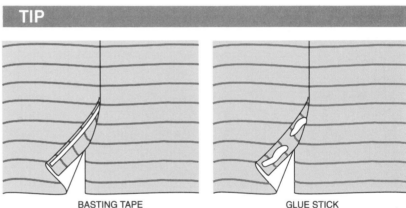

TIP

BASTING TAPE   GLUE STICK

To match a stripe, a plaid or other repeating motif along a seamline:

● Press one seam allowance under at the seamline, then do one of the following:

—Position the basting tape so that the sticky side is against the right side of the seam allowance, about ⅛″ (3mm) from the fold. Remove the protective covering from the tape.

—Apply glue stick to the right side of the seam allowance.

● Lap the pressed seam allowance over the unpressed one, matching both the seamline and the fabric design.

● Turn the project sections to the wrong side, open out the folded seam allowance and stitch along the creased line.

Another alternative is to use the fusible thread matching technique described on page 35.

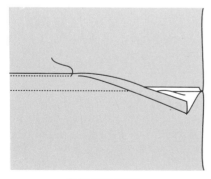

FLAT-FELL SEAM

The *mock flat-fell seam* combines the overlock and the conventional seam.

STITCHING TERMS

Slipstitch. A good choice for securing turned-under edges by hand. The stitches are invisible on both the inside and outside of the project.

● Fasten the thread in the fold of the fabric.

● Working from right to left, pick up a single fabric thread just below the folded edge.

● Insert the needle into the fold directly above the first stitch and bring it out 1/4″ (6mm) away.

● Pick up another single thread in the project directly below the point where the needle just emerged.

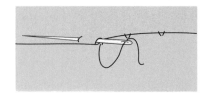

Understitch. A row of machine stitching that keeps an inside layer of fabric, such as a lining, from rolling to the outside.

● Press the seam allowances toward the underside of the project.

● Working from the right side, stitch 1/8″ (3mm) from the seamline, through the lining and the seam allowances only.

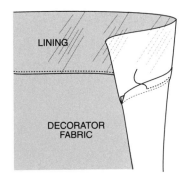

Staystitch. A row of machine stitching, placed just inside the seamline, which prevents curved or bias edges from stretching out of shape as they are handled. It is also used as a "roadblock" where the seam allowance needs to be clipped before the seam is stitched.

Edgestitch. An extra row of machine stitching placed approximately 1/8″ (3mm) or less away from a seamline or a foldline, or close to a finished edge. It is similar to *topstitching* but is usually less noticeable.

Topstitch. A row of machine stitching used to apply one layer of fabric to another. Note that, in home dec sewing, the terms *edgestitching* and *topstitching* are used interchangeably.

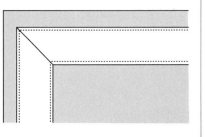

Loosen the needle-thread tension slightly and lengthen the stitch. (The heavier the fabric, the longer the stitch.) Then:

● On the right side of the fabric, stitch along the seamline. Stitch again, 1/4″ (6mm) away, within the seam allowance. Leave long thread tails at both ends of the stitching. If you're working on a very long area, divide the gathers into sections, leaving long tails at each marking.

● With right sides together, pin the two sections together, matching the markings. Gently pull the bobbin threads at each end, sliding the fabric along until the gathered section fits the shorter section. Distribute the gathers evenly and pin at frequent intervals between the markings.

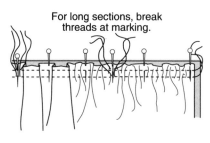

For long sections, break threads at marking.

● Working with the gathered side up, stitch just next to the first row of gathering stitches. Use the tips of your fingers to hold the fabric on either side of the presser foot. This will keep tucks from forming along the seamline.

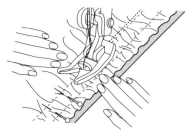

Gathering Over a Cord

Use this fast method when the gathering stitches are concealed in a seam.

- Cut a piece of strong, thin cord, such as perle cotton, button and carpet thread or lightweight packing string, slightly longer than the edge to be gathered.

- Set your machine for a zigzag stitch wide enough to cover the cord without catching it. Position the cord within the seam allowance so the left swing of the needle falls just short of the seamline. Stitch.

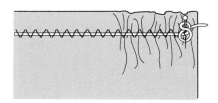

- Wrap one end of the cord around a pin in a figure eight to secure it.

- Pin the sections together, matching markings. Distribute the gathers by holding the cord taut and sliding the fabric along it.

- Working with the gathered side up, stitch along the seamline, being careful not to catch the cord. Depending on the weight of the fabric and the thickness of the cord, you may find it easier to use the machine's zipper foot.

- When you're finished stitching, just pull out the cord.

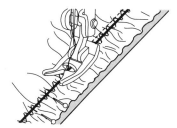

Gathering on the Overlock

This is a great gathering method for light- to medium-weight fabrics. However, because the overlock will trim the seam allowance to $1/4''$ (6mm), heavyweight fabrics may be difficult to handle. To be sure, test this technique on a scrap of your fabric.

- Adjust your machine for a wide, balanced, 3-thread overlock stitch.

- Serge a chain at least $6''$ (15cm) longer than the edge to be gathered. Gently run your fingers along the thread chain to smooth it out. Do *not* cut the chain.

- Raise the presser foot and bring the thread chain around to the front, under the back of the presser foot, then up over the toe, to the left of the knife. Lower the presser foot. Serge along the edge to be gathered, encasing the thread chain in the new stitches.

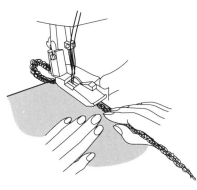

- To gather, simply pull up on the thread chain.

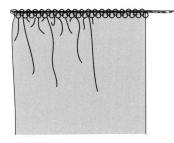

Hems

Double Hem

This is the most popular hem for home decorating items. It helps projects such as curtains, drapes and dust ruffles hang smoothly because it adds a little bit of weight at the lower edge. It also provides a clean finish on both the right and wrong sides of the project. And because the raw edge of the fabric is "buried" inside the hem allowance, it is extremely durable.

If you plan on using a double hem, the cutting dimensions of your project must include a hem allowance that is twice the depth of the finished hem. For example, a $4''$ (10cm) double hem requires an $8''$ (20.5cm) hem allowance; a $1''$ (2.5cm) double hem requires a $2''$ (5cm) hem allowance.

To make a double hem:

- Press the lower edge up the prescribed amount.

- Press up again the same amount.

- Machine-stitch the hem in place close to the first fold or, for a custom look, hand-sew or machine-blindstitch the hem in place.

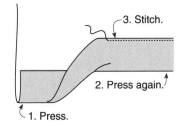

3. Stitch.
2. Press again.
1. Press.

TIP

For information on how to blindstitch on your conventional machine, consult your owner's manual.

Narrow Double Hem

This hem is similar in appearance to the double hem, but because the hem allowance is narrower, the construction process is slightly different. It is used frequently on items such as napkins and tablecloths, or for decorative details such as ruffles, when a wider hem would be too bulky.

On a straight edge:

● Machine-stitch ¹/₂″ (1.3cm) from the raw edge.

● Working on the wrong side, fold the raw edge up to meet the stitching; press.

● Fold up along the stitching line and press again.

● Edgestitch close to the inner fold.

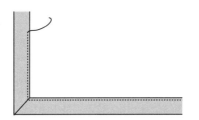

1. Stitch.
2. Press.
3. Press again.
4. Stitch.
¹/₂″ (1.3cm)

To miter a corner:

● Machine-stitch ¹/₂″ (1.3cm) from the intersecting edges, crossing the stitching at the corner.

● At the cross-point, fold the fabric diagonally to the wrong side; press. Trim the corner seam allowance to ¹/₄″ (6mm).

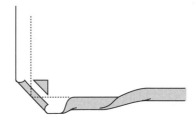

● Fold and press twice, then edgestitch as for a straight edge.

On a curved edge, such as a round tablecloth:

● Loosen the needle tension slightly and adjust your machine to sew with a longer (3mm, or 8–10 stitches per inch) stitch. With the project wrong side up, stitch ¹/₄″ (6mm) from the raw edge. This is called ease stitching.

● Press the edge to the wrong side along the stitching line.

● Fold the edge up another ¹/₄″ (6mm). If necessary, use a pin to draw up the bobbin thread wherever there is extra fullness; press.

● Machine-stitch close to the inner fold.

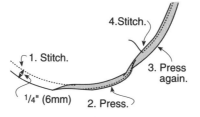

1. Stitch.
2. Press.
3. Press again.
4. Stitch.
¹/₄″ (6mm)

Serger Rolled Hem

This type of hem creates the beautiful and durable finish often found on the edges of commercially made napkins and tablecloths. Use a contrasting thread to add a splash of color at the edges of the project.

The mechanics of creating this hem depend on your overlock machine. Some machines require that you change the foot and the throat plate. On other overlocks, you can convert the machine to the rolled hem setting via built-in adjustments. Check your machine's manual for complete information.

The right combination of fabric and thread is important for good results. Fabrics that are too crisp or too heavy will not roll satisfactorily.

On a serger rolled hem, the upper looper thread is the one that's visible; the lower looper and needle threads are hidden inside the roll.

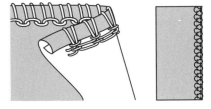

ROLLED HEM

Generally, you'll get the best results with woolly nylon thread in the upper looper and polyester overlock thread in the needle and lower looper. If woolly nylon isn't available in your desired color, use the same polyester overlock thread in the upper looper . . . or, for a more "filled in" effect, use the heavier-weight thread designed for home dec sewing on the overlock.

Self-Fringed Hem

This almost no-sew technique is wonderful at the edges of napkins, tablecloths and placemats. For successful results, choose a loosely woven fabric that will ravel easily, such as linen or challis.

● The edge to be fringed must be a straight edge, cut exactly on grain. To be sure the edges are straight, cut the project slightly larger than its finished size (including the depth of the fringe). Then pull a thread to mark the finished edge of the project. Trim off the excess fabric.

● Pull a second thread to mark the depth of the fringe. Machine-stitch along the pull, using either a straight stitch or a narrow zigzag. This will lock the edges so your project will not fray away during future laundering or dry cleaning.

● Clip the fabric every 2″–3″ (5cm–7.5cm), just up to the stitching. Pull out the crosswise threads between the clips.

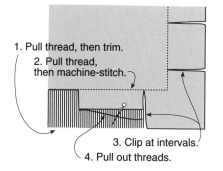

1. Pull thread, then trim.
2. Pull thread, then machine-stitch.
3. Clip at intervals.
4. Pull out threads.

If your fabric isn't suitable for a rolled hem, a narrow serged hem may work just as well. Experiment, increasing the stitch length and adjusting the looper tensions so the loops meet on the edge of the fabric.

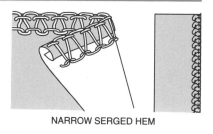

NARROW SERGED HEM

Clean-Finish Border

With this technique, you can add a border and hem the edge, both at the same time.

● Cut strips of fabric equal to the finished depth of the border plus 1″ (2.5cm).

● Fold one long edge under ½″ (1.3cm) and press.

● Pin the border to the project, right side of border to wrong side of project, raw edges matching; stitch a ½″ (1.3cm) seam.

● Press the border away from the project and then to the right side along the seamline. Topstitch along the folded edge of the border.

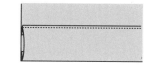

To miter a corner:

● Start with strips of fabric equal to the length of each edge of the project plus 1″ (2.5cm).

● Place one strip wrong side up; fold the end diagonally, forming a 45° angle; press. Trim, leaving a ½″ (1.3cm) seam allowance. Press under ½″ (1.3cm) along the shorter of the two long edges.

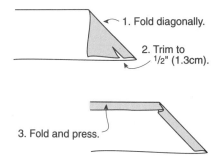

1. Fold diagonally.
2. Trim to ½″ (1.3cm).
3. Fold and press.

● On the intersecting strip, press one long edge under ½″ (1.3cm).

● Open out the folds. Pin the two strips together, as shown below. Stitch along the diagonal line, just to the point where the folds intersect; backstitch to secure.

● Trim the diagonal seam allowances to match; press the seam open.

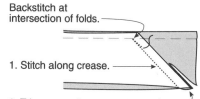

Backstitch at intersection of folds.
1. Stitch along crease.
2. Trim seam allowances to match.

● Re-press the long, folded edges. Apply the mitered border as on page 41.

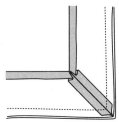

Hook-and-Loop Fasteners

These flexible, two-part fasteners have tiny, stiff hooks and soft loops that interlock when you press them together. Although they are available in precut dots or squares, the strips are the most popular form for home dec sewing.

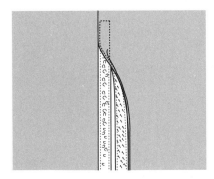

This type of fastener can be used in place of a zipper. (See "Easy-On/Easy-Off Closures" in Chapter 8, PILLOW PIZZAZZ.) It can also be used to attach soft fabric treatments to wood or metal surfaces. In the latter case, the loop side of the fastener tape is stitched to the wrong side of the fabric; the hook side is glued to the receiving surface. (See "Drapery/Pleater Tapes" in Chapter 11, TIMESAVERS.)

Most brand names, including Velcro®, are available in two versions:

● *Sew-on hook-and-loop tape* comes with a light adhesive backing to "baste" it in place for permanent stitching. To attach, machine-stitch along both long edges of the tape. For a no-sew application on vinyl, wood, cardboard, pressed board and similar surfaces, purchase the clear adhesive that's specially designed for this purpose.

● *Pressure-sensitive hook-and-loop tape* is designed for hobby and craft needs on smooth surfaces, such as glass, walls, tile and porcelain. Just peel off the paper backing and press the tape in place. *Never, never* try to machine-stitch this tape in place. The adhesive will cause major damage to your machine. If you have the need, and the patience, you can hand-sew it to the project along the long edges.

Zippers

Zippers are an easy-on/easy-off option for pillows, cushions, duvet covers and slipcovers.

Some sewers prefer the center application because it is a bit faster and easier. Others prefer the look of the lapped application because there's only one row of stitching on the outside of the project. Most of the time, the decision is up to you. However, when the zipper is installed along an edge, be sure to use the lapped method. (See "Traditional Slipcovers" in Chapter 9, SITTING PRETTY, and "Contemporary Box-Edge Pillow" in Chapter 8, PILLOW PIZZAZZ).

The standard seam allowance for the projects in this book is ½″ (1.3cm). However, if a zipper will be incorporated in the seam, increase those seam allowances to 1″ (2.5cm) when you cut out your project. The extra width ensures an easier, more secure installation.

Center Application

Step 1: Pin the two fabric sections, right sides together; mark along the seamline for the zipper opening. Stitch up to the first marking, backstitch for a few stitches, lengthen to a basting stitch and stitch just past the next marking. Shorten the stitch, backstitch to the marking and then stitch forward to the end of the seam. Clip the bobbin thread at regular intervals so the basting stitches will be easy to remove later on.

Step 2: Press the seam open. Use basting glue to secure the seam allowances between the markings.

Step 3: Center the zipper facedown over the seamline, between the markings. Baste in place with glue stick.

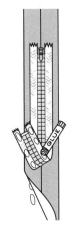

TIP

If desired, substitute double-faced basting tape for the two applications of glue stick. Just be sure to position the basting tape so you won't stitch through it.

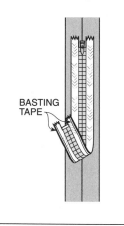

BASTING TAPE

Step 4: Turn the project over to the right side. Using a zipper foot and beginning at the seamline, topstitch across the bottom of the zipper, up one side and across to the seamline. Repeat for the other side. Pull the thread tails to the wrong side and tie in a knot.

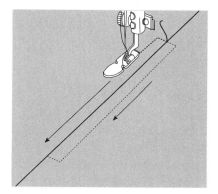

Lapped Application

Step 1: Prepare the opening as for "Center Application," Step 1.

Step 2: Position the project wrong side up with the right-hand seam allowance extended. Open the zipper. Place it facedown on the seam

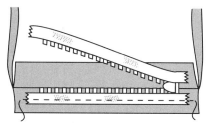

allowance, between the markings, with the zipper teeth just next to the seamline. (If the seam is piped, crowd the teeth against the piping.) Machine-baste along the woven guideline on the zipper tape, through the tape and seam allowance only.

Step 3: How you handle this step depends on whether the seam includes piping. Close the zipper. Then:

● For a plain seam, turn the zipper faceup so the seam allowance folds under. Bring the fold close to, but not touching, the zipper teeth. Starting at the bottom of the zipper, stitch along the fold, through both the tape and the seam allowance.

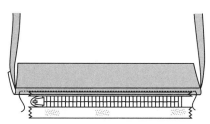

● For a piped seam, turn the project right side up so it is flat. Mark the top and bottom of the zipper with a pin. Stitch from the bottom to the top marking, crowding the stitches next to the piping.

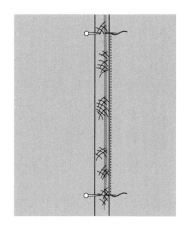

Step 4: Open out the project, so the fabric is flat and the zipper is facedown. Note that a small pleat will form along the folded edge. Hand-baste or machine-baste the remaining zipper tape in place, through all thicknesses.

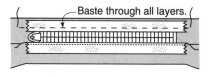

Baste through all layers.

TIP

To shorten a too-long zipper, close the zipper. Measure down from the top of the slider to the desired length; mark. Using a double thread, and working from one side to the other, stitch tightly across the teeth, eight to ten times, at the mark. Cut the zipper 1/2″ (1.3cm) below the stitches.

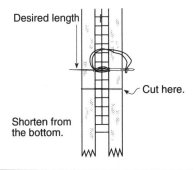

Desired length

Cut here.

Shorten from the bottom.

Step 5: Turn the project right side up. Starting at the seamline, top-stitch across the bottom of the zipper, up the side, then across the top, to the seamline. Backstitch at the beginning and end. Pull the thread tails to the wrong side and tie in a knot.

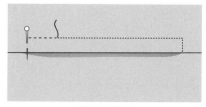

PLAIN SEAM

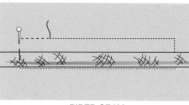

PIPED SEAM

For more information on zipper installations, see "Easy-On/Easy-Off Closures" in Chapter 8, PILLOW PIZZAZZ, and "Traditional Slipcovers" in Chapter 9, SITTING PRETTY.

SPECIAL TOUCHES

Applied Trims

Ribbon, braid or any other trim with two finished edges can be applied almost anywhere on the right side of a project. Create borders by applying them in parallel rows. Use narrow, flexible trims around a curved edge or to create intricate, scrolled designs.

Where possible, apply flat trims, such as ribbon, early on in the project so the ends will be caught in a seam or turned under with a hem allowance. Trims with a raised surface, such as narrow braid, may be too bulky to do this. Instead, seal the cut ends with a bit of seam sealant, then topstitch the trim in place.

For a professional, ripple-free appearance:

● Baste the trim securely in place. Fuse basting and glue basting are two great methods.

● Machine-stitch both long edges in the same direction.

● Some narrow trims look best if applied with one row of stitching, positioned down the center.

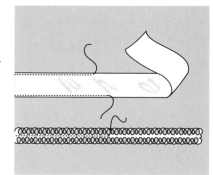

Mitering a Corner

Applied trims require mitering anytime they turn a corner. If you are applying the trim anyplace except along the edge of the project, mark the trim placement line so it is visible on the right side.

TRIMS WITH TWO STRAIGHT EDGES. Use either the marked line or the edge of the project as the trim placement line. Note that the trim will be applied to the left of the placement line; press.

TIP

For a perfect zipper installation:

● *Always* use the zipper foot for machine basting and permanent stitching.

● To make it easy to remove the basting threads later on, clip them at regular intervals before pressing the seam open.

● Transparent tape that is ½″ (1.3cm) wide makes a great topstitching guide.

● To avoid bumpy topstitching around the tab and slider, stop stitching just before you get to the slider. Leaving the needle in the fabric, raise the presser foot and pull the slider down below the needle. (If necessary, remove some of the basting that is holding the seam closed.) Lower the presser foot and continue topstitching.

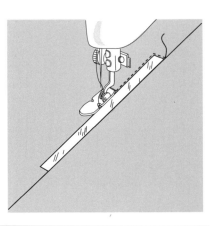

- Pin the trim along the placement line. Topstitch both edges, ending the stitching when you reach the corner.

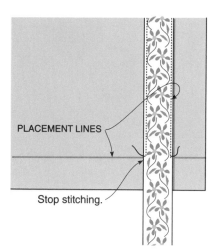

PLACEMENT LINES

Stop stitching.

- Fold the trim back up on itself and press. Then fold the trim diagonally so that it meets the intersecting placement line.

- Refold the trim back on itself and stitch along the diagonal crease, through all layers.

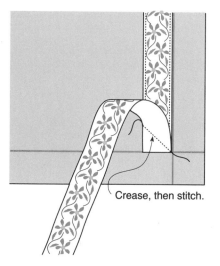

Crease, then stitch.

- Fold the trim back down along the diagonal stitching and press. Then continue topstitching along both edges of the trim.

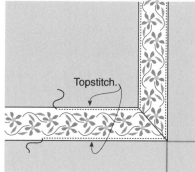

Topstitch.

TRIMS WITH ONE STRAIGHT AND ONE DECORATIVE EDGE. Use either the marked line or the edge of the project as the placement line. Note that the trim will be applied to the right of the placement line.

- Pin the straight edge of the trim along the placement line. Topstitch all the way to the corner.

- Take the project to your ironing board. Fold the trim back up on itself, positioning the fold slightly be-

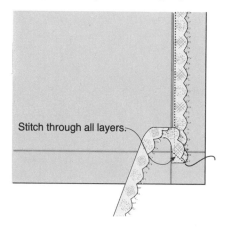

Stitch through all layers.

low the placement line. Then fold the trim back down so it meets the intersecting placement line. Secure the trim to the ironing board with a few straight pins; press the corner.

● Open out the trim and stitch through the diagonal crease, through all the layers.

● Fold the trim back down and continue topstitching.

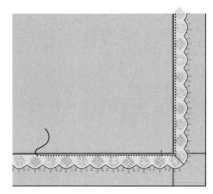

Appliqués

Appliqués are a great way to embellish the surface of your project. You can create your own appliqués or use motifs cut from interesting printed fabrics.

Pillows, bedcoverings, table linens and bath towels are particularly good canvases for appliqués.

Secure basting, using glue stick or fusible web to guarantee the least amount of shifting, is the key to a smooth application.

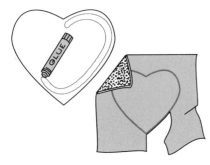

Once the appliqué is basted in place, it is permanently secured with a narrow- to medium-width zigzag stitch. Experiment on scraps of fabric, shortening the stitch length until you get a smooth, even satin-stitch effect. Then:

● Position the project so the appliqué is just to the left of the needle when the needle is in the right-hand position. Stitch slowly.

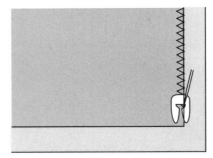

● For outside corners, stitch all the way to the end of the appliqué's edge. Stop stitching with the needle in the fabric at the far-right position. Raise the presser foot, pivot the fabric, lower the foot and continue stitching.

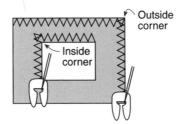

● For inside corners, stitch past the corner into the appliqué for a distance equal to the width of the zigzag stitch. Stop stitching with the needle in the fabric at the far-left position. Raise the presser foot, pivot the fabric, lower the presser foot and continue stitching.

● For outside curves, stop stitching with the needle in the background fabric, in the far right position. Raise the presser foot, swivel the fabric slightly, lower the presser foot and continue stitching.

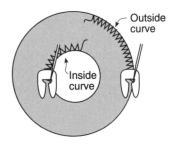

● For inside curves, stop stitching with the needle in the appliqué, in the far left position. Raise the presser foot, swivel the fabric slightly, lower the presser foot and continue stitching. Deeper curves require more frequent swiveling.

TIP

Fusing is often an excellent alternative to machine stitching, particularly when you are applying a heavy trim to a lighter-weight fabric.

Two colors of rickrack can be intertwined to form a bicolor trim that can be applied flat or used as an edging.

For smoother stitching on many fabrics, particularly towels, knits and lightweight wovens, place a layer of stabilizer underneath the project as you machine-stitch. Use a nonwoven tear-away stabilizer that can be gently ripped away from your finished appliqué. If your project is washable, consider a water-soluble stabilizer. This product is a plastic-like sheet that dissolves in cold water.

Bias Binding

Bias binding is a beautiful, decorative edge finish. Make it easy by using purchased double-fold bias tape. For a custom touch, make your own printed or plain bias binding, to match or contrast with your decor.

Purchased Bias Tape

PIECING THE BIAS TAPE. Open out the folds. Place the ends of the tape, right sides together, to form a right (90°) angle; pin. Stitch a ¼" (6mm) seam. Press the seam open; trim away the points that extend beyond the edge of the binding.

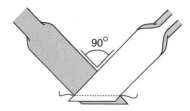

APPLYING PURCHASED BIAS TAPE. NOTE: Purchased double-fold bias tape is folded so that one side is slightly wider than the other. Apply the tape to the project in Step 1, below, so that the wider side will end up on the underside of the fabric.

Step 1: Open out the tape. With right sides together, pin the tape to the fabric, matching cut edges. Stitch along the foldline. Press the tape up, toward the stitching. Then fold the tape over, encasing the cut edge, and pin or glue-baste in place.

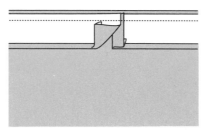

Step 2: Working on the right side of the fabric, "stitch in the ditch" (in the groove where the binding joins the fabric), catching the underneath layer of tape in the stitching.

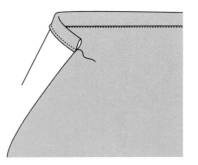

At an outside corner, use this technique to achieve a perfect miter:

● Use a fabric marking pen or dressmaker's pencil to mark where the seam allowances intersect at the corner.

● Pin and stitch the binding or bias tape to the right side of the fabric, as described previously, ending the stitching where the seamlines intersect at the corner. Backstitch a few stitches and cut the thread.

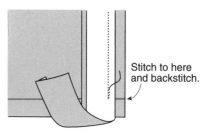

Stitch to here and backstitch.

● Fold the binding over on itself, creating a diagonal crease at the corner. Then fold the binding back on itself to make a fold that is parallel to, and even with, the edge of the binding on Side A, as shown on the next page. The cut edges of binding and fabric match on Side B.

Whether applying custom or purchased binding, handle it gently so you won't distort the shape or width as you stitch.

- Insert the needle exactly at the corner marking and continue stitching.

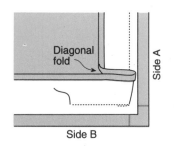

Diagonal fold

Side A

Side B

Custom-made Binding

CUTTING AND JOINING THE BIAS STRIPS. The easy *continuous bias method* eliminates the need for piecing individual strips.

- Cut a rectangle of fabric. The longer side can follow either the lengthwise or the crosswise grain of the fabric. Trim each side of the rectangle so that it *exactly* follows a thread of the fabric.

- To determine the true bias, fold one corner of the rectangle so that the crosswise and the lengthwise edges meet; press, then open out the rectangle.

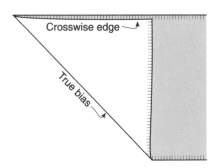

Crosswise edge

True bias

- Cut a cardboard template that is four times the width of the finished binding. For example, a ¼″ (6mm) finished binding requires a 1″ (2.5cm) wide template; a ½″ (1.3cm) finished binding requires a 2″ (5cm) wide template. Beginning at the crease, use the template to pencil-mark parallel lines across the width of the fabric until you reach a corner.

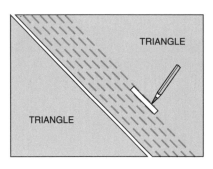

TRIANGLE

TRIANGLE

- Cut off the triangles of unmarked fabric at either end of the rectangle.

- With right sides together, fold the fabric into a tube. Match the pencil lines so that one width of binding extends beyond the edge on each side. Sew a ¼″ (6mm) seam and press open.

- Starting at one end, cut along the pencil line, working your way around the tube until there is one continuous strip.

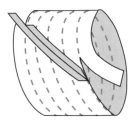

Applying the Binding

Step 1: Fold up and press along one long edge of the binding. On 1″ (2.5cm) wide strips, fold up ¼″ (6mm); on 2″ (5cm) wide strips, fold up ½″ (1.3cm).

Step 2: With right sides together, pin the unfolded edge of the binding to the fabric, matching the cut edges. On 1″ (2.5cm) wide strips, stitch a ³⁄₁₆″ (5mm) seam; on 2″ (5cm) wide strips, stitch a ³⁄₈″ (1cm) seam. Press the binding up, toward the stitching. Fold the binding over so that it encases the cut edge and covers the stitching by approximately ⅛″ (3mm); pin or glue-baste in place.

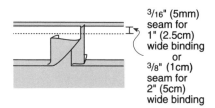

3/16″ (5mm) seam for 1″ (2.5cm) wide binding or 3/8″ (1cm) seam for 2″ (5cm) wide binding

Step 3: Working on the right side of the fabric, "stitch in the ditch" (in the groove where the binding joins the fabric), catching the underneath layer of binding in the stitching, the same as for purchased binding.

To apply custom binding to an outside corner, follow the technique for *purchased bias tape*.

Here's how much binding can be obtained from ¼ yard (.3m) of fabric:

FABRIC WIDTH	BINDING	
	1″ (2.5cm) strips	2″ (5cm) strips
45″ (115cm)	7⅞ yd (7.2m)	4 yd (3.6m)
54″ (138cm)	10⅛ yd (9.3m)	5 yd (4.5m)

Edgings

An edging is a trim with at least one decorative edge, such as fringe, piping, ruffles, rickrack, caterpillar fringe and twisted cord with a lip.

How the trim is applied depends on where it is located on the project.

In a Seam

To insert an edging in a seam, follow the instructions for applying piping on page 51. If the trim is flat, you will not need to use the zipper foot. If desired, use the overlock when joining the two seam allowances.

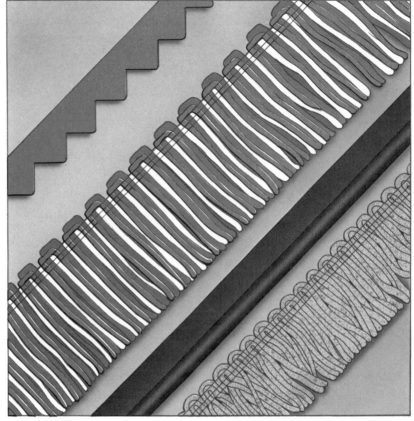

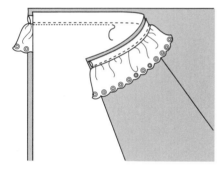

• Press the seam allowances to one side. If desired, turn to the right side of the project and edgestitch close to the seamline, through all layers. Edgestitching is particularly recommended if you are trimming piecing seams in projects such as bedcoverings or tablecloths.

Along an Edge

TOPSTITCH METHOD. Before applying the trim, the edge should be hemmed or folded under and pressed. Then lap the finished edge over the straight edge of the trim; topstitch in place. For rickrack, position the finished edge so only one set of points is visible.

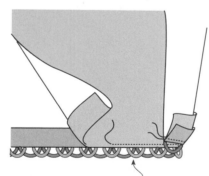

Overlap, then topstitch.

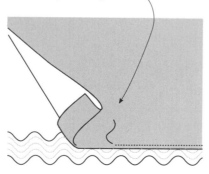

OVERLOCK METHOD. With this method, you can finish the edge and attach the trim, all in one operation, using a 3- or 4-thread overlock stitch. This technique works best with lace and other lightweight trims. Plan on a ½" (1.3cm) hem allowance along the edge of the project.

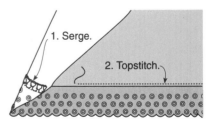

1. Serge.

2. Topstitch.

• Place the trim and the fabric right sides together, with the straight edge of the trim parallel to, and ³⁄₈"

(1cm) from, the raw edge of the fabric. Use glue stick or pins to hold the trim in place.

● Lift the presser foot and place the project, trim side up, so that the straight edge of the trim is aligned slightly to the left of the knife; serge.

● Press the seam allowance toward the garment. If desired, topstitch on your conventional machine.

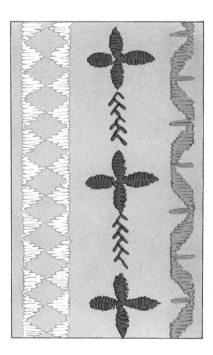

Machine Embroidery

If your sewing machine has programmed embroidery stitches, home dec sewing is a great place to put them to work. Use them singly or in rows on placemats, napkins and tablecloths, or to create borders on larger items like dust ruffles and curtains.

For best results, use a #11/80 or #14/90 needle and machine embroidery thread in all cotton, cotton-covered polyester or, for more luster, rayon. These threads are all lighter in weight than regular sewing thread, thus preventing thread buildup.

Consult your machine's manual for any adjustments in pressure and tension. Test first on scraps of fabric. If necessary, put strips of a tear-away or water-soluble stabilizer underneath your work.

Machine Quilting

Quilting does more than decorate the surface of your project. It also adds durability and warmth. Bed-coverings, placemats and table runners, pillow tops, tiebacks and crib bumpers are just a few of the items that lend themselves to quilting.

Of course, the easiest way to achieve a quilted surface is to purchase prequilted fabric. However,

since your fabric selection will be limited, you might want to consider other alternatives.

Quilt Your Own

Quilted fabric consists of three layers: fashion fabric for the top, batting for the inside layer and a backing fabric for the bottom layer.

The backing can be another fashion fabric (making the quilted fabric reversible), or it can be a lightweight lining fabric, such as muslin or batiste.

Because the quilting process tends to "shrink up" the fabric, quilt first, before cutting the section to its final dimensions.

Choose a simple quilting pattern: rows of parallel stitches (called "channel quilting") or intersecting rows of stitches that form squares or diamonds. Mark the pattern on the quilt top before assembling the layers, using chalk, a sliver of soap or a water-soluble fabric marking pen.

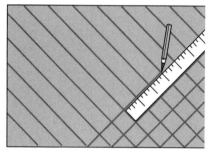

To assemble, work on a large, flat surface. Pin the layers together in order: backing fabric, then batting, then fashion fabric. Be sure each layer is smooth and flat. Hand-baste the layers together with long, diagonal stitches.

Before quilting, test your technique on a sample (at least 12″, or

If your fabric has a large, fairly simple motif, you might want to consider outlining some of the shapes with machine quilting.

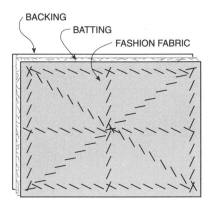

BACKING
BATTING
FASHION FABRIC

To cover the cord:

● Wrap the bias strip, right side out, around the cord, so that the raw edges are even.

● Using a zipper foot and a machine basting stitch, stitch just next to the cord. Do not crowd the stitches against the cord or stretch the bias as you stitch.

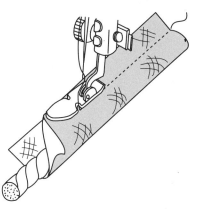

To apply the piping:

The covered piping is basted in place along one seamline; then the two sections of the project are permanently stitched together. Here's how to do it:

● Position the piping so the raw edges are within the seam allowance and the basting stitches are just to the right of the seamline.

For square corners, clip the piping seam allowances just to the basting stitches, at the point where the piping turns the corner.

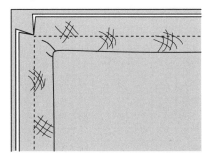

30.5cm, long) that duplicates the layers of the project:

● Use a #11/80 or #14/90 machine needle and a slightly longer stitch length. Stitch continuously, with as few stops and starts as possible.

● If tucks or puckers occur on either side, or the bottom layer is longer than the top, reduce the pressure on your machine's presser foot. If this doesn't help, you may need a special attachment, called an even feed foot, or a walking foot, which allows both the upper and lower layers to move through the machine at the same rate.

As you stitch, support the weight of the quilt so it doesn't hang over the back or side of the sewing table. For large projects, roll up the portion you are not working on. Secure the roll with T-pins or large safety pins.

For more information on batting, see Chapter 7, SLEEPING BEAUTY. For information on tufting, see "Tufted Comforter with Ruffled Edges," also in Chapter 7.

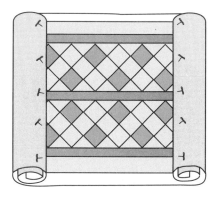

Piping

Whether it's called piping, piping cord or welting, this is a wonderfully versatile trim. Use it to accent the shape of the project, to strengthen and embellish seams, or to add a touch of color between the edge of the fabric and another, wider trim, such as ruffles.

You can purchase covered piping in a variety of colors or purchase the plain cord and custom-cover it with your own choice of fabric.

The cover is made from bias strips of fabric. To cut and join the bias strips, use the same method as for *bias bindings*. For cord that is up to 1/4" (6mm) in diameter, you will need 1 1/2" (3.8cm) wide strips. For thicker cord, measure the cord's circumference, then add 1" (2.5cm) for the seam allowances.

For a slightly curved corner, clip the piping seam allowance 1½" (3.8cm) on either side of the point.

For curved areas, clip the piping seam allowance at frequent intervals until the trim lies flat.

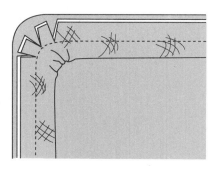

● Using the zipper foot, baste the piping in place over the first row of basting stitches.

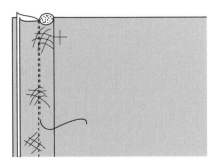

● Pin the two sections together so that the section with the piping is on top. Stitch the seam, crowding the zipper foot up next to the piping so that all of the previous stitching is concealed in the seam allowance.

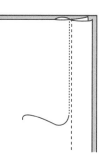

Resist the temptation to overlap the ends of the piping. The result is bulky and unprofessional. Instead, use this technique to join the ends so there's a continuous strip of piping:

● Plan the joining to fall on a long edge, in a place that will be fairly inconspicuous on the finished project. Do not start it on a zipper edge, at a corner or on a deep curve. Lightly mark the joining point.

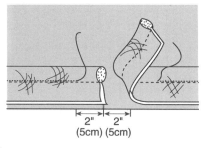

2" (5cm) 2" (5cm)

● Match one end of the piping to the mark. Baste the piping in place, beginning 2" (5cm) from the mark. Stitch around the project, stopping 2" (5cm) before the mark. Leave the needle in the fabric and the presser foot down. Trim the piping so the end will overlap the mark for 1" (2.5cm).

● Remove 1½" (3.8cm) of basting stitches from the overlap. Pull the bias cover back; trim the cording only so it will butt up against the other cording at the mark.

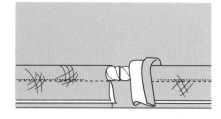

● Turn the end of the bias cover under ½" (1.3cm). Wrap it around the exposed cord and the beginning

of the piping. Complete the stitching.

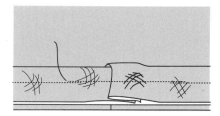

Variation

Shirred Piping

Cut and piece strips of fabric equal to two to three times the length of the piping cord. For this technique, cut strips on the crosswise grain, rather than on the bias. The strips should be wide enough to wrap around the cord, plus 1" (2.5cm) for seam allowances.

● Wrap the strip, right side out, around the cord so the cut edges are even. Using a regular-length stitch, stitch back and forth across the end, through both the cover and the cord.

● Using a zipper foot and a machine basting stitch, stitch just next to, but not crowded up against, the cord. Stitch for about 6" (15cm). Stop with the needle in the fabric.

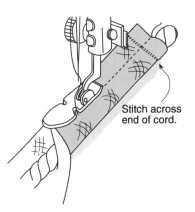

Stitch across end of cord.

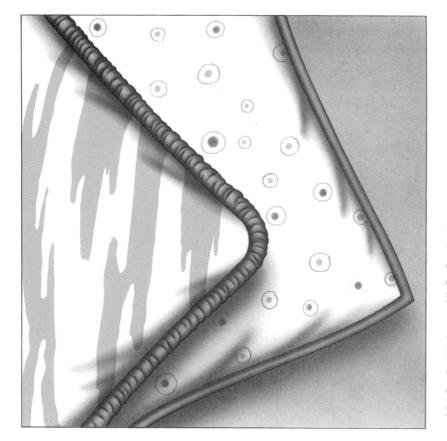

Double Welting

Double welting is an applied trim that is glued in place on upholstered projects, such as fabric-covered walls (see "The Stapled Wall" in Chapter 5, WONDERFUL WALLS AND CEILINGS) and drop-in seat covers (see page 210 in Chapter 11, TIMESAVERS).

It is made by covering double welt cord, which is available where upholstery supplies are sold. The double cord is actually two lengths of size 0 ($^5/_{32}$", or 4mm) piping cord knitted together.

To cover the double cord:

● Cut and piece 3" (7.5cm) wide bias strips of fabric—enough to cover the amount of welting needed.

● With the bias strip wrong side up, place the welting on top of the strip

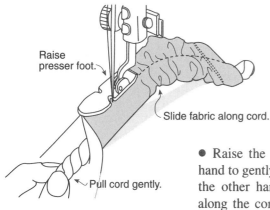

Raise presser foot.

Slide fabric along cord.

Pull cord gently.

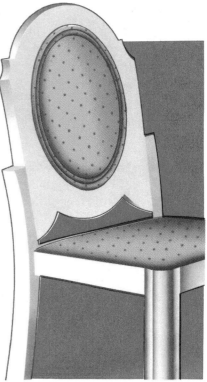

● Raise the presser foot. Use one hand to gently pull on the cord. Use the other hand to slide the fabric along the cord, behind the needle, until it is tightly shirred.

● Continue stitching and shirring in 6" (15cm) intervals until the entire cord is covered.

so that the right edge of the welting is aligned with the right edge of the strip. Stitch down the center of the welting.

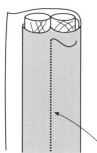

Stitch to bias strip.

- Wrap the left side of the bias strip over the front of the welting and around to the back. Stitch down the center of the welting, through all the layers.

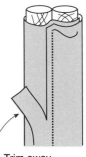

Wrap fabric around to back; stitch down middle again.

- Trim the excess fabric close to the stitching.

Trim away excess on back.

Pleats

Normally, pleats require a great deal of careful measuring. Happily, here are two painless techniques—one for box pleats and one for small knife pleats.

Box Pleats

Use this technique to create items like a box-pleated dust ruffle, a box-pleated valance or a box-pleated skirt on your slipcovers. The "secret" is Gosling® Folding Tape, a sew-in drapery tape that creates 3″ (7.5cm) deep pleats. And when you're finished making the pleats, you still have the tape for another project.

- Cut the section to be box-pleated 2½ times the finished length, piecing, if necessary. The width should be equal to the finished width plus hem allowance plus 1½″ (3.8cm).
- Hem the lower edge.
- On the wrong side of the fabric, machine-baste the folding tape along the unfinished edge. Pull up the cords, forming the pleats.

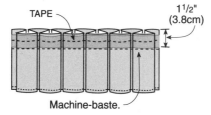

TAPE

1½" (3.8cm)

Machine-baste.

- Press the pleats. Machine-baste across the top of the project, just below the folding tape. Pull out the basting stitches, removing the tape. Trim 1″ (2.5cm) from the upper edge, then complete the project.

BOX PLEATS

KNIFE PLEATS

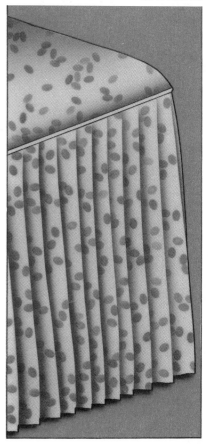

Knife Pleats

Substitute pleated trim for ruffles . . . or create a pillow with a beautifully pleated top . . . or transform a plain tieback into one with an interesting surface texture.

The Perfect Pleater™ is a stiff, fabric-covered board fashioned into tiny louvers. Following the manufacturer's instructions, simply tuck the fabric into the board at the required intervals. Press to set the pleats, using a steam iron and a press cloth soaked in a solution of one part white vinegar to nine parts water. Let dry. Remove the fabric and machine-baste close to the raw edges to secure the pleats.

If you can't find this item at your local fabric store, check your favorite sewing publication for a mail order source.

1. Tuck.

2. Press.

3. Stitch.

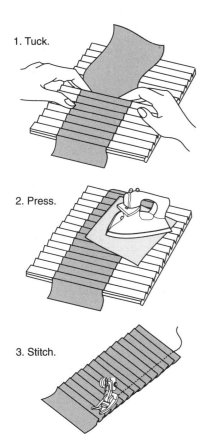

Ruffles

There are two types of ruffles:

● A *single ruffle* has one finished edge; the other edge is gathered and then incorporated into a seam or attached to an edge.

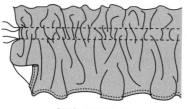

SINGLE RUFFLE

● A *double ruffle* has two finished edges. It is gathered at the center or near one edge and then topstitched in place.

DOUBLE RUFFLE

Cutting and Hemming

Ruffles are cut two to three times the length of the edge to which they are attached. The wider the ruffle or the more sheer the fabric, the fuller the ruffle should be. The width is equal to the finished depth of the ruffle, plus hem allowance and seam allowance (single ruffle) or two hem allowances (double ruffles).

Ruffles can be cut on the straight grain (more economical) or on the bias (for a softer effect). If necessary, piece the ruffle.

Hem the ruffle before gathering it. The preferred hemming techniques are the *narrow double hem* or the *serger rolled hem*.

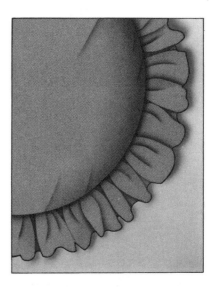

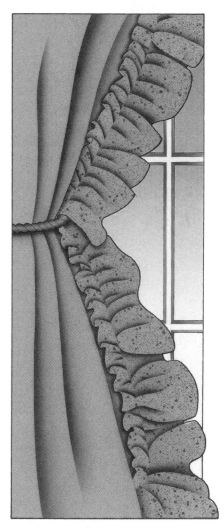

Gathering

For a single ruffle, use any of the gathering techniques described earlier in this chapter. For a double ruffle, use the *straight stitch gathering* technique on page 37.

Attaching

To attach a single ruffle in a seam or along the edge of a project, follow the instructions for *edgings* in this chapter.

To attach a double ruffle:

● Divide and mark the ruffle and placement line on the project into eighths or sixteenths.

● Pin the wrong side of the ruffle to the right side of the project, matching all the markings. Adjust the gathers to fit.

● Topstitch over the gathering stitches. Then remove the gathering stitches or hide them under a flat trim, such as ribbon or rickrack, topstitched in place.

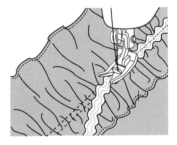

TIPS

On a single ruffle, eliminate the hem by cutting the strips twice the finished width plus 1″ (2.5cm). Piece, then fold in half lengthwise, wrong sides together. Gather ½″ (1.3cm) from the raw edges.

Since this technique will create extra bulk at the piecing seams (especially on mid- to heavyweight fabrics), here's another tip:

● Diagonally trim the ends of the ruffle sections before piecing.

When the ruffle is folded in half, the seams won't match because they're on the bias.

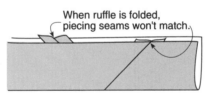

When ruffle is folded, piecing seams won't match.

● Trimming diagonally will shorten each ruffle section. Therefore, to maintain your fullness ratio, you'll need to cut longer strips. The total extra amount equals the number of piecing seams times the width of the ruffle.

When determining the finished length of projects like dust ruffles or curtains, be sure to take the depth of the ruffle into account.

CHAPTER 5

Wonderful Walls and Ceilings

Wonderful Walls and Ceilings

Walls, ceilings and floors are potentially the largest areas of color and texture in a room. These three surfaces can serve as the background canvas for your decorating scheme or as the focal points.

While the surfaces of your walls and ceilings can be changed fairly easily, floors are usually a more permanent investment. It's generally wise to concentrate on selecting a carpet, floor tile or finish that will adapt easily to new decorating schemes. Then, when the redecorating bug strikes, other details, such as window treatments, wall coverings, paint, accessories or even the furniture arrangements, can be the vehicles for change.

Thanks to new tools and types of paints, wallpapers and fabric-installation systems, walls are wonderful places to try out your do-it-yourself decorating savvy. This chapter concentrates on three different ways to enhance your walls with fabric.

As a wall covering, fabric offers several distinct advantages over wallpaper or paint.

- Because you can unroll the fabric and view a larger expanse, it is often easier to visualize exactly how a particular fabric will look when applied to a wall. Wallpaper, on the other hand, often seems to undergo a personality change once it is applied to the wall.

- As a camouflage for a less-than-perfect wall, fabric can hide years of paint, peelings and putty. By stretching or pasting a glorious print fabric taut across a span, the minor bumps and imperfections on the wall seem to disappear. By stapling a batting underneath that fabric, you can achieve a padded, upholstered look. Plus, if your fabric is light in color and the surface behind it is dark, batting is an easy way to whitewash the wall. More now-you-see-it-now-you-don't magic can be created by shirring or gathering fabric across the area.

- Fabric-covered walls will absorb sound better than painted ones, particularly if the surface is padded first with a layer of batting.

- Fabric, unlike wallpaper or paint, is a portable investment. If you should decide to move, it can come with you. If you get tired of it, you can take it off the wall and give it a new role in life.

GENERAL INSTRUCTIONS

In the pages that follow, there are three different methods for covering walls with fabric—the shirred wall, the pasted wall and the stapled wall. No matter which one you choose, some of the basic techniques are the same:

- For easiest handling, select a fabric that is lightweight and firmly woven. See Chapter 11, TIME-SAVERS, for special considerations when working with sheets.

● Press out any wrinkles or folds.

● Look for fabrics that are printed "on grain." However, if the fabric you love is a bit askew, go with the design, not the grain, when the stapling or pasting method is used.

● When covering a whole room with fabric, you can be almost certain that it will be impossible to match a motif at the final seam. Therefore, plan the start/stop point to occur at the least conspicuous vertical place in the room. A door located near a corner of the room would be a particularly good choice, since only the short distance above the door would be unmatched. Another idea is to "bury" the mismatched seam in a corner where it will be concealed by furniture.

● The method you choose for covering your walls will depend on the look you wish to achieve and the condition of your walls. Each technique has its own advantages and limitations. Use the chart on page 62 to help you decide.

● Since techniques for matching and joining the seams vary slightly, they will be explained under each wall-covering method.

● Correct any leaks, mildew or other plumbing or moisture problems on walls, air conditioners or around windows. Fabric will only highlight such defects if they are not repaired. Plus, if the problem persists, it might damage your fabric.

● Do any necessary painting on moldings, trim and windows before hanging the fabric. If desired, moldings can be removed, painted and replaced after the fabric is installed.

● Remove switch plates, vent covers, old window-curtain hardware, etc.

● To clean fabric-covered walls, vacuum them occasionally, using the wand attachment. With the shirred method, it's easy to remove and reinstall the fabric when it requires laundering or dry cleaning.

The Plumb Line

Regardless of the method, your first order of business is to determine the plumb, or true vertical, of each wall. Even if your fabric is true to grain, your walls often are not. If you simply align a vertical motif with the corner of the room, the result may be a very biased view by the time you've worked your way around to meet that corner. If you live in a crooked little (or big!) house, allover prints are often a better choice than stripes or plaids.

To create a plumb line:

● Tie a weight to a piece of string equal to the height of the wall. While the pros use a plumb bob, a fishing sinker, scissors or a gym lock is each a great substitute. Rub the string with soft carpenter's chalk; then thumbtack it to the top edge of the wall, about 4″ (10cm) in from the corner.

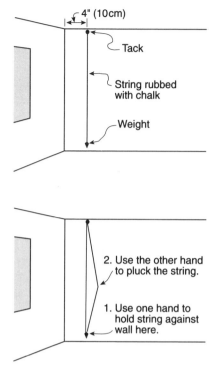

● When the weighted string stops swaying, use one hand to hold the string flat against the wall, just above the weight. Use the other hand to "pluck" the cord. The mark that the chalk dust leaves on the wall will be the alignment line your design motif should follow.

Repeat this plumb process on every wall. Then check to see how far "off" each corner is from its plumb

TIP

If you prefer wallpaper, remember that many wallpaper lines have fabric coordinates that can be used to create matching soft furnishings and accessories. Even sheet manufacturers are cross-merchandising their patterns. Designs that are mated to, or coordinated with, bed linens can be found in wallpaper books as well as in the linen, china, lighting and accessory departments of many retail stores and mail-order catalogs.

If wallpapering a whole room seems an overwhelming challenge, consider using a border design around the edge of the ceiling, to outline a window or as a chair rail.

line. If your walls are very crooked, repeat the plumb-line process at intervals equal to the width of your fabric.

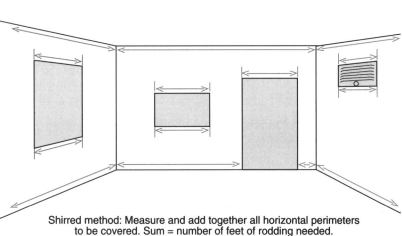

Plumb-line

Be sure same repeat lines up
with plumb line guide.

Now that you have established the true vertical—caused by the pull of gravity on the weighted string—use that line to chart your course. If your fabric has a geometric design, align the lengthwise stripe or motif with the plumb line. On other types of prints, look for a motif that repeats vertically on the fabric. Once that vertical repeat is tacked in place, stretch or paste the remaining fabric out and away from that guide.

TIP

Before investing your time and energy in painting a large expanse of walls and/or ceilings, purchase just one quart of the desired color of paint. Apply it to the wall or ceiling, then live with it for a few days. The type and amount of lighting in the room can change the color significantly once it is on the wall. Note, too, the different effects of daylight and nighttime lighting.

✤
THE SHIRRED, OR GATHERED, WALL

This treatment is a wonderful way to cover a multitude of sins. And exact matching, although always effective, is not as critical as with flat or smooth wall treatments.

Shirred walls require a lot of fabric, generally 2½ to 3½ times the width of each wall. In a small room, you may find covering all four walls a bit overpowering. But covering just one wall can create the desired dramatic impact without overextending your budget.

Supplies:

● *Fabric.*

● *Shirring rods*, *cord* or *wire*, as detailed below.

● *Eye hooks*, *staples*, *cup hooks* or *curtain brackets*, as determined by the choice of rod.

Measure the horizontal perimeters of all the areas to be covered with fabric, including tops of doors, tops and bottoms of walls, windows and any significant obstructions. The sum of these lengths is the amount of rodding needed to hold the shirred fabric.

Half-round wood molding, lattice strips, café-curtain rods, polyvinyl chloride (PVC) pipe (available at plumbing-supply stores), clothesline, wire or heavy cord are all options. If wire, cord or any other flexible item is used, staples or screw eyes must be installed along the horizontal perimeters to hold the cord taut.

For a designer look, consider using a thicker rod. Wood or brass works fine, but since you're covering the rod with fabric anyway, why not try this inexpensive idea? Do a little scavenging at the fabric, track lighting or carpet store. Those sturdy, throw-away fiberboard tubes can serve as a nice plump rod. Because they are hollow, you can thread a strong string through one end and out the other. The cardboard rod will rest on the string, which is then tied to cup hooks, curtain-rod brackets or even a few nails. To cover a wide space, use a series of

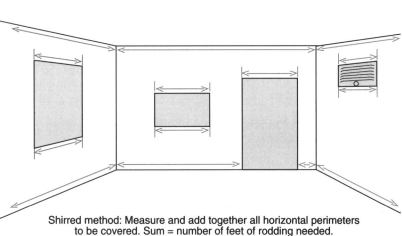

Shirred method: Measure and add together all horizontal perimeters
to be covered. Sum = number of feet of rodding needed.

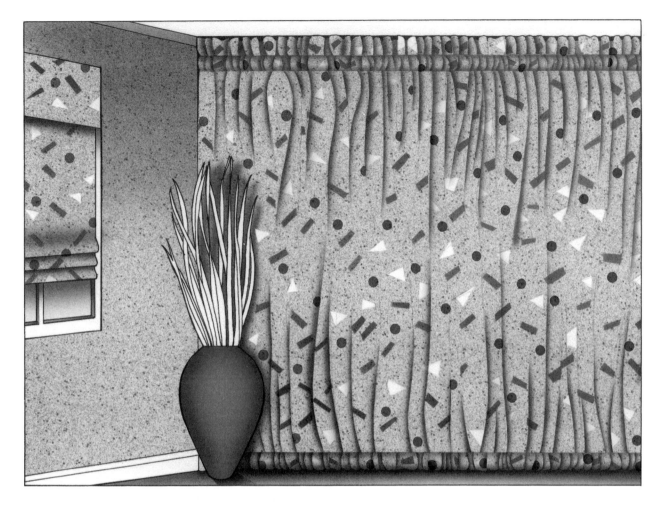

tubes. Just hang each tube on its own string. The ends of the tubes are easily concealed by the fullness of the fabric.

PVC pipe is installed the same way. On wide spans, it has a tendency to droop. Therefore, a sup-port bracket, nylon fishing line or string, tied to ceiling or wall, should be added as necessary. If you have some thinner curtain rods on hand, use them instead of string as the inner support for the PVC pipe or cardboard tubes.

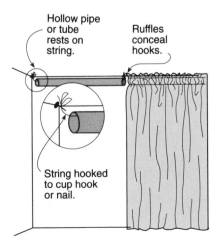

Hollow pipe or tube rests on string.

Ruffles conceal hooks.

String hooked to cup hook or nail.

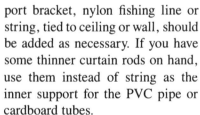

TIP

You may be able to subtract some yardage for doors and windows, depending on how large the openings, where the seams will fall and the size of the repeat. It's easier to ignore these openings in your initial calculations and then use the "leftovers" for pillows and other small projects.

How Much Fabric?

Review "Fabric Basics" in Chapter 4, THE SEWING BASICS. Then:

● To determine your total width, measure your wall width(s), then multiply by $2\frac{1}{2}$ to $3\frac{1}{2}$, depending on the weight of your fabric. Light-weight fabrics can generally accommodate more fullness than heavier ones. The fuller the allowance, the more luxurious the effect.

● Determine where your rods will be installed. Measure from the top of the upper rod to the bottom of the lower rod. Add allowances for casings, with or without a header. (See "Curtains: General Directions" in Chapter 6, WINDOWS: A DIFFERENT VIEW.) This total is the length of each panel.

FABRIC-COVERED WALLS

SITUATION	THE BEST METHOD				Notes
	Shirred	Pasted	Stapled (directly to wall)	Stapled (to lattice strips)	
Tight budget, least expense		X	X		
Damaged walls	X			X[1]	[1] Adding batting will help conceal damage.
Smooth Sheetrock walls	X	X	X		
Conceal stucco or siding	X[1]			X[2]	[1] Hang from ceiling in front of wall. [2] Use lattice as "thick" as necessary. Batting will help cover the texture.
Drafty room/ poor insulation	X		X[1]	X[1]	[1] Batting will provide additional insulation.
Quick, temporary fix	X[1]				[1] Gather on fiberboard tubes. Run string through tubes and tie to cup hooks.
Noisy room	X		X[1]	X[1]	[1] Batting underneath will help absorb more sound.
Covering paneling	X		X[1]	X[1]	[1] Add batting to help conceal dark color and fill in grooves.
Staples can't penetrate the walls	X	X		X	
Dirt	X[1]				[1] Panels can be removed easily for cleaning.
Extreme humidity changes (as in bathroom)	X[1]	X[1],[2] possibly			[1] Correct any mildew problems first. [2] Add staples to ceiling fabric if necessary.
Covering cinder-block walls				X[1]	[1] Use additional adhesive to secure strips to wall.
No-sew method		X	X	X	
Easiest to replace or change	X				
Limited yardage		X[1]	X		[1] Easiest to piece, no hems to tuck.
College dorm or rental apartment	X[1]	X[2]			[1] Only need a few nails at ceiling. [2] Pulls right off, paste washes away.

- To determine how many panels are needed, divide the total width (2½ to 3½ times the wall widths) by the fabric's usable width.

- To determine total yardage, multiply the number of panels by the length of each panel, then divide by 36″ (91.5cm) to convert inches (centimeters) to yards (meters).

Wall Preparation

Gather up the fabric in your hand; then check to see if it will conceal any color or pattern already on the wall. If it does, you're ready to begin. However, if the color does show through, either paint your walls an unobtrusive white or staple a layer of white batting on top of the existing wall. The latter is ideal for severely damaged walls or to preserve certain surfaces, such as real wood paneling or rough stucco.

Method

- Install the hardware of choice—cup hooks, screw eyes, sash brackets, etc.—along the horizontal perimeters. If you're using a flexible cord or wire as your rod, and it is difficult to staple or screw into the actual wall, it may be necessary to glue or nail lattice strips along these perimeters before installing the

Shirred walls usually are installed on a rod at the top and bottom of the wall. If you prefer, fabric can just hang from the top rod to the floor, like a long curtain, rather than be pulled taut.

Make a sample casing to check on the tightness and proportion.

hardware. Refer to "The Stapled Wall" on pages 68–69 for information on attaching the lattice strips.

- Cut the fabric into panels equal to the total length.

- Hem or serge-finish the sides of each panel. If you are using sheets, which have no selvage markings, this step is optional.

- Make casings across the top and bottom edges of each panel.

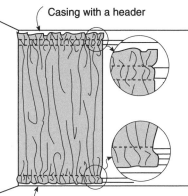

Casing with a header

Casing without a header

- Insert the rod or cords through the casings.

- Hang the rods or cords, then adjust the fullness.

❀

THE PASTED WALL

Pasting, which requires no sewing, is one of the quickest methods of applying fabric to walls. The fabric adheres directly to the existing surface. Therefore, to achieve the best results, the walls must be smooth, light in color and crack-free. While slightly textured surfaces can also be covered this way, every bump will show through. On such walls, a busy, allover print would be the best choice. Always do a "patch test" to

see if your choices of fabric and glue are compatible (see supplies just below). Let the patch dry thoroughly, then check the fabric for any discoloration.

Supplies:

- *Fabric.*

- *Glue.* Choose one of the following:

  Powdered cellulose or *wheat paste.* Check the manufacturer's instructions and claims. Look for a nonyellowing, mildew-resistant product whose label states that it is suitable for hanging fabric.

  Premixed vinyl paste. Check the color of the paste. Some are dark and may distort your fabric's coloring. Check, too, that it's labeled "mildew-resistant" and suitable for hanging fabric.

- *Liquid starch.*

- *Drop cloth* or *plastic sheets* to protect the floor.

- *Plumb line* or *level.*

- *Tacks and hammer.*

- *Straight-edge ruler* or *yardstick.*

- *Wallpaper cutter/knife* with snap-off blades.

- *Paste* or *painter's brushes* or *sponge brushes.*

- *Wallpaper smoothing brush.*

- Several *café-curtain clip-on rings, large safety pins* or *artist's clamps.*

How Much Fabric?

Review "Fabric Basics," in Chapter 4, THE SEWING BASICS. Then:

- To determine the total width, measure your wall width(s). Do not adjust for window and door openings.

● To determine how many panels are required, divide the total width by your fabric's usable width.

● To determine the length of each panel, measure the height of the wall. Add 3″–6″ (7.5cm–15cm) for waste allowance.

● To determine total yardage, multiply the number of panels by the length of each panel. Then divide that number by 36″ (91.5cm) to convert inches to yards (centimeters to meters). If you have selected a fabric with a repeat, an extra repeat may be required for each panel, depending on how the repeat relates to the wall's height.

Wall Preparation

● Clean the walls. If painted, wash with a mild detergent; if wallpapered, vacuum thoroughly. If the walls are dark—and your fabric is light—apply an undercoat of white paint. If you're covering new Sheetrock walls, prime them with paint. Otherwise, when you remove the

fabric sometime in the future, the glue may pull the paper covering away from the wall. This primer will also help ensure good adhesion. It is particularly important for new walls. Without the protection of a primer, the glue may be absorbed into the wall, resulting in a spotty paste job.

● Remove all switch plates and vent covers.

● Draw a plumb line on each wall to be covered.

Method

Matching and piecing are done right on the wall. The technique is simple: Overlap the design motifs slightly; then, working through both fabrics, cut away the overlap.

● Cut the first fabric panel equal to the height of the wall plus 4″–6″ (10cm–15cm).

● Apply the paste smoothly to the wall, using a wide paste or painter's brush and covering the upper third of the wall. Cover an area slightly wider than the width of your fabric.

If your fabric is very heavy, clips or clamps may not be strong enough to hold it. If this is the case, large safety pins may be the best choice.

If your fabric is hard to cut, wait until the paste dries.

● Align a motif (not necessarily the selvage) with the plumb line and allow a 2″–3″ (5cm–7.5cm) margin at the top. If you're covering more than one wall, position the first panel so the left side wraps around the start-up corner for 1″–2″ (2.5cm–5cm). Using the smoothing brush, straight-edge ruler or rag, smooth the fabric in place on the wall. Brush out from the plumb line and up toward the top. If the fabric is very heavy, use a few sharp tacks to temporarily hold the fabric in place along the upper edge.

● Carefully lift the remaining fabric away from the wall. Apply paste to the middle third of the wall. Working with a buddy helps—you have someone to hold the fabric out of the way while you apply the glue. No helper? Catch the fabric up with a curtain clip or an artist's clamp. Hook it to a nail tapped in along the upper edge of the wall.

● Smooth the fabric in the just-pasted area, working out from the plumb line and down from the previously pasted area.

● Repeat, pasting and smoothing the fabric over the lower third of the wall.

● With a razor-sharp craft knife and straight edge, cut away the excess fabric on the top and bottom edges.

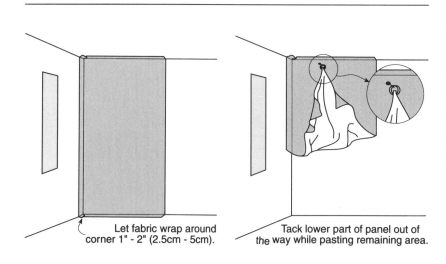

Let fabric wrap around corner 1″ - 2″ (2.5cm - 5cm).

Tack lower part of panel out of the way while pasting remaining area.

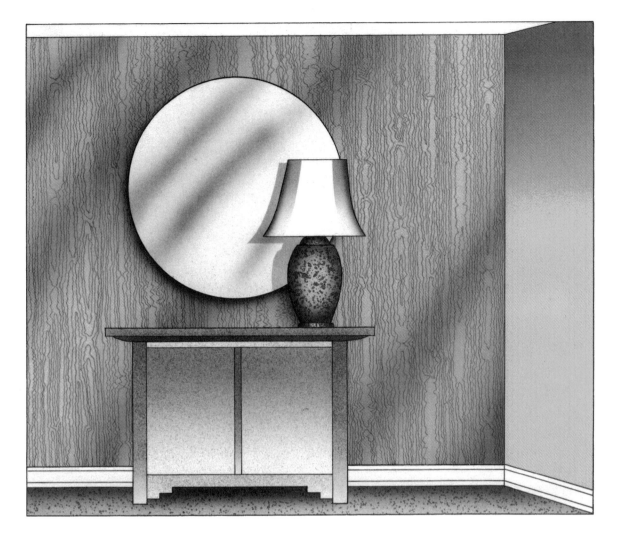

Since the knife blades dull easily, they should be changed after every few cuts.

• Cut the fabric for the second panel. Plan on a 1″–2″ (2.5cm–

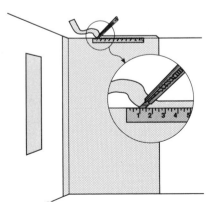

Use yardstick or straight-edge ruler to trim away excess fabric at top and bottom.

5cm) side margin for overlapping the design match. Apply paste to the upper third of the wall, including the underlap (right margin) of the first panel. Smooth the fabric in place, making sure the design matches exactly at and under the overlap. Repeat, pasting and smoothing the rest of the panel in place.

• Hold a straight edge firmly in place against the wall, midway between the overlap and the underlap. Using a craft knife, and working from top to bottom, slash through both layers of fabric.

• Remove the fabric strips on the overlapping edge. Then gently peel back the fabric and remove the un-

derlapping strip. Smooth the second panel back in place. If necessary, brush a little more paste on the wall along the seam.

TIPS

Check to see if the chalk line will show or bleed through your fabric. If so, either wash it away just before you permanently paste the fabric down or tack a weighted string to the ceiling so it hangs along the wall, just in front of the area where you are working.

For more ideas, see "Decorating with Sheets" in Chapter 11, TIMESAVERS.

- Trim the top and bottom allowances as for the first panel.

- Repeat, pasting, smoothing and trimming the remaining panels.

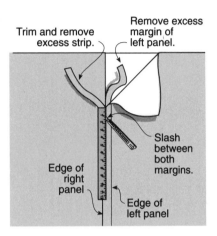

Trim and remove excess strip.

Remove excess margin of left panel.

Slash between both margins.

Edge of right panel

Edge of left panel

- Air bubbles can be stubborn, refusing to go away or appearing only after you think you're all done. If this happens, prick the area with a pin or make a small slash and rework the area, smoothing the fabric to the wall. Be sure the room is well lit, especially if you are working at night. Otherwise, air bubbles may mysteriously appear once daylight arrives.

TIPS

If the edges of your fabric should loosen from the wall, this problem is much easier to correct on fabric than on wallpaper. Gently pull the fabric partially away from the wall, apply glue to the wall and smooth the fabric back in place.

As an alternative, apply a thin solution of glue right on top of the affected area. As the fabric softens again, the glue will be absorbed through the fabric and onto the wall. Smooth the area with a rag or brush.

Depending on the fabric and glue, tiny air bubbles may appear under the fabric. If this occurs, finish one wall, then brush on a thin coat of liquid starch. This "sizing" seems to help eliminate the bubbles, as well as to add a protective layer to help ward off dust and dirt.

THE STAPLED WALL

Another method, favored by decorators, is to staple the fabric directly to the wall or to lattice strips that are secured to the wall. Seaming can be done directly on the wall with staples, or several panels can be joined at the sewing machine and then hung on the wall. If you choose the latter method, be aware that handling, and hanging, more than two or three widths of fabric is difficult. For wide walls, a combination of preseamed and direct on-the-wall seaming may best suit your needs.

For a luxurious look, as well as clever camouflage for poor walls, staple a layer of polyester batting to the wall before hanging the decorative fabric. This will also provide additional insulation benefits, reducing both drafts and noise.

If you have Sheetrock walls, or another covering that will accept the staples, there is no need to add lattice strips. If you have difficult-to-staple walls, such as plaster or cinder block, then you must first attach strips of wood. Once they are in place, the fabric can be stapled to the strips. The best way to tell if your walls will accept the staples is simply to test this method out on several different spots. If the staples adhere securely, eliminate any reference to lattice strips in the instructions that follow.

Supplies:

- *Fabric*.

- *Polyester batting* (optional). It's preferable to purchase this as continuous yardage rather than in prepackaged sizes.

- *Lattice wood strips* (optional), approximately 1″ × ¼″ (2.5cm × 6mm) times the length needed.

- Hand or electric *staple gun*. Be sure the gun can reach into a corner when held flush against the wall and that the staples eject from the very edge of the stapler. An electric gun makes the job a lot easier.

- *Staples*—⁵/₁₆″ (7.5mm) chisel point.

- If using *lattice strips*, choose one of the following for securing the strips to the wall:

  Nails—6d finishing nails, 2″ (5cm) long.

  Construction adhesive. Use if wood cannot be nailed to the wall. *Liquid Nails*™ or *a nonflammable contact cement* could be used.

- *Carpet or upholstery tacks*. Use to "blind tack" the final seam or areas around the doors and windows.

- *Upholsterer's tape*. This is a ³/₈″ (1cm) wide strip of cardboard, sold on a roll and available from upholstery-supply sources. The tape

provides a sharp, straight edge along seams and prevents the fabric from pulling or gapping when stretched. An excellent alternative is *clear packing tape*, the type used on heat-shrunk parcel wrappings. Check an office-supply or packaging store for these items.

● White or light-colored *masking tape* (optional). Use it to cover the upholsterer's tape if it shows through light-colored fabric. Available at art-supply stores.

● *Pushpins*. Long, sharp-pointed ones work best, ½″ (1.3cm), 100 per box. These are available from upholstery-supply stores or art-

supply shops. You'll need one or two boxes.

● *Leather thimble* or *a few bandages*. Either is an invaluable finger-saver when pushpinning into walls.

● *Plumb line*.

● *Model toy paint*, matched to a predominant color in the fabric. Use it to cover the backs of staples before loading them into the gun. Color only those staples that will not be covered later by trim.

● Squeeze-type *café-curtain rings* or *large safety pins*. Use a few to grip and hold the fabric to temporary nails placed along the ceiling line.

● *Carpenter's level*. An additional aid in checking the "plumb" of the fabric.

● *Wallpaper cutter* with a snap-off blade.

● *Air-soluble marking pen* and/or *chalk marking pencils*.

● *Scissors*.

● *Yardstick*.

● *Tape measure*.

● *Hammer, nails, pliers* and *screwdriver* may all be needed at some point during your project.

● *Cording, trim* or *other finishing treatments* (optional).

How Much Fabric?

For batting and fabric:

See "The Pasted Wall/How Much Fabric?" on pages 63–64. When calculating the amount of batting, there is no need to allow extra for matching.

For welting, cord or trim:

Measure the lengths and heights of walls, windows, doors and other areas you wish to outline with trim. Add these measurements together.

Wall Preparation

Review the "General Instructions" at the beginning of this chapter.

Method

To Apply the Lattice Strips

● Cut the strips to the lengths required to outline the perimeters of the walls, doors and windows, as well as other obstructions, such as switch plates, air conditioners, wall vents, etc. Since the wood is thin, it is easy to cut. A saw, garden clippers or even a serrated knife will work fine. Do not be concerned with mitering the corners or getting a tight fit.

● Run a bead of adhesive down the middle of the wrong side of each

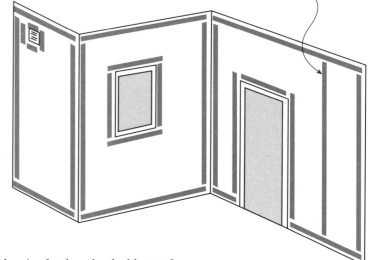

May need additional strips for batting and/or fabric, depending on width of fabric, and if not preseamed.

strip. Apply the glued side to the wall and hold in place by tapping 2″ (5cm) finishing nails every 12″–24″ (30.5cm–61cm) along the strip.

● You will need to attach vertical lattice strips under the fabric seams and any batting seams. Because fabric and batting widths may be different, the placement of these seams usually will not match.

If you are preseaming two or more fabric panels, it is not necessary to place lattice strips under these seams.

If you are seaming the fabric on the walls, wait until you are ready to hang each panel before attaching the corresponding wood strip. Then make a vertical slash through the

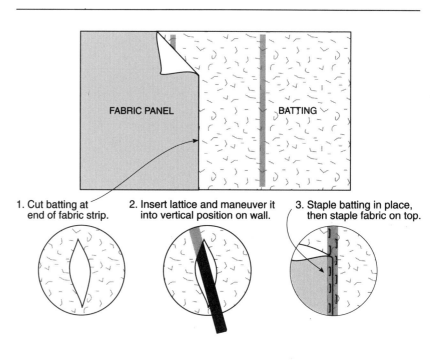

FABRIC PANEL   BATTING

1. Cut batting at end of fabric strip.

2. Insert lattice and maneuver it into vertical position on wall.

3. Staple batting in place, then staple fabric on top.

batting, where the seam will fall, about two-thirds of the way down the wall. Apply glue to the back of the wood strip, insert it between batting and wall, then wiggle it into place. Staple the batting to this new strip.

● For strips not adjacent to a corner or an edge (for example, the vertical strips under a seam), use a level to mark a guideline on the wall before applying the strips.

To Apply the Batting

● Cut the batting to the height of the area to be covered. Pushpin in place.

● Staple the batting around the perimeters of the area directly to the wall or onto the lattice strips. Place the staples every 8″–12″ (20.5cm–30.5cm) apart. Butt the edges of the batting to form the seams.

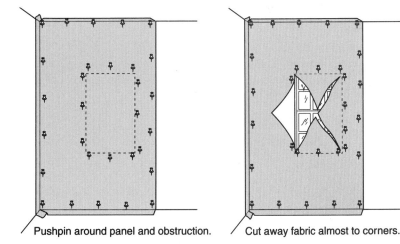

Pushpin around panel and obstruction. Cut away fabric almost to corners.

To Apply the Fabric

● Drop or mark a plumb line a few inches (centimeters) away from the left corner of the first wall to be covered. (See the "General Instructions" at the beginning of this chapter.)

● Allow a few extra inches (centimeters) of fabric on the left side as a margin to wrap around the adjacent corner or to be trimmed and turned under. Match the motif repeats to the guideline and pushpin the fabric in place along the top, then sides, then bottom edges. Allow a few inches (centimeters) of margin at the top and bottom. Pull the fabric as taut as possible.

● If there is an obstruction, pushpin around it. When you're sure of the panel placement, cut away the fabric almost to the corners, leaving a margin for error and for a turn-under. For more information, see "Special Problem Areas" on pages 72–73 of this chapter.

● Trim the top and bottom allowances, leaving ½″ (1.3cm) margins for turning under. For a neat, sharp appearance, insert a piece of upholsterer's tape inside each fold, then staple the edge in place.

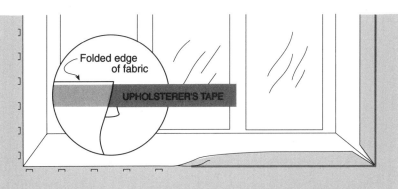

Folded edge of fabric

UPHOLSTERER'S TAPE

Fold fabric under. Insert upholsterer's tape inside fold, then staple to wall.

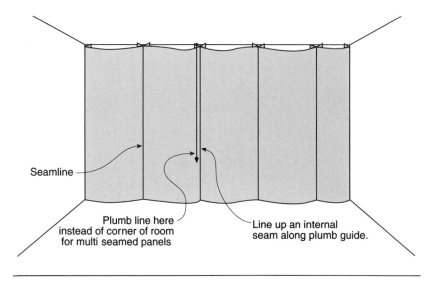

Seamline

Plumb line here instead of corner of room for multi seamed panels

Line up an internal seam along plumb guide.

If you're working alone, tap a few nails along the ceiling line and use safety pins or café-curtain clip-on rings to help support the weight of the fabric.

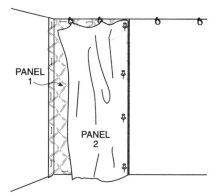

PANEL 1

PANEL 2

On vertical seams, pull a bit of the batting over the staples to conceal the dimples.

If the cardboard strip shows through the fabric, cover with a thin strip of white masking tape.

- If applying preseamed panels, drop the plumb line at one of the internal seams, then work from the plumb line out. (See Chapter 4, THE SEWING BASICS, for information on how to match seams.)

To Join the Seams Directly on the Wall

- Attach the first panel as explained above. Staple the right edge of the fabric to the wall or lattice strip, pulling taut, without turning the edge under.

- Hold the next panel to the right of the first panel (overlapping at least ½" [1.3cm]) and select a matching detail for a guide. Press a crease down the overlapping edge, along the length of the panel, using the matching motif as your guide. If necessary, trim the turned-under seam allowance to ½" (1.3cm). If needed, loosely tack the panel in place with pushpins or small nails as you work.

- With right sides together, pushpin the second panel over the first

along the vertical seam. Check the design match and adjust, if necessary.

- Position a strip of upholsterer's tape over the seam allowance, so the left edge abuts the crease. Staple

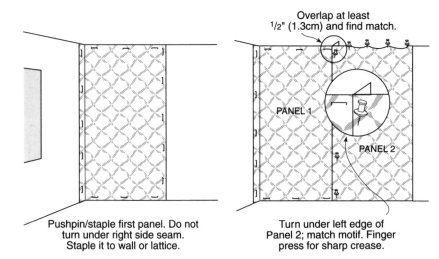

Pushpin/staple first panel. Do not turn under right side seam. Staple it to wall or lattice.

Overlap at least ½" (1.3cm) and find match.

PANEL 1

PANEL 2

Turn under left edge of Panel 2; match motif. Finger press for sharp crease.

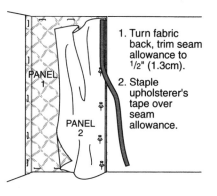

PANEL 1

PANEL 2

1. Turn fabric back, trim seam allowance to ½" (1.3cm).

2. Staple upholsterer's tape over seam allowance.

TIPS

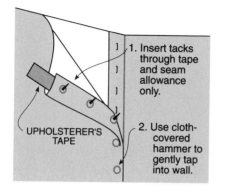

1. Insert tacks through tape and seam allowance only.

UPHOLSTERER'S TAPE

2. Use cloth-covered hammer to gently tap into wall.

To avoid seeing staples at the last seam or around any obstruction, blind-tack the edge. To do this, turn the seam allowance under and insert upholsterer's tape into the fold. Working from inside the fold, push flathead carpet tacks through the tape, then through the seam allowance. Align the fold with the edge of the wall or the obstruction and, using a cloth-covered hammer, gently tap the tacks in place.

For information on how to create your own piping or double welting, see "Special Touches" in Chapter 4, THE SEWING BASICS, page 51.

● When gluing double welting in place, be sure the trimmed edge is against the wall.

● To conceal the seam allowance on the piping, remove the staples or pushpins, slip the seam allowance under the folded edge of the fabric and then staple the fabric back in place through all layers.

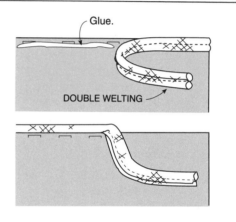

Glue.

DOUBLE WELTING

Tuck seam allowance of welting under top folded edge of fabric panel.

every 2″ (5cm) through the tape and both layers of fabric.

● Flip the second panel to the right, smooth and pushpin in place. Staple the top, bottom and right edges of the panel.

● Repeat for the remaining panels.

● If possible, plan seam joints at the corners. If not, run the fabric around the corner, staple the fabric to hold it into the corner and cover later with a decorative trim.

● For the final seam, trim the panel, leaving a ½″ (1.3cm) seam allowance. Turn the seam allowance

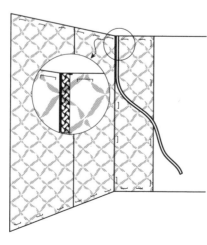

Finish corners with molding or trim.

under, insert upholsterer's tape and staple in place.

For the Finishing Touches

Cover the top and bottom edges with single or double welting, braid or other trim. Apply with white, clear-drying craft glue or a hot glue gun.

To create a border on the pasted or stapled wall, use ribbon or cut out bands of coordinating fabric. Fuse in place directly on the wall, using a fusible web with release paper. For inspiration, see the dining room in the color section of this book.

SPECIAL PROBLEM AREAS

Large Obstructions: Windows, Doors, Wall-Mounted Air Conditioners, etc.

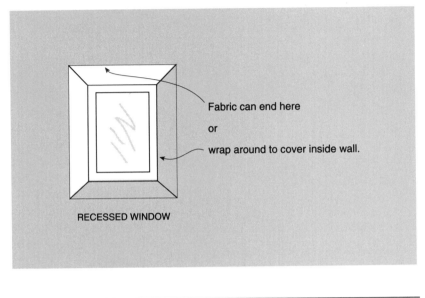

Fabric can end here

or

wrap around to cover inside wall.

RECESSED WINDOW

In general, it is best to hang full panels of fabric and then cut away the areas for doors, windows and built-ins. Somehow, when you cut first, these obstructions seem to "move," sneakily changing their size or their position!

● Paste or staple the best you can over the area.

● Then, when you're sure of the match to the previous panel, cut through the areas to be removed. Cut away as large a piece of fabric as possible, while allowing a few extra inches (centimeters) to cover the inner edges of the opening and for any adjustments before the final cut.

If windowsills or moldings protrude, it will be necessary to readjust the fabric below. Make small diagonal cuts into the fabric at these corners.

● For stapled methods, turn the edges under.

● For pasted methods, use a razor to cut the fabric to meet the moldings.

On recessed windows, the fabric can end at the outer edges or wrap around to cover the inside walls as well. If you choose to cover these walls, you need to be aware that it's impossible to slash into the fabric so that the one panel completely covers all four inside walls.

Slash the fabric diagonally from the center of the opening to the outside corners. Wrap it to the inside of the window frame. Add a well-matched fabric patch at the corners where the bare spots occur.

If a cornice or other window treatment will be installed to cover the upper portion of the window, you have the option of leaving the inside top wall bare. This will eliminate the need to patch at those corners. To do this, slash the fabric at the center of the window opening up to the edge of the wall. Cut straight across along the edge of the wall until you reach the corner. Wrap the fabric to the inside and trim, as necessary.

If raveling is a problem, apply a few drops of seam sealant to any of these cut edges.

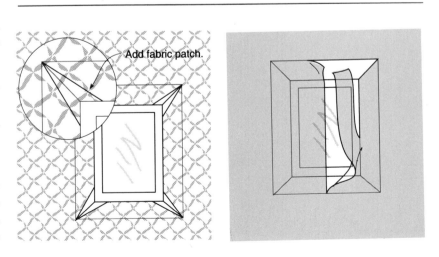

Add fabric patch.

Small Obstructions: Switch Plates, Vents, etc.

If the fabric is shirred and projects a distance from the wall, the easiest method may be simply to make a vertical slash at the plate area, apply seam sealant to the cut edges and

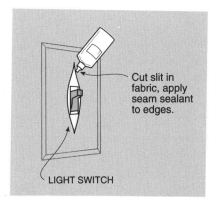

Cut slit in fabric, apply seam sealant to edges.

LIGHT SWITCH

"fish" for the outlet or switch when needed.

● If a dimmer dial is used, consider slashing the fabric so that only the dial is visible on the wall.

● If the switch or outlet is used frequently, it may soil easily. In this case, consider using the method that follows for the stapled or pasted wall.

CAUTION: Before doing any work around the switch plates or other electrical outlets, be sure to disconnect the power source.

If the fabric is stapled or pasted taut against the wall, remove all switch plates and vent covers before hanging the fabric. After the fabric is applied, locate the plate area and

Trim fabric, reapply switch plate.

carefully make a small slash in the fabric. Trim the fabric within the obstructed area. Make sure the fabric clears any wires under the plate, but that sufficient fabric remains so that the switch plate will cover the slashed edges. Apply seam sealant to the cut edges, then replace the plate.

TIP

For a custom touch, cover the switch plate to match your wall.

● Cut a rectangle of fabric 2″ (5cm) larger all around than the plate. For a perfect match, trace the shape of your plate onto a piece of lightweight tracing paper. Position the tracing paper

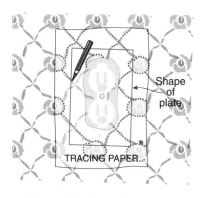

Shape of plate

TRACING PAPER.

Trace plate, then put paper over opening and trace fabric motif.

over the plate opening and trace the motif of the fabric underneath. Pin this pattern to the right side of your fabric, matching the traced motif to the fabric underneath. Cut the cover, adding 2″ (5cm) all around.

● Center the plate on the wrong side of the fabric. Fold the edges in and temporarily secure them with masking tape. Turn the plate over and use the paper pattern to check the position of the motif or check by holding the plate in position on the wall. Trim the excess fabric on the back of the plate to ½″ (1.3cm) and secure with masking tape.

● Cut an X in the switch or outlet openings. Fold the triangular flaps in to the wrong side of the plate; secure with masking tape.

Fold fabric to back of plate, tape in place.

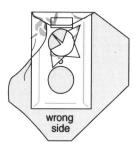

wrong side

● Use your seam ripper or the tip of your scissors to pierce the fabric at the screw holes. Apply seam sealant to all the cut edges.

● If the cover plate will be vulnerable to soil and wear, spray the area with a fabric protector, add a see-through cover plate or save your fabric remnants for follow-up re-covering, as needed.

✽

CEILINGS

Ceilings are particularly susceptible to damage, especially peeling paint, water stains and general cracks and fissures. Fabric is a wonderful way to camouflage these headaches. Depending on the installation method and the extent of the damage, you may be able to hide these defects without much additional surface preparation. A word of caution, however: If the original damage was caused by water, be sure the problem is corrected before you apply fabric to the ceiling. Otherwise, sooner or later, your fabric-covered ceiling will show evidence of water damage.

Since ceilings are usually out of reach of curious touch-and-feel guests, and gravity works a bit like a natural dustcloth, fabric-covered ceilings actually stay soil-free much longer than fabric-covered walls do.

Special Tips

All three of the wall techniques described in this chapter—shirring, pasting and stapling—can be utilized to cover a ceiling. While covering a ceiling does not require establishing a plumb line, there are some other considerations to keep in mind.

Unless you are working with a solid or an allover print, you will need to consider the direction of your motif. In any room, one wall

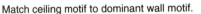

Match ceiling motif to dominant wall motif.

Divide ceiling into four triangles.

tends to be more dominant visually than the others. Often, it is the wall that is directly opposite the doorway. Generally, you'll want to position the ceiling fabric so that the motif matches, and continues to follow, the direction established on the dominant wall.

Another solution is to divide the ceiling into four triangles that meet at the center of the room. Each triangular section can be matched to its corresponding wall. This solution works best when the fabric is pasted to the ceiling. With the staple method, it's all too easy to stretch and distort the bias edges of the triangles.

Still another solution is to choose a coordinating solid or allover print. Nowhere does it say that your walls and ceiling must be covered in the exact same fabric!

Handling Gravity

One drawback to applying fabric to the ceiling is the weight of the fabric. Gravity, of course, compounds the problem. Here's where you need a friend, preferably a tall one, to help you. Together, you can put one of the following ideas to good use:

● Temporary tacks or nails can support the fabric while you are stapling or pasting it in place.

Secure to chair.

TIP

When a stripe or border print is sectioned into triangles, the result is a wonderful tent-like feeling. Note how changing the direction of the stripes alters the finished effect.

Stripes radiate out
from center of ceiling.

Stripes run up wall
to center of room on ceiling.

T-bar supports fabric.

● If your room is quite large, or the ceilings are higher than usual, a simple T-bar, secured between two chairs, will save everyone's arms from constant strain. To make one, start with a plank of plywood or scrap lumber at least 6″ (15cm) wide and as long, or slightly longer, than the width of your fabric. Nail the plank to an upright that is slightly shorter than the height of the room. Brace the upright between two straight-back chairs, or have your helper hold it where needed.

- Once the fabric is pressed, it can be rolled back onto one of the fabric tubes. With your helper holding the tube, the fabric can be gradually unrolled as needed.

- If the room is small, preseaming the panels may be a viable option. However, as a general rule, the pull of gravity makes working with more than one width of fabric a formidable task. In the case of the stapled application, the awkward stapling stance makes it even more difficult.

- On a shirred ceiling, consider installing additional rods across the span. The extra crosspieces will help support the weight.

If you want to conceal the extra rod(s), cut a strip of fabric long enough and wide enough to form the casing, plus 1″ (2.5cm) for seam allowances. Press the edges under ½″ (1.3cm). Then stitch the casing in place on the wrong side of the fabric, topstitching the long edges.

If you've selected a decorative rod, consider installing the rod so that the fabric merely rests on it. To achieve a bit of drama, cut the fabric slightly longer than the length of the ceiling so that it will drape in graceful swags between the rods.

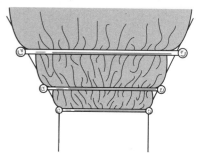

❁ ❁ ❁

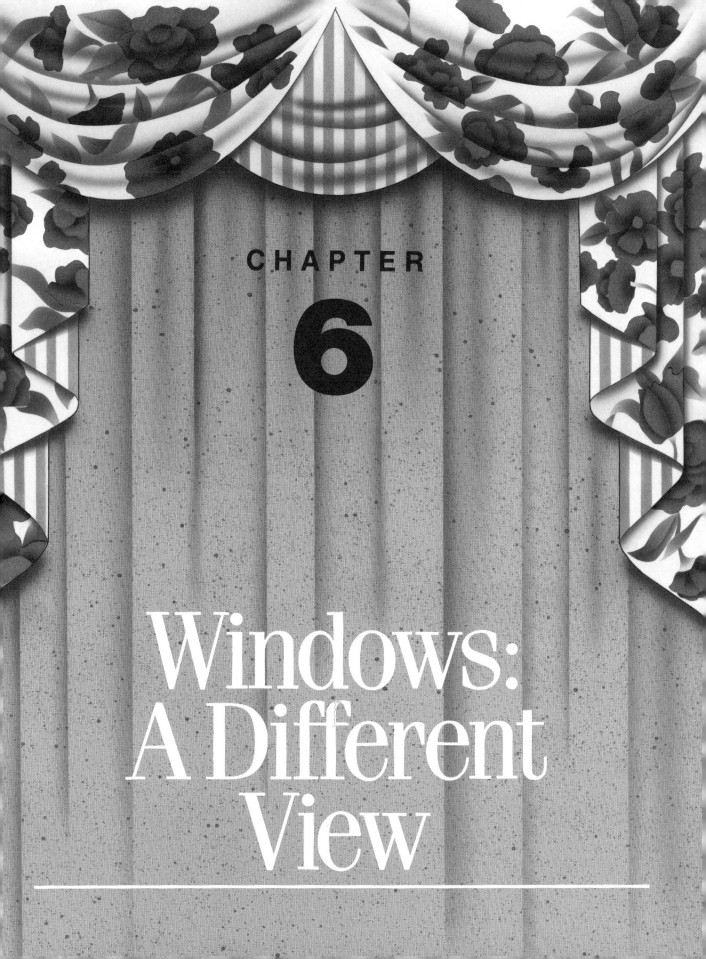

CHAPTER

6

Windows:
A Different
View

Windows: A Different View

In the hierarchy of decorating, windows rank right up there with walls in terms of their impact on a room. Whether tailored or frilly, minimal or opulent, they are the standard-bearers for the personality of the room.

When it comes to the actual sewing, window treatments are extremely easy to make. What sets the best-dressed windows apart are the small details: fine-tuning the placement of the hardware; using deep header, side and bottom hem allowances, as well as drapery weights, to ensure the treatment hangs properly; taking the exterior, as well as the interior, view into consideration; using linings, where appropriate; and determining the fullness that best suits your fabric. In this chapter, we've gathered our favorite tips, many direct from some of the finest custom workrooms, to help you create simply the best window treatments.

PRACTICAL CONSIDERATIONS

Since most windows are adaptable to a variety of treatments, how do you zero in on the best solution for your room? And how do you decide if a treatment that catches your eye in a magazine will be equally at home in your home?

Before you make any decisions regarding style, color and fabric, there are several factors to consider.

THE VIEW. Does the window have a view that you would like to incorporate into your decorating scheme? Then the window should be simply dressed, so that it functions as a frame for the view.

Consider plain drapes, matched to the wall color, which, when opened, stack back to expose the entire glass. If privacy is not an issue, a cornice with stationary side panels or a swag and jabot treatment are also possibilities.

WHEN THE ROOM IS USED MOST. Not all rooms are used all the time. Heavy daytime traffic calls for a treatment that admits maximum natural light. At night, however, the blackness of an open window can be chilling. In a room that is used primarily after dark, a heavily textured fabric or a layered window treatment can warm the atmosphere. Rooms that are used both day and night should have window treatments that strike a happy medium.

THE SUN FACTOR. A window with a northern exposure admits little or no direct sunlight. An eastern exposure admits strong morning sun, and a western exposure is flooded with strong, late-afternoon sun. A southern exposure creates the greatest problem because it is subject to direct sunlight most of the day. Unless heavily exposed windows are properly shaded with trees or awnings, fabrics may fade and/or the room may simply get too hot. Lined draperies, blinds or shades, which can be raised and lowered, or sun-filtering sheers should be considered.

WINDOW CONFIGURATIONS. Are the existing windows the same size? . . . the same shape? In many homes, living room and dining room windows may be the same length but may vary in width. In bedrooms, windows may be different widths *and* lengths. Plan the treatment for the largest window first, then dress the smaller ones in a scaled-down version. To unify the look, install all the hardware at the same height.

NOISE. Heavily textured fabrics and/or lined treatments help muffle street noises and absorb interior sounds.

HEATING SOURCES. For safety and efficiency, fabric should never touch or block radiators, vents or heating units. Consider heat deflectors, where appropriate, or choose a window treatment that clears the heat source.

HISTORIC INFLUENCES. The room's decorating scheme can be an important consideration. If the decor is heavily influenced by a particular era—for example, Victorian, eighteenth-century French or Early American—then you will probably want your window treatments to be compatible with the period.

MATCHING WINDOW TREATMENT TO WINDOW STYLE

The window treatment must also be compatible with the style of the window. It should not interfere with the way the window operates, and if the window is used for ventilation, it should not block the airflow.

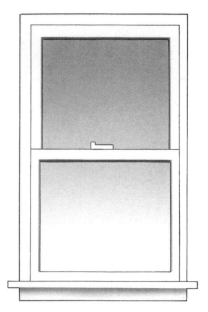

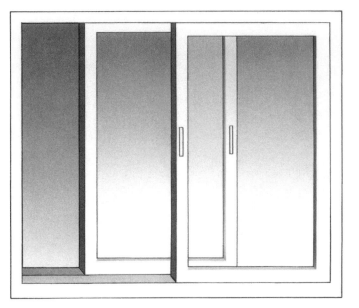

Double-hung windows are the most common. They consists of an upper and a lower sash. Both sashes can move up and down, allowing the window to open at the top or the bottom. These windows may consist of a single unit or multiple units separated by a common vertical wood casing.

Horizontally sliding windows generally have one stationary pane and one movable pane. Allowing for proper ventilation is the primary consideration.

W I N D O W S : A D I F F E R E N T V I E W

Picture windows consist of a large center window, alone or flanked by one or more fixed panes with movable sashes. With the latter, the window treatment should be able to clear the sashes for ventilation purposes.

Casement windows swing inward or outward. If they swing inward, the window treatment should be installed so that the fabric doesn't interfere with the operation of the window. If they swing outward, the only consideration is easy access and operating clearance for the crank.

Bay and bow windows are generally considered the most charming. Since they allow for little or no wall space, both types require special care when installing rod hardware. Many require ceiling mounts.

A *bay window* consists of three or more windows, usually double-hung, which are set at an angle to create a recess.

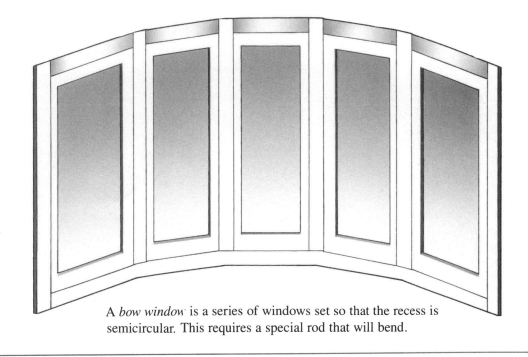

A *bow window* is a series of windows set so that the recess is semicircular. This requires a special rod that will bend.

Corner windows consist of two of any type of window. The key is that they meet in a corner, creating two different exposures to the elements and two different views. For best results, treat both windows as a single unit.

Awning windows have horizontal glass panels that can be opened out at any angle, offering good ventilation. The windows may each have one such movable panel or many. The only concern with this type of window is that ventilation will be blocked.

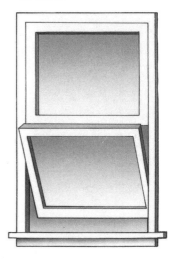

Dormer windows are small vertical windows, recessed into a gable or alcove. Because the area is generally narrow, there is often very little wall space for installing the treatment. If the windows swing inward, your best bet is to install the treatment directly on the frame. If the windows slide up and down, you have more options.

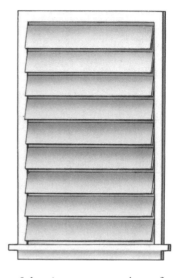

Sliding glass doors function as both a window and a door, creating two concerns: protection against the elements and easy access to the door. If the wall space is limited, drapes installed on a one-way traverse rod are a practical solution.

Jalousies are a series of narrow, adjustable glass strips. Considerations are the same as for awning windows.

French doors generally function as a pair, although you may encounter a lone French door. Because the door(s) usually swing inward, the most practical solution is to install the treatment directly on the door(s).

Ranch windows, also called *strip windows,* are wide strips of encased glass placed high on the wall. Because they're up high, the main concern is to bring the window into proportion with the rest of the room. Treatments that blend into the background, such as shutters, shades or blinds, are usually good solutions.

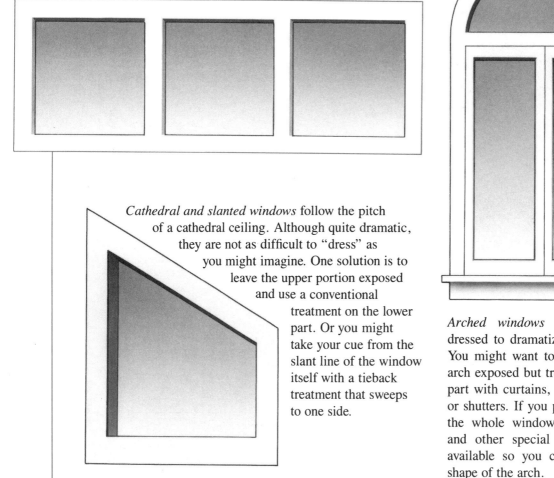

Cathedral and slanted windows follow the pitch of a cathedral ceiling. Although quite dramatic, they are not as difficult to "dress" as you might imagine. One solution is to leave the upper portion exposed and use a conventional treatment on the lower part. Or you might take your cue from the slant line of the window itself with a tieback treatment that sweeps to one side.

Arched windows generally are dressed to dramatize their shape. You might want to leave the top arch exposed but treat the bottom part with curtains, blinds, shades or shutters. If you prefer to cover the whole window, shaped rods and other special hardware are available so you can follow the shape of the arch.

Clerestory windows are narrow strips of glass or glass blocks placed along the ceiling line. Generally, these windows are left uncovered so they can admit light without drawing attention to themselves.

CHOOSING A FABRIC

Fabrics for window treatments can be solid or multicolored, plain or patterned, textured or smooth, transparent or opaque. They can match or coordinate with upholstered pieces or existing wallpaper.

Solids that blend in with the wall treatment are restful to the eye; solids that contrast add a direct design accent. If in doubt, tone down your color choice. You can always brighten it up by adding trim, tassels, fringe, ribbon, lace, braids, borders or interesting tiebacks. Adding trim at a later stage is easier and more economical than replacing a finished window treatment because the fabric or color is too much.

Patterns and prints can be used to draw the eye away from any unappealing design features in the room, or they can be used to unify a collection of solids.

● To give your decor a unified look, consider repeating the print somewhere else in the room. For dramatic effect, repeat it in another large area, such as wall coverings,

slipcovers or bed linens. For a more subtle effect, use leftover fabric to trim one of these large areas or for small accent pieces, such as throw pillows.

● If the fabric has a motif that must be matched and you have used a companion wall covering, be sure to plan the window treatment so that the motif matches in an unbroken repeat around the room.

Fabrics, like people, have personalities. Some are very formal, while others impart a more casual air. Think about the impression you want the room to convey, then choose a fabric for your window treatment that is compatible with its message. In Chapter 3, CHOOSING FABRICS, you'll find a list of fabrics that are commonly used in formal, informal and casual settings.

MEASURE FOR MEASURE

If you were to hire a professional designer to dress your windows, the first thing he or she would do is take a set of measurements that are flexible enough to cover almost all the possibilities. Armed with this shopping list of measurements, you'll be able to determine the style of the treatment, the placement of the hardware and the amount of fabric you need. This information also will give you the luxury of changing your mind, without going back to the tape measure.

Taking measurements and deciding on the appropriate window treat-

ment and hardware is a "Which comes first—the chicken or the egg?" situation. If you are absolutely sure about the style and placement of your chosen treatment, skip ahead to "Hardware Basics" on page 87 to be sure that your hardware will be properly installed. Then you can zero in on the few measurements that are important to you.

Length Measurements

These measurements indicate the placement of curtain and drapery rods, as well as the finished length of the treatment, from the top of the rod to the hem.

Fabrics most commonly used for lightweight treatments and undercurtains include:

> **Austrian shade cloth**
> **Batiste**
> **Dimity**
> **Dotted swiss**
> **Filet lace**
> **Lawn**
> **Marquisette**
> **Net**
> **Ninon**
> **Organdy**
> **Piqué**
> **Plissé**
> **Point d'esprit**
> **Voile**

Match the weight of the fabric and the scale of the print to the overall size of the window treatment. Heavy fabrics and large prints usually overwhelm short curtains.

When selecting fabric, color and trim for your window treatment, pay particular attention to how your choices coordinate with three elements in the room: the wall treatment, the floor covering and the largest piece of upholstered furniture.

Start with these basic length measurements:

A. Floor to ceiling.*
B. Top of outside frame to floor.*
C. Ceiling to top of outside frame.
D. Top of outside frame to sill.
E. Top of outside frame to bottom of apron.
F. Top of inside frame to sill.
G. Top of inside frame to meeting rails.
H. Top of meeting rails to sill.
I. Top of meeting rails to bottom of apron.
J. Top of meeting rails to floor.*
K. Top of outside frame to bottom of inside frame.

If your window has grids, take these length measurements, too:

L. Top of upper grid to sill.
M. Top of upper grid to bottom of apron.

*If you want your curtains or drapes to "puddle" on the floor, add at least 6"–8" (15cm–20.5cm) to these measurements.

Width Measurements

These measurements will help you determine the length of the curtain or drapery rod, as well as where to install it. In several cases, they will also help you decide if there is enough wall space for your desired window treatment.

AA. Width, from outside frame to outside frame.
BB. Width between the outer edges of the brackets. (NOTE: You will not be able to determine this measurement until your hardware is installed.)
CC. Width, from inside frame to inside frame.
DD. Width of exposed glass.
EE. Width of outside frame.
FF. Width from outside frame to wall or adjoining window.

If the distance between two windows is less than 12" (30.5cm), it is a good idea to treat the two as one large expanse of window.

If the distance from window to wall or other vertical obstruction is less than 7" (18cm), you won't have enough room to mount your drapes so that they will open up to completely expose the window.

CURTAINS AND DRAPERIES

Because they suit almost any shape window, and because they easily adapt to any style decor, curtains and drapes are the most popular window treatments.

• *Curtains* are installed on stationary rods and generally have gathered, smocked or ruffled headings.

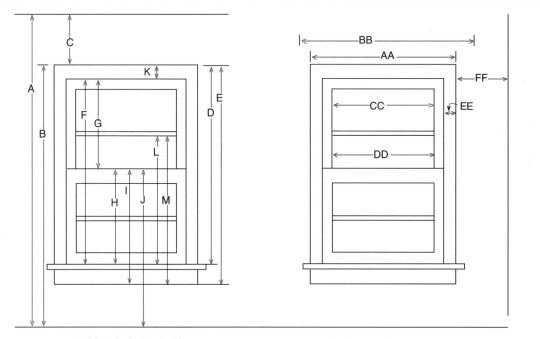

LENGTH MEASUREMENTS   WIDTH MEASUREMENTS

• *Draperies* are more tailored and have pleated, smocked or gathered headings. They are attached to traversing rods with special pin hooks. They also can be installed on flat curtain rods by hooking the pins over the rod. This type of window treatment is constructed like a drape, but it functions as a stationary curtain.

CONVENTIONAL CURTAIN RODS

CONTINENTAL RODS

To Line or Not to Line

Adding a lining to either of these treatments is both a practical and an aesthetic decision.

• Medium- and heavyweight fabrics have a richer appearance if they are lined. The folds appear softer and deeper.

• Linings cut down on the amount of light, noise and dust that filter through a window.

• Linings give windows a unified appearance on the outside.

• As a general rule, unlined curtains and drapes should be cut fuller than lined versions.

The most common lining fabric is white or off-white sateen. However, any plain fabric of similar weight, such as sheeting or unbleached muslin, can also be used.

SPRING TENSION RODS

SASH RODS

CAFÉ RODS

HARDWARE BASICS

There are adjustable tracks and rods that will accommodate any style curtain or drape or any weight of fabric you desire.

• *Curtain rods* are the easiest to install and work with.

Conventional curtain rods are narrow, flat metal rods used for outside mounts. The rod should be completely hidden in the pocket casing. For sheer curtains, look for special clear or translucent plastic versions.

Continental rods are wide, flat curtain rods that add depth and interest to rod pocket treatments. Common widths are 2½" (6.3cm) and 4½" (11.5cm).

Spring tension rods are used to install curtains or valances inside the window frames. They do not require any type of brackets or mounting screws.

Sash rods are flat or round rods with shallow mounting brackets. They are most often used on doors and other areas where a sheer or lightweight curtain is installed close to the glass.

Café rods are decorative curtain rods, with or without rings, and available in many finishes, including wood, brass and enamel.

TIP

Buy the best-quality fabric that your budget will allow. Your window treatment will last longer and look better.

● *Cord-controlled traverse rods* are available in both decorative and conventional styles.

Conventional traverse rods may be purchased as two-way draw (for drapes that part from the center), one-way draw and in sets for layered window dressings, such as drapes with sheer undercurtains. These last use one set of brackets for both rods and are spaced far enough apart so both treatments fall freely.

CONVENTIONAL TRAVERSE ROD

Decorative traverse rods are all two-way draw. However, you can convert them to one-way draw by following the manufacturer's directions included in the package.

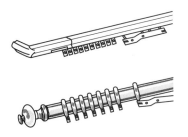

DECORATIVE TRAVERSE RODS

● *Ring and pole sets* are decorative rods, generally wood, designed so that curtains or drapes can be hand-drawn across the window.

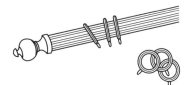

HAND-DRAW WOOD POLE SET

Ceiling Installations

A *ceiling mount* refers to any rod installation on the wall above the window frame or, in the case of some special traverse rods, when the rod is literally hung from the ceiling. The result is a curtain or drape that brushes the top of the ceiling and extends down to the desired finished length. Rods should be installed so the inner edge of the bracket clears the window frame.

When installing drapes, set the pin hooks so that the top of the drapery rides 1/4″ (6mm) above the rod.

Although curtain rods can be hung close to the ceiling, there needs to be enough clearance between the ceiling and the top of the bracket to install the rod and the actual window treatment.

● Minimum clearance is equal to the rod projection (i.e., the distance the rod extends out from the wall). For rods with a rounded projection, add another 1/2″ (1.3cm).

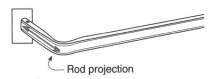

Rod projection

● When you are ready to make your curtains, the header should be the same depth as the clearance measurement. That way, there will be no gap between the ceiling and the top of the curtains.

For Full Glass Exposure

For *two-way draw traverse rods*, divide measurement AA by 6 to determine how far out from the edge of the window frame the brackets should be installed. For example, if the window is 42″ (107cm) wide across the frame, the brackets should be installed 7″ (18cm) out from the frame.

For *one-way draw traverse rods*, divide measurement AA by 3 to determine how far out from the edge of the window frame on the stacking side of the window the return bracket should be installed. For example, if the window is 42″ (107cm) wide across the frame, the return bracket should be installed 14″ (35.5cm) out from the frame on the side where the drapes will stack, or "pile up." The support bracket should be installed on the wall, just above the window frame.

TIPS

If you want to hang a valance directly above a curtain or drape, look for double curtain rods and combination traverse and valance rods. These rods are installed on one set of brackets and have the necessary clearance built in. In a similar vein, triple rods are the easy way to hang valance, drapes and undercurtains.

Although it was once necessary to purchase custom-made rods for bay, bow or corner windows, today you can purchase rods that will adapt to almost any shape window. Virtually every rod and hardware manufacturer has a book available for free or at a nominal cost to help you decide what will work best for your special windows. Inquire at your local fabric store or drapery shop.

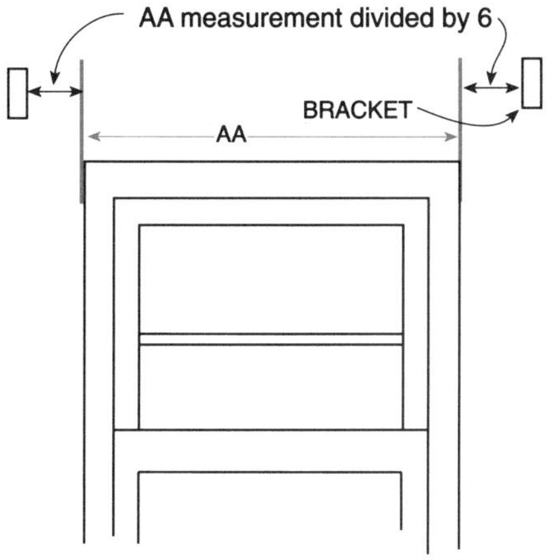

TWO-WAY DRAW TRAVERSE ROD

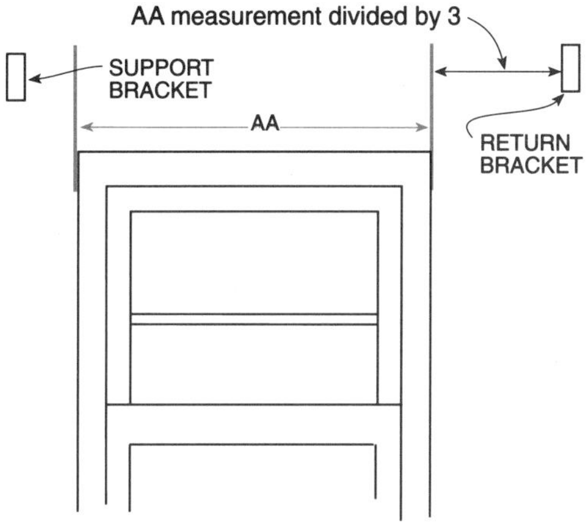

ONE-WAY DRAW TRAVERSE ROD

Special Tips for Window Installations

Most windows have outside frames, or moldings, with mitered corners. If the rods are installed directly into the moldings, you run the risk of splitting or damaging the wood. To avoid this possibility, install the brackets on the wall. They are usually positioned so the inner edge of the bracket just clears the window frame.

Here are some other tips for specific situations:

- For *curtain rods* and *conventional traverse rods*, generally the best installation is one where the top of the rod rides even with the top of the molding.
- For a *decorative rod with rings*, install the brackets so that the rod will be parallel with the top of the window frame and the lower edges of the rings are 1/4″ (6mm) above the top of the molding. When the window treatment is installed, the molding will be completely covered.
- For *inside lengths* where the rod will be hidden by the fabric (length measurements H, I, J, L and M), install the rod so it is even with any exposed wood.

CURTAINS: GENERAL DIRECTIONS

Since our goal is to help you make the very best possible curtains, we've adapted the cutting and sewing processes that are used by some of the finest custom workrooms. The resulting window treatments will have the "extra something" your decor deserves.

Measuring

With the rods installed, determine the finished width and finished length of the curtains (refer to the "Measure for Measure" diagrams on page 86):

- *Finished length*. Measure from the top of the rod to the point on the window where you want the curtain to end. Then, depending on where your curtains will hang, adjust this measurement as follows:

From ceiling or top of window to floor (length measurements A, B and J), subtract 1/2″ (1.3cm) for floor clearance.

TIP

Since it isn't pretty to see drapery pins from the outside of the window, check your K measurement. For no-show hooks, there should be at least 4″ (10cm) of wood (inside frame plus outside frame) at the top of the window. If not, measure up at least 4″ (10cm) from the top of the exposed glass and install the rod at this point on the wall above the window.

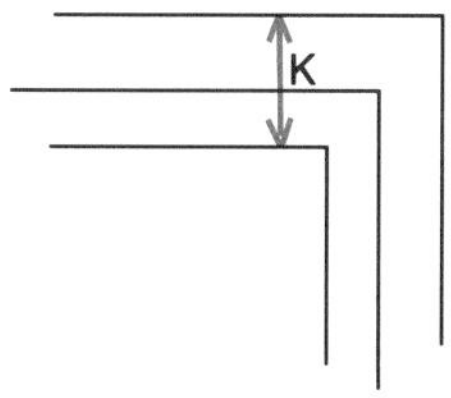

From top of window to bottom of apron (length measurements E, I and M), add 1½″ (3.8cm).

From top of window to sill—or for any inside frame installation—(length measurements D, F, G, H and L), do not make any adjustment.

NOTE: The finished length does not include any header. You will add it in when you determine the cutting length.

● *Finished width.* Add the following:

The outer bracket to outer bracket measurement.
+
The depth of the rod projection multiplied by 2. Then, if the rod has a rounded projection, add 1″ (2.5cm).

Cutting Length

To determine the cutting length of the curtain, add the following:

Finished length
(including any adjustments)
+
Header depth, multiplied by 3

For most curtains, 2″ (5cm) is an attractive depth for the header.

For a ceiling installation, the header should be the same depth as the clearance measurement.

For a standard curtain rod with rounded projections, the clearance measurement is usually 3″, or 7.5cm.
+
Rod pocket depth, multiplied by 2

A 2″ (5cm) deep rod pocket creates a pleasing proportion that works well with most curtain rods. However, continental rods and some decorative rods require a deeper rod pocket. If so, measure the rod's circumference, divide by 2, then add ½″, or 1.3cm, for easy insertion.
+
8″ (20.5cm) for a 4″ (10cm) double hem at the bottom
+
1″ (2.5cm) straightening allowance

How Much Fabric and Lining?

Custom workrooms don't spend time on tedious fabric calculations. Instead, they rely on some simple formulas. The following is based on the three most common fabric widths. Each fullness ratio allows for 1¼″ (3.2cm) double side hems and seam allowances for any piecing seams.

Step 1: Decide how full you want your curtains to be. The weight of your fabric, or the presence of a lining, affects the fullness of your window treatment.

● For heavyweight fabrics, or treatments that will be lined, use a fullness ratio of 2 to 1.

● For medium-weight fabrics, use a fullness ratio of 2½ to 1.

● For sheer and lightweight fabrics, use a fullness ratio of 3 to 1.

Step 2: On the chart below, locate where your fullness ratio intersects with your fabric width. That number is your fullness factor.

Have you ever thought you were carefully measuring for curtains, only to find out they ended up too short? This is because up to a ½″ (1.3cm) of length "disappears" in the gathering process. Our adjustments for finished length take this "shrinkage" into account.

Don't skimp on fullness. An expensive fabric will lose its richness if the treatment is not full enough. An inexpensive fabric will look lusher if the fullness is generous or if the curtains or drapes are lined.

To determine the number of widths (panels) of fabric you will need, divide the finished width of the curtains by the appropriate fullness factor.

Step 3: To determine the amount of fabric, multiply the cutting length by the number of panels. Divide by 36″ (91.5cm) to determine the number of yards (meters).

NOTE: If you are dealing with a fabric that has a motif that must be matched, measure the distance between the repeats, then multiply this distance (i.e., the size of the repeat) by the number of panels. That's how much extra fabric to buy.

Step 4: To determine the amount of lining, follow Steps 2 and 3.

FULLNESS FACTOR			
FABRIC WIDTH	FULLNESS RATIO		
	2:1	2½:1	3:1
45″ (115cm)	20	16	14
48″ (122cm)	22	18	15
54″ (138cm)	25	20	18

Cutting Width

Although the cutting width has been accounted for in the fullness factor, you need an exact measurement to construct the curtain.

To determine the cutting width of each curtain, multiply half the finished width by the fullness ratio (2, 2½ or 3). Add 5″ (12.5cm) for side hems.

NOTE: Curtains are usually in pairs. However, where a single curtain spans the window, use the full finished width.

BASIC UNLINED CURTAINS

Step 1: Cut and piece the curtain. Using the cutting width and cutting length as your dimensions, cut the fabric for the curtain. If necessary, piece the panels, using ½″ (1.3cm) seams.

Step 2: Hem the lower edge.

● After the panels are joined together, lay the fabric wrong side up on a large, flat surface. Press the lower edge up 4″ (10cm), then 4″ (10cm) again to form a double hem.

● At the location of each piecing seam, hand-tack a drapery weight to the inner hem allowance, ½″ (1.3cm) from the hemline.

● Topstitch or, for a custom look, hand-sew or machine-blindstitch the hem in place.

Step 3: Hem the sides.

● Press the sides in 1¼″ (3.2cm), then 1¼″ (3.2cm) again to form a double hem.

● At each bottom corner, hand-tack a drapery weight to the inner hem allowance, ½″ (1.3cm) from the side hemline and ½″ (1.3cm) from the bottom hemline.

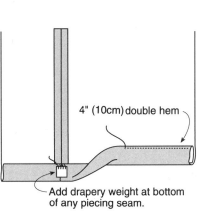

4″ (10cm) double hem

Add drapery weight at bottom of any piecing seam.

● Topstitch or, for a custom look, machine-blindstitch the hems in place.

Step 4: Make the header and rod pocket.

● Measure up from the bottom hem and mark a distance equal to the cutting length, minus the 8″ (20.5cm) that became the bottom hem. Trim off the excess fabric.

1. Double hem sides.

2. Measure up and mark cutting length minus 8″ (20.5cm); trim.

Add drapery weights at both bottom corners.

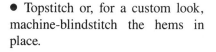

When cutting and assembling your curtain:

● **Work on a large, flat surface. The padded cutting board that's described on page 33 works great!**

● **Always press and mark the fabric on the wrong side.**

● **Measure from bottom to top and mark each bottom edge with a piece of masking tape. When joining panels, treat the fabric as if it has a nap. Then there will be no nasty surprises later on.**

● **When working with a motif that must be matched, be sure the pattern repeats line up across the width of the fabric as each subsequent panel is measured and cut.**

● **If the selvages do not shade through or are not so tightly woven that they pull the fabric, you can use them as piecing seam allowances. For more information on dealing with the selvages, see "Fabric Basics" in Chapter 4, THE SEWING BASICS.**

● **Always stitch from bottom to top. This way, if your motif begins to lose its match, the problem area will fall into the header, where it will be the least noticeable.**

WINDOWS: A DIFFERENT VIEW

BASIC CURTAINS STYLED AS CAFÉ CURTAINS

• Press the upper edge down a distance equal to the header depth plus the rod pocket depth. Fold down again the same amount, forming a double hem; press again.

• Edgestitch along the edge of the hem allowances.

• Measure down from the top of the curtain a distance equal to the header. Machine-stitch, creating the header and the rod pocket.

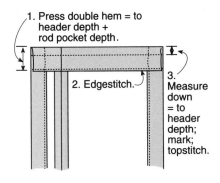

1. Press double hem = to header depth + rod pocket depth.

2. Edgestitch.

3. Measure down = to header depth; mark; topstitch.

Variation

Unlined Ruffled Curtains

When a soft, gentle aura is your decorating goal, ruffled curtains just can't be beat. Make your own ruffles or use pregathered trim. Contrast or color-match them to the main fabric. *Priscilla curtains* are ruffled curtains made from sheer fabric.

This special technique encases both the raw edge of the ruffle and the raw edge of the curtain. As a result, everything is as attractive on the outside of the window as it is on the inside. Plus, there's no worry about fraying seam allowances or ugly, cut-edge show-through on sheers. Another bonus: Although the ruffle extends to the top of the curtain, the rod pocket does not ex-

tend across the ruffle. The result is a neat, professional finish.

To determine the cutting length of the curtain, add the following:

Finished length
minus the depth of the ruffle

+

Header depth, multiplied by 3

+

Rod pocket depth,
multiplied by 2

+

1½" (3.8cm) for seam allowance
at lower edge

Determine the cutting width as in "Curtains: General Directions" on page 91, subtracting the width of the ruffle.

Step 1: Cut and piece the curtain, following "Basic Unlined Curtains," Step 1. Round off the lower inside corner.

Step 2: Hem the outside edge only, following "Basic Unlined Curtains," Step 3.

Step 3: Prepare the header.

• Press the upper edge down a distance equal to the header depth and the rod pocket depth.

• Fold down again the same amount, forming a double hem; press.

Step 4: Prepare and attach the ruffles.

• Construct a double-layer, single ruffle, as in Chapter 4, THE SEWING BASICS.

• Divide and mark the edge of the ruffle and the inside and lower edge of the curtain into sixteenths.

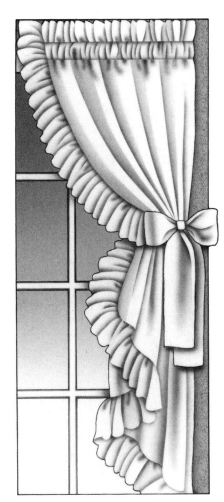

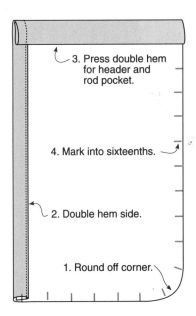

3. Press double hem for header and rod pocket.

4. Mark into sixteenths.

2. Double hem side.

1. Round off corner.

● Unfold the header. Starting at the pressed line that indicates the top of the header, pin the ruffle to the curtain, right sides together, so that the raw edge of the ruffle is 1″ (2.5cm) from the raw edge of the curtain. Match the markings and draw the ruffle up to fit. Stitch ½″ (1.3cm) from the raw edge of the ruffle. Trim the ruffle seam allowance *only* to ¼″ (6mm).

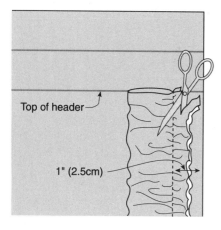

Top of header

1" (2.5cm)

● Fold the raw edge of the curtain over ½″ (1.3cm) and press.

● Fold the raw edge over again so the pressed edge just covers the stitching line; pin and press. Edgestitch close to the first fold, through all thicknesses.

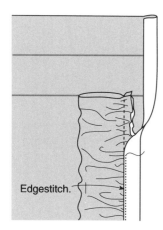

Edgestitch.

● Press the encased seam allowance (including the portion that extends into the header and rod pocket allowances) flat, then toward the curtain.

Step 5: Finish the header and rod pocket.

● Refold and re-press the double hem at the top of the curtain.

● Edgestitch along the lower edge of the double hem.

● Measure down from the top of the curtain a distance equal to the header. Machine-stitch, creating the header and rod pocket.

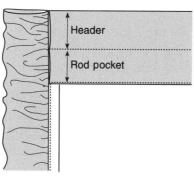

Header

Rod pocket

Variation

Two-Rod Curtain—
Tied in
the Center

This variation is nothing more than an unlined single curtain with a header and rod pocket at both the top and bottom. It is particularly attractive in sheers, laces or other lightweight fabrics. Its smooth, yet snug, fit is achieved by changing the basic rectangular shape to accommodate the center tie. It is generally installed close to the glass on a sash

or spring tension rods. If desired, add a ruffle to the outer edge, using the technique in "Variation: Unlined Ruffled Curtains", described previously on this page.

To determine the cutting length, install both the rods; then measure and add the following:

Finished length from the
upper edge of the top rod
to the lower edge
of the bottom rod

+

Header depth,
multiplied by 6

+

Rod pocket depth,
multiplied by 4

+

5″ (12.5cm) for curve allowance
and gathering ease

Determine the amount of fabric and the cutting width as in "Curtains: General Directions" on pages 90–91.

Step 1: Cut and piece the curtain as in "Basic Unlined Curtains, Step 1." Then:

● Fold the curtain lengthwise in half. At the fold, mark 2″ (5cm) down from the top and 2″ (5cm) up from the bottom. Draw a diagonal line from each mark to its corre-

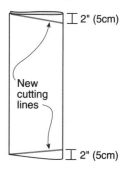

2" (5cm)

New
cutting
lines

2" (5cm)

sponding outside corner, smoothing it out to form a gentle curve at the center front. Trim along the line.

Step 2: Hem the sides, as in "Basic Unlined Curtains," Step 3.

Step 3: Make a header and rod pocket at the top and bottom of the curtain, as in "Basic Unlined Curtains," Step 4, gently easing in the fullness at the curve.

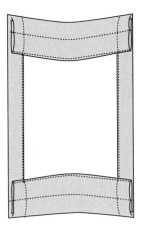

Step 4: Install the curtain, adjust the gathers and secure at the center with a ribbon or a tieback.

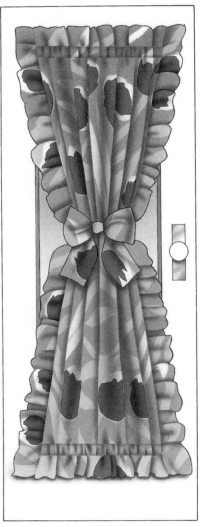

TWO–ROD CURTAIN—TIED
IN THE CENTER

TWO–ROD CURTAIN—TIED
TO THE SIDE

Variation

Two-Rod Curtain— Tied to the Side

Follow the instructions for the _two-rod curtain—tied in the center_, making two curtains, but with this adjustment in Step 1:

● On the outside edge of each panel, mark 2″ (5cm) down from the top and 2″ (5cm) up from the bottom. Draw a diagonal line from each

mark to its corresponding inside corner. Trim along the line.

2″
(5cm)

New
cutting
lines

New
cutting
lines

2″
(5cm)

2″
(5cm)

2″
(5cm)

Variation

One-Piece Pouf Valance and Curtain

Use this variation as one curtain across the window, or make two side panels and add the _basic valance_ in the center. The secret is a second curtain rod, mounted just underneath the first one.

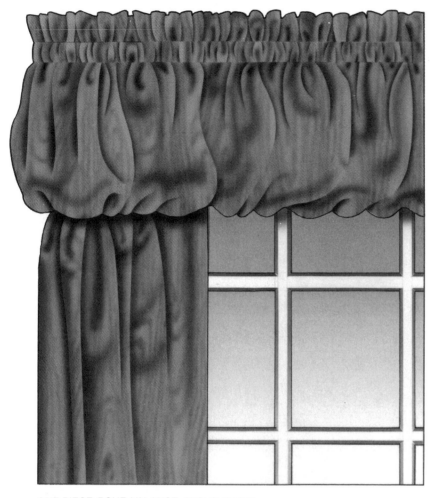

ONE-PIECE POUF VALANCE AND CURTAIN

Step 1: Determine the cutting dimensions:

● First, determine the curtain's cutting length, as in "Curtains: General Directions" on page 90. Then, to this measurement, add the desired valance depth (10″–14″, or 25.5cm–35.5cm) multiplied by 2, plus 3″ (7.5cm). That is your total cutting length.

● Determine the amount of fabric and the cutting width, as in "Curtains: General Directions" on pages 90–91.

Step 2: Cut and construct the cur-

tain, as in "Basic Unlined Curtains," Steps 1–4.

Step 3: Make the extra rod pocket.

● Working on the right side of the curtain, measure down from the bottom of the rod pocket a distance equal to twice the valance depth plus

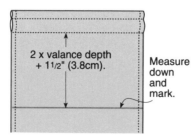

2 x valance depth + 1½″ (3.8cm).

Measure down and mark.

1½″ (3.8cm) and mark across the width of the curtain.

● Fold the curtain, right sides together, along this marked line. Stitch 1½″ (3.8cm) from the fold, forming the second rod pocket.

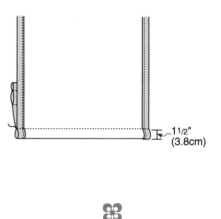

1½″ (3.8cm)

BASIC LINED CURTAINS

Follow the directions for the *basic unlined curtains*, Steps 1–3. Measure and press, but do *not* stitch the side hems.

Step 4: Prepare the header.

● Measure up from the bottom hem and mark a distance equal to the cutting length, minus the 8″ (20.5cm) that became the bottom hem. Trim off the excess fabric.

● Press the upper edge down a distance equal to the header depth and the rod pocket depth. Fold down again the same amount, forming a double hem; press again.

Step 5: Cut, piece and hem the lining.

● To determine the cutting length of the lining, add the finished length of the curtain plus the header depth plus 6″ (15cm).

- To determine the cutting width of the lining, add the cutting width of the curtain plus 2½" (6.3cm).

- Cut the fabric for the lining. If necessary, piece the panels, using ½" (1.3cm) seams.

- Press the lower edge of the lining up 3" (7.5cm), then 3" (7.5cm) again to form a double hem; stitch.

Step 6: Attach the lining.

- Place the curtain, wrong side up, on your work surface. Place the lining, right side up, over the curtain, so that the bottom of the lining is 1" (2.5cm) above the bottom of the curtain. Offset the lining slightly so any piecing seams in the lining and curtain are parallel and a scant ½" (1.3cm) apart. This will eliminate bulk in the header. Pin the hem allowances together at the bottom.

- Working from center to side, and bottom to top, smooth, press and pin the lining to the curtain. (See illustration A, below.)

- When you reach the top of the curtain, trim the lining so it corresponds to the top of the header. Lift up the double hem and tuck the lining under it; pin.

- As you reach each side hem, unpin the hem, open it out and trim the lining to correspond to the inner foldline. Fold the side hems back over the lining; repin.

- When you get to the top, unpin the header area just enough to allow you to finish trimming and securing the lining under the side hems. (See illustration B, below.)

- Topstitch or hand-sew the side hems—or use strips of fusible web to secure the side hems to the lining. Then repin the header area.

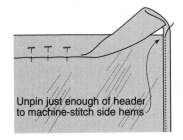

Unpin just enough of header to machine-stitch side hems

Step 7: Finish the header and rod pocket.

- Edgestitch along the lower edge of the header area, through the curtain and the lining.

- Measure down from the top of the curtain a distance equal to the header. Machine-stitch, creating the header and rod pocket.

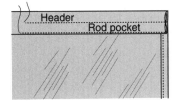

Header
Rod pocket

A

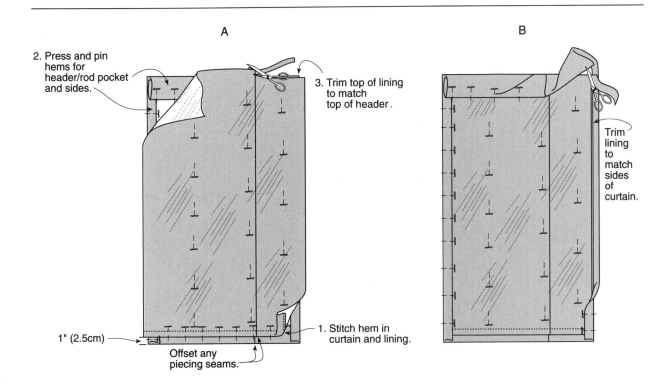

2. Press and pin hems for header/rod pocket and sides.

3. Trim top of lining to match top of header.

Trim lining to match sides of curtain.

1" (2.5cm)

Offset any piecing seams.

1. Stitch hem in curtain and lining.

B

DRAPERIES: GENERAL DIRECTIONS

The process for making draperies is similar to making curtains. There are, however, a few differences.

Measuring

With the rods installed, determine the finished length and the finished width of the drapes (refer to the "Measure for Measure" diagrams on page 86).

- *Finished length*. Where the measurement is taken depends on the type of rod. Measure down to the point where you want the drapes to end. Then, for *floor-length draperies* only, subtract 1/2″ (1.3cm) for floor clearance.

For *conventional traverse rods*, measure from the top of the rod. Add 1/2″ (1.3cm) so the top of the drape will extend slightly above the rod.

For *decorative traverse rods*, measure from the bottom of the ring.

For *ring and pole sets*, measure from the pinholes in the rings.

For *conventional curtain rods* (a stationary installation), measure as for *conventional traverse rods*.

- *Finished width, one-way draw drapes*. Add the following:

Length of the rod
+
Depth of the rod projection
+
2″ (5cm) for the overlap

- *Finished width, two-way draw drapes*. Measure as for one-way draw drapes; then add 4″ (10cm) for the center overlap. Since you need two drapes, divide by 2. This is the finished width of *each* drape.

NOTE: Although there is no overlap when two-way draw drapes are installed on a curtain rod (a stationary installation), the extra width will be eased in along the rod.

NOTE: Finished width means the amount the curtain or drape must cover in its closed position. Because this width does not include fullness, it is *not* a cutting measurement.

Cutting Width

The type of header you choose will determine the cutting width of your draperies.

Drapery tapes are the secret to easy pleated, shirred or smocked headers.

- *Conventional pleater tape* is a wide, firmly woven tape with long, skinny pockets. When special pronged hooks are inserted into the pockets, the tape accordion-folds into pleats.

Most pleater tapes, including standard *pinch pleat tapes*, pleat up to a 2 to 1 ratio. That means your cutting width will be twice your finished width plus 5″ (12.5cm) for side hems.

A few *novelty pleater tapes* will pleat up to 2 1/4 to 1 or 2 1/2 to 1. Check the manufacturer's information to be sure.

- *Pull-cord tapes*, including *smocking and shirring tapes*, have draw cords running through the header. When the cords are pulled up, a gathered, shirred or pleated header is formed.

For medium- and heavyweight fabrics, plan on a 2 to 1 ratio. That means the cutting width will be twice your finished width plus 5″ (12.5cm) for side hems.

For lightweight and sheer fabrics, plan on a 3 to 1 ratio. That means the cutting width will be three times your finished width plus 5″ (12.5cm) for side hems.

For more information on various styles of drapery tapes, including illustrations of the finished effect, see "Drapery/Pleater Tapes" in Chapter 11, TIMESAVERS. Many of the iron-tapes described in that section are also available in sew-on versions.

Cutting Length

To determine the cutting length of the drapes, add the following:

Finished length
(including any adjustments)
+
Header: depth of the drapery tape + 1/4″ (6mm), multiplied by 2
+
8″ (20.5cm) for a 4″ (10cm) double hem at the bottom
+
1″ (2.5cm) straightening allowance

How Much Fabric and Lining?

To calculate quickly how much fabric and lining you will need, refer to "Curtains: General Directions" in the earlier part of this chapter. Follow Steps 2–4.

How Much Drapery Tape?

For *smocking, shirring* and other *draw-cord tapes*, the amount of tape you purchase should equal your cutting width.

Pleater tape has pockets that are used to create alternating pleats and spaces. For drapes with that custom look, the pleater tape should be positioned so you start and end with a space.

To be certain you have enough tape to ensure proper placement on your drapes, purchase an amount equal to the cutting width of both drapes plus four extra spaces. For two-way draw drapes, purchase eight extra spaces.

If you are using a tape with evenly spaced pockets, you must first determine how many pockets equal the space between your pleats. Check the manufacturer's information.

Before constructing your drapes, check to see if you need to adjust their cutting width to correspond to the tape.

● Divide the cutting width by half the length of the spaces. (For pleats that will be spaced 4″, or 10cm, apart, divide by 2; for pleats spaced 3½″, or 9cm, apart, divide by 1.75.) This will tell you how many spaces there will be on each panel.

(Any fractions count as whole spaces.)

Length of space between pleats

● Next, count off this number of spaces on your pleater tape and measure from the start of the first space to the end of the last space. This distance, plus 5″ (12.5cm) for side hem allowances, should be equal to the cutting width of your drapery. If it is not, increase your cutting width accordingly. The extra width will be "eased in" across the top of the rod when the drapes are installed.

✵ LINED DRAPES

Whether you choose a sew-on or iron-on drapery tape, the construction process is the same.

Follow the directions for *basic unlined curtains*, Steps 1–3, but do *not* stitch the side hems.

Step 4: Prepare the header.

● Measure up from the bottom hem and mark a distance equal to the cutting length, minus the 8″ (20.5cm) that became the bottom hem. Trim off the excess fabric.

● Press the upper edge down a distance equal to the depth of the drapery tape plus ¼″ (6mm). Fold down again the same amount, forming a double hem. Pin and press.

Step 5: Cut, piece and hem the lining, following "Basic Lined Curtains," Step 5, but with the following adjustment:

● To determine the cutting length of the lining, add the finished length of the drape plus 6″ (15cm).

Step 6: Attach the lining, following "Basic Lined Curtains," Step 6.

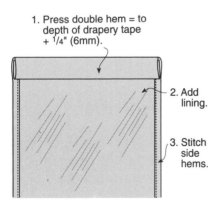

1. Press double hem = to depth of drapery tape + ¼″ (6mm).

2. Add lining.

3. Stitch side hems.

Step 7: Apply the drapery tape.

● For *smocking, shirring* and other *draw-cord tapes*:

Cut the tape to match the length of the header, plus 2″ (5cm). Fold the ends of the tape under 1″ (2.5cm) and press. Use a pin to pull out the draw cords so they are free of the folded end.

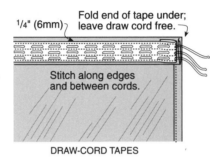

¼″ (6mm)

Fold end of tape under; leave draw cord free.

Stitch along edges and between cords.

DRAW-CORD TAPES

● For *pleater tapes*:

If your rod has a return, measure in from the side(s) of the header a distance equal to the return.

Next, lay the tape across the header, adjusting its position so there is a space at each end. If there is a return, make sure the last pleat falls at the corner of the return. (You will not be forming any pleats in the return.)

Cut the tape to correspond to the length of the header plus 1″ (2.5cm). Fold the ends of the tape under ½″ (1.3cm) and press.

● Position the tape, right side up, over the header allowance, ¼″

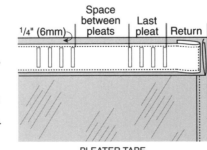

¼″ (6mm)

Space between pleats

Last pleat

Return

PLEATER TAPE

(6mm) from the top of the drape; pin. Stitch across the tape, ½″ (1.3cm) from the top edge and ½″ (1.3cm) from the bottom edge. Stitch the sides close to the fold, keeping any draw cords free of the stitching. For draw-cord tape, stitch again, next to each cord line, being careful not to catch the cord.

Step 8: Install the drapes.

● For *pleater tapes*:

Insert the pronged hooks in the pockets of the tape, forming the pleats. Add a single hook at each end of the drape. Hang the drapes on the rods.

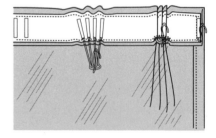

Pull the drapes back into a stacked position. If you're using a traverse rod, crease the space between the pleats forward, away from the window. If you're using a ring and pole set, crease the space to the back, toward the window. Work all the way down the pleat, following the grainline of the fabric so the pleats are perpendicular to the floor.

To "set" the pleats, loosely wrap the drape with an approximately 4″ (10cm) wide strip of muslin or self-fabric. Overlap the ends of the strip and pin or staple together. Do this midway between header and hem and again just above the hemline. After wrapping, steam gently, using your steam iron or a hand-held steamer. Leave the drapes undisturbed for two or three days, then remove the wrapping strips.

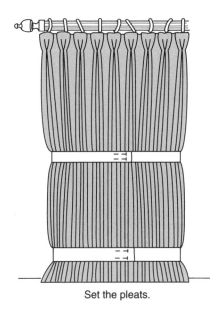

Set the pleats.

● For *draw-cord tapes*:

The easiest way to gather these headers is with the assistance of a doorknob and a friend. Tie the cords together securely at one end. Then have the friend hold that end of the drapery. Tie the cords on the other end to a doorknob. Using the palms of your hands, gently ease the fabric up to the desired length. Once the drape is the desired width, tie the cords. Cut the ends or wrap the excess cording around an embroidery floss holder and tuck it into the folds of the drapery.

Insert the hooks, per the manufacturer's instructions, and hang the drapes.

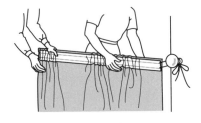

✵ BASIC UNLINED DRAPES

To retain the light-filtering properties of sheer or very lightweight fabrics, you may choose to leave your drapes unlined. These are also the perfect undercurtains for heavier draw drapes or formal swags and jabots.

Steps 1–3: Cut and piece the drape, hem the lower edge and hem the sides, following "Basic Unlined Curtains," Steps 1–3.

Step 4: Prepare the header, following "Lined Drapes," Step 4.

Step 5: Apply the drapery tape, following "Lined Drapes," Step 7.

Step 6: Install the drapes, following "Lined Drapes," Step 8.

--- *Variation* ---

Flat Drapes Installed on Ring and Pole Sets

Follow the instructions for *lined drapes* or *basic unlined drapes*, with these adjustments:

● When you determine the cutting length, substitute a 3″ (7.5cm) double hem—6″ (15cm) in all—for the header. In Step 4, make a 3″ (7.5cm) double hem and omit any subsequent references to drapery tapes.

● Use a 2 to 1 fullness ratio when determining the finished width and cutting width.

● To install the drapes, sew a ring or hook at each corner, then in

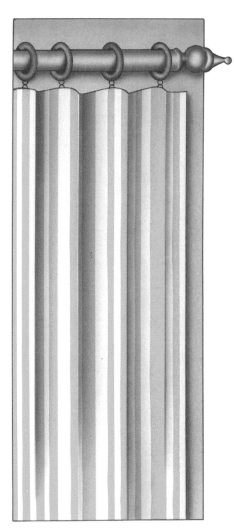

evenly spaced intervals across the top of the drapes. As a no-sew alternative, use café clips.

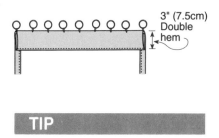

3″ (7.5cm) Double hem

TIP

To permanently secure draw cords after the header is gathered, add a dab of glue to the center of each knot.

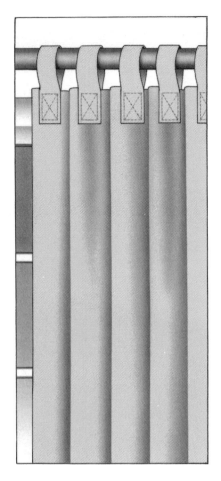

___ *Variation* ___

Flat Drapes with Tab Tops

These drapes should be installed on a decorative café rod or pole rod.

Follow the instructions for *lined drapes* or *basic unlined drapes*, with these adjustments:

● To determine the finished length, install the rod, then make a test tab with a strip of fabric. Pin-mark the tab the desired distance from the pole. Use that point as the starting point for measuring the finished length.

● When you determine the cutting length, substitute a 2″ (5cm) double hem—4″ (10cm) in all—for the header. Then, in Step 4, make a 2″ (5cm) double hem and ignore any subsequent references to drapery tapes.

TO MAKE THE TABS:

● Decide how far apart you want to place the tabs. As a guideline, try spacing them 5″ (12.5cm) apart on short drapes, 8″–10″ (20.5cm–25.5cm) apart on floor-length drapes. Measure the width of your finished drape by the spacing distance. This number plus 1 is how many tabs you'll need to make.

● Measure the loop of the test tab; then add 5″ (7.5cm). This is the tab cutting length.

● For each tab, cut a strip of fabric 3½″ (9cm) wide by the tab cutting length.

● Fold one strip in half, right sides together. Stitch a ½″ (1.3cm) seam. Press the seam open and turn the tab right side out. Center the seamline in the middle of the tab; press. Tuck the raw edges in ½″ (1.3cm) and press.

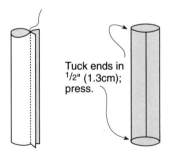

Tuck ends in ½″ (1.3cm); press.

● Divide and mark the upper edge of the curtain to correspond to the number of tabs.

● At one upper corner of the drape front, pin one end of the tab in place over the hem allowance. Pin or glue-baste. Position the other end of the tab in the corresponding position on the drape back; pin or glue-baste. To attach the tab, stitch in a box, then in an X, as shown, through all layers.

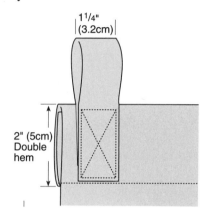

1¼″ (3.2cm)

2″ (5cm) Double hem

● Repeat, attaching the remaining tabs at the markings, with the last tab at the opposite upper corner.

TO CHANGE THE PERSONALITY OF THESE DRAPES:

● Add a covered button, a bow or a fabric flower (see Chapter 10, DECORATIVE ACCESSORIES) to the end of each tab.

● Substitute ribbons for the tabs; then tie the drape onto the rod.

● Instead of tabs, apply grommets across the top of the drape. To hang the drape, loop decorative cording over the rod and through the grommets.

TIP

A shower curtain is simply a flat curtain or drape with grommets. Add a separate, clear plastic liner and install with shower clips.

TIEBACKS

Tiebacks can be dramatic or inconspicuous. They can repeat an existing design detail or bring an entirely new dimension to your curtains or drapes.

Hang the curtains first; then decide on the style and placement of the tiebacks.

● Wrap a tape measure or 3″ (7.5cm) wide strip of fabric around the curtain until you achieve the desired effect. The depth of the angle of the tieback can vary from 3″–12″ (7.5cm–30.5cm). As a guideline, fuller and/or heavier curtains require a deeper angle.

● For a custom look, the finished tiebacks should be 3″–6″ (7.5cm–15cm) wide.

Mark lightly on the window frame or wall for the placement of the tieback holders.

Generally, the tieback is made as one long piece with a ring sewn to each end. Then it is installed in one of the following ways:

● Both rings are looped onto the same cup hook or drapery tieback wedge. This is a common installation for light- to medium-weight curtains that do not extend past the window frame.

● Each ring is looped onto a separate cup hook or tieback wedge. This is a common installation for medium- to heavyweight curtains or for window treatments that extend beyond the window. In the former case, the hooks or wedges are spaced 2″ (5cm) apart on the molding. In the latter case, one hook or wedge is installed on the wall, the other on the molding.

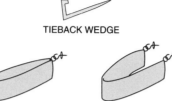

CUP HOOK

TIEBACK WEDGE

Installed on same hook

Installed on two hooks

● For perfect alignment, the outside cup hook or wedge is always installed so that it is directly in line with the outside edge of the bracket that holds the rod in place at the top of the window.

Standard Tiebacks

FOR EACH TIEBACK:

● Cut a strip of fabric equal to the desired length plus 1″ (2.5cm) and double the width of the tieback plus 1″ (2.5cm).

● Fold lengthwise in half, right sides together. Stitch ½″ (1.3cm) from the raw edge, leaving an opening for turning. Clip corners, then

---

TIP

If you want to add piping or other insertion trim to the shaped tieback:

● Make the pattern and cut the tiebacks as above.

● For the tieback lining, convert the foldline to a center seam, adding a ½″ (1.3cm) seam allowance.

● Baste the piping to the front of the tieback. Press the center seam allowances under on the lining

---

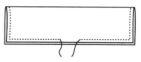

turn and press. Slipstitch the opening closed.

The rings should be attached so that, when the tieback is installed, both the rings and the cup hook or wedge are hidden from view.

● On the end that will be closest to the window or wall, sew the ring at the upper outside edge.

● On the other end, sew the ring at the inside, ½″ (1.3cm) from the edge.

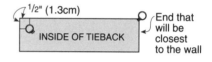

½″ (1.3cm)

INSIDE OF TIEBACK

End that will be closest to the wall

——— *Variation* ———

Shaped Tiebacks

Draw a rectangle equal to the desired width and half the basic length of the tieback. Then:

● Raise the end so it is 1½″–2½″ (3.8cm–6.3cm) higher than the

sections. Pin lining and tieback, right sides together, and complete as for a *standard tieback*. Stitch again, over the stitching that crosses the lining seam. Turn right side out through the open seam in the lining.

If desired, interface the front of the tieback for stability. Choose a fusible or sew-in interfacing designed to provide firm, crisp support.

center. Draw two arcs to connect the new end with the original center. Round off the lower outside corner.

● Leave the lower edge plain or add scallops.

● Add ½" (1.3cm) to the curved edges for seam allowances. Mark the straight edge as a foldline.

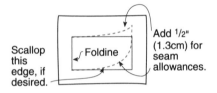

Scallop this edge, if desired.

Foldine

Add ½" (1.3cm) for seam allowances.

● Use as a pattern to cut tiebacks and tieback linings.

● Pin tieback and lining, right sides together. Complete as for a *standard tieback*.

Here are some great ideas for no-sew tiebacks: heavy cord, ribbon, chains, ropes of beads, bandannas and bolero ties. Drapery shops and fabric stores also carry a wide variety of decorative holdbacks.

Tassels and soft fabric flowers can add new dimensions to any of these tiebacks. For information on how to make these embellishments, see Chapter 10, DECORATIVE ACCESSORIES.

_____ *Variation* _____

Ruffled Tiebacks

● For each tieback, cut a fabric rectangle equal to the desired length plus 1" (2.5cm) and 5" (12.5cm) wide.

● For each ruffle, cut a strip of fabric twice as long as the body of the tieback and 7" (18cm) wide.

● Fold the ruffle, right sides together, lengthwise in half. Stitch the ends. Trim, turn and press. Machine-gather along the raw edge.

● Pin the ruffle to one long edge of the tieback, right sides together, with the finished ends of the ruffle ½" (1.3cm) from the cut ends of the tieback. Draw up the gathers to fit; stitch. Press the seam allowances toward the tieback.

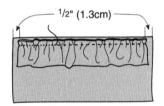

½" (1.3cm)

● Press the other long edge of the tieback under ½" (1.3cm). Fold the tieback lengthwise in half, right sides together, matching the pressed edge to the ruffle seam. Stitch the ends, keeping the ruffle seam allowance free. Trim, turn and press.

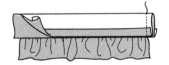

● Fold the pressed edge over the ruffle seam allowance; edgestitch.

_____ *Variation* _____

Bows

Here's how to make a luxurious bow that hangs smartly at the window.

Make *standard tiebacks*, adding 36"–45" (91.5cm–115cm) to the basic length. Use 10" (25.5cm) as the cutting width. Do not interface.

To install with the bow in the forward position, use a 1" × 3" (2.5cm × 7.5cm) strip of chipboard to prevent the bow from falling forward. This will also give the tieback a nice clean edge at the outside of the window.

● Establish the center of the tieback by folding it crosswise in half and creasing lightly with your fingernail. Position the crease at the tieback marking and secure on the side nearest the window with thumbtacks, as shown.

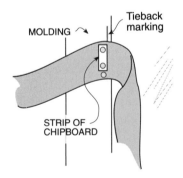

MOLDING

Tieback marking

STRIP OF CHIPBOARD

● Butt the cardboard strip up against the crease and secure to the molding or wall, through the tieback, with two thumbtacks.

● Wrap the tieback around the curtain and fashion into a bow.

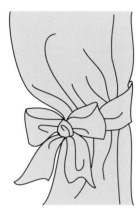

To install with the bow at the outside edge:

• Establish the crosswise center of the tieback.

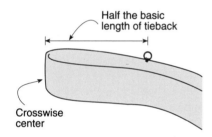

Half the basic length of tieback

Crosswise center

• Measure out from the center a distance equal to half the basic length of the tieback; mark at the upper edge. Sew a ring at this mark.

• Loop the ring onto the tieback holder. Wrap the tieback around the front of the curtain. Tie into a bow at the outside edge.

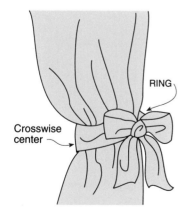

RING

Crosswise center

VALANCES: GENERAL DIRECTIONS

Used alone or in combination with another treatment, valances can add the finishing touch to your windows. Consider a valance as a topper for full-length curtains or drapes, or coordinated with a custom-made shade. A valance can also provide visual continuity to curtains that cover only part of the window, soften the look of miniblinds or shutters, or simply add a touch of color to an otherwise unadorned window.

Rod Placement

Most valances are hung on a conventional curtain rod installed across the top of the window. Usually, the rod is hung so the top of the rod rides even with the top of the molding. The hardware can be installed at the outer edges of the molding or on the wall. Continental rods, spring tension rods and café rods are also suitable. To explore your options, review "Hardware Basics" on page 87.

If the valance is installed directly over curtains or draperies, consider a double rod, which requires only one set of hardware. Triple rods can

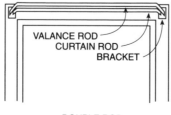

VALANCE ROD
CURTAIN ROD
BRACKET

DOUBLE ROD

accommodate valance, drapes and undercurtains.

If you are using two different rods, there should be a minimum of 2″ (5cm) clearance between the two rods. For example, if the curtain rod has a 1½″ (3.8cm) return, then the valance rod must have at least a 3½″ (9cm) return.

Valance rods should also be installed so that the edge of the valance extends slightly beyond the curtain that's underneath. Take a look at the measuring diagram in "Measure for Measure" on page 86.

• If you use width CC for curtain rod placement, use width AA for valance rod placement.

• If you use width AA for curtain rod placement, use width BB for valance rod placement.

Length

Most valances have a finished length of 10″–16″ (25.5cm–40.5cm). This includes a 2″ (5cm) header. The exact length depends on where you are installing the valance. For example, a valance that is installed inside the window frame (on a spring tension rod) would be shorter than one that is installed at the top of the window over a pair of floor-length drapes.

TIP

If you're unsure how long to make your valance, here's how to visualize the finished product: Cut open a large brown grocery bag; then trim it to the desired depth. Tape in place across the top of the window and analyze the proportions.

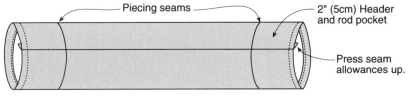

Piecing seams — 2" (5cm) Header and rod pocket

Press seam allowances up.

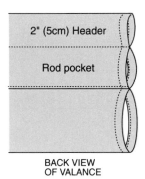

2" (5cm) Header

Rod pocket

BACK VIEW OF VALANCE

BASIC VALANCE

This super-easy method eliminates the need for a separate lining. Although it is made entirely from decorator fabric, eliminating the double hems at top and bottom means minimal extra yardage.

Step 1: Determine the cutting dimensions.

● For the cutting length, add together the finished length (including 2", or 5cm, for the header) plus ½" (1.3cm) seam allowance; then multiply by 2.

● For the cutting width:

    Measure from outer bracket to outer bracket.

Add the depth of the rod projection multiplied by 2. Then, if the rod has a rounded projection, add 1" (2.5cm).

Multiply this total by your fullness ratio (2, 2½ or 3). Add 5" (12.5cm) for the side hems.

Step 2: To determine how much fabric you need, see "Figuring Fabric" in Chapter 4, THE SEWING BASICS.

Step 3: Assemble the valance.

● Cut out the valance, piecing, if necessary, using ½" (1.3cm) seams.

● Hem the sides, using a 1¼" (3.2cm) double hem.

● Fold the valance lengthwise in half, right sides together. Stitch a ½" (1.3cm) seam.

● Decide how deep the rod pocket should be. Turn the valance right side out and reposition the seam until its distance from the top of the valance is equal to 2" (5cm) plus the depth of the rod pocket. Press, directing the seam allowances toward the top of the valance.

TIP

If your valance requires piecing, avoid having a seam fall at the center of the valance. Instead, split the second panel and join to each side of the full panel. Press the seams toward the outside of the valance.

● To form the rod pocket, stitch along the seamline, through all thicknesses. Measure down 2" (5cm) from the top of the valance and stitch again.

● If desired, add ribbon or other trim to the lower edge of the valance. Conceal the ends of the trim between the layers of the valance, then topstitch the trim through all layers.

_____ *Variation* _____

Ruffled Valance

If you want to add a ruffle or other type of insertion trim to the lower edge of the valance, follow the instructions for the *basic valance*, with these adjustments:

● Before figuring the cutting length in Step 1, subtract the depth of the ruffle from the finished length.

● Cut out the valance and hem the sides as in Step 3. Then:

    With right sides together, pin or

baste the trim to one long edge of the valance.

Fold the valance lengthwise in half, right sides together. Stitch a ½″ (1.3cm) seam.

Turn the valance right side out, with the trim at the lower edge; press. Edgestitch.

Measure down from the top of the valance, and mark for the 2″ (5cm) deep header and for the depth of the rod pocket. Stitch along both lines.

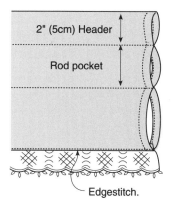

Edgestitch.

For more information on ruffles and insertion trims, see Chapter 4, THE SEWING BASICS.

——— *Variation* ———

Pouf Valance

Follow the instructions for the *basic valance.* Then lightly stuff it with fiberfill or tissue paper.

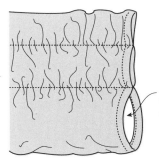

Stuff with fiberfill or tissue paper.

POUF VALANCE

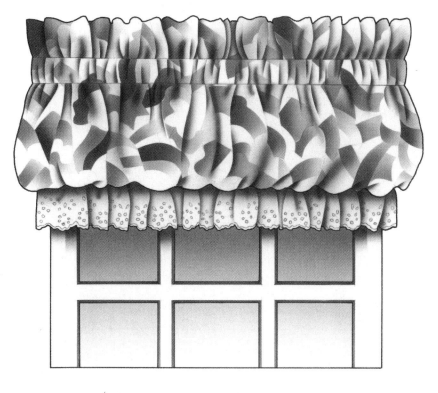

——— *Variation* ———

Pouf Valance with Eyelet Underlay

This window treatment is particularly pretty if you use a 2½″ (6.3cm) wide continental rod for the pouf valance. The underlay is hung on a conventional curtain rod, installed just below the continental rod.

Construct the *pouf valance* as described above, using 15″ (38cm) for the finished length of the valance. Install the pouf valance at the window. The curtain rod for the underlay will be installed later.

To make the underlay, purchase enough 14½″ (37cm) wide eyelet to equal 2½ times the length of the curtain rod, including projections. Then:

● Hem the sides, using a ½″ (1.3cm) double hem.

● Press the upper edge under ½″ (1.3cm); press under again 1½″ (3.8cm). Machine-stitch close to inner fold, forming the rod pocket.

● Insert the curtain rod into the rod casing. Then hold the rod up to the window, under the pouf, to determine how much eyelet should show; mark for the bracket positions. Remove the valance and install the hardware for the curtain rod. Hang the underlay; then rehang the valance.

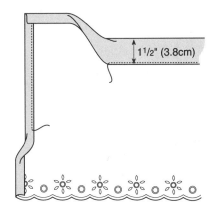

1½″ (3.8cm)

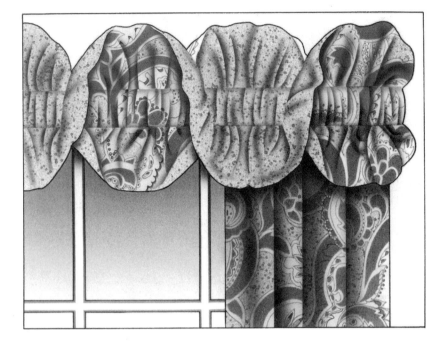

✿ EASY TWIST VALANCE

Made from two contrasting colors or prints, this valance adds a light-hearted twist above miniblinds, shutters, roller shades and café curtains. It is particularly effective in a crisp, medium-weight fabric, such as chintz or polished cotton.

Use a 2½″ (6.3cm) continental rod. When determining the rod placement, allow for a 5″ (12.5cm) header.

Step 1: Determine the cutting dimensions:

● The cutting length is 14″ (35.5cm).

● For the cutting width:
Measure from the outer bracket to the outer bracket.
Add the depth of the rod projection, multiplied by 2.
Multiply this total by 2½.

Step 2: To determine how much fabric and contrasting lining you need, see "Figuring Fabric" in Chapter 4, THE SEWING BASICS.

Step 3: Assemble the valance.

● Cut out the valance and lining, piecing, if necessary, using ½″ (1.3cm) seams.

● On the right side of the lining, measure down 5½″ (14cm) and mark lightly across the width of the valance. Measure down 3″ (7.5cm) more and mark again for the rod pocket. Turn the lining to the wrong side and mark the rod pocket placement at the side edges only.

● Pin the valance and the lining right sides together. Stitch, using a ½″ (1.3cm) seam, leaving an opening between the rod pocket markings.

● Turn the valance right side out through one rod pocket opening; press.

● To form the rod pocket, stitch across the valance on both marked lines.

Step 4: Install the valance.

● Gather the valance onto the rod and hang it at the window.

● Adjust the gathers, then twist the valance back and forth so the contrasting fabrics are alternately exposed across the top of the window.

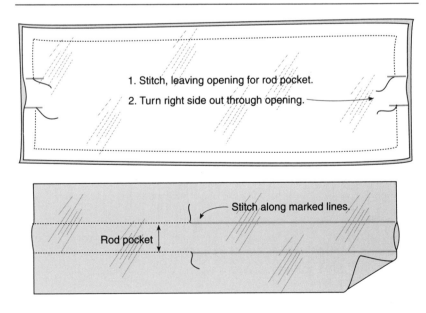

1. Stitch, leaving opening for rod pocket.
2. Turn right side out through opening.

Stitch along marked lines.

Rod pocket

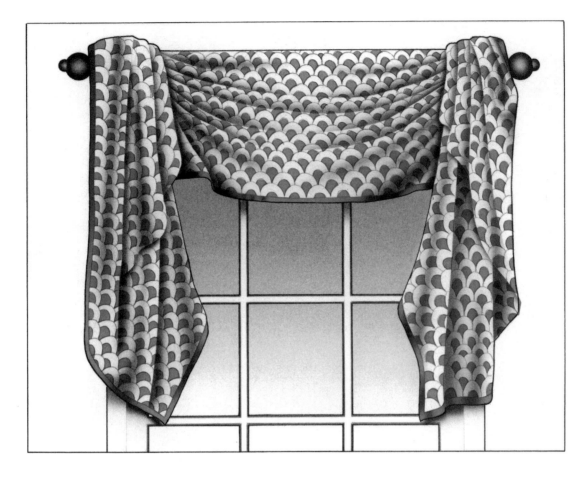

ONE-PIECE SWAG AND JABOT VALANCE

This lined, all-in-one mock swag and jabot looks great on its own or as a valance for floor-length curtains or drapes. The outer edges are bound with ½" (1.3cm) wide bias tape. Use purchased tape or make your own (see Chapter 4, THE SEWING BASICS).

For this window treatment, you need a decorative wood rod that is at least 1⅜" (3.5cm) in diameter and measures 7" (18cm) longer than the width of the window at the top of the molding or above it on the wall (width AA or BB on the "Measure for Measure" diagram on page 86), not including the finials.

You will also need 2½ yards (2.5m) of two-cord shirring tape, two 3" × 3" (7.5cm × 7.5cm) angle brackets and a stapler.

Step 1: Determine the cutting dimensions.

● For the cutting width, add the rod measurement (between the finials) plus 52" (132cm).

● The cutting length is 48" (122cm).

Step 2: Determine how much fabric, lining and bias tape you'll need.

● For fabric and lining, see "Figuring Fabric" in Chapter 4, THE SEWING BASICS.

● For the bias tape, you need an amount equal to the cutting width plus 96" (244cm).

Step 3: Assemble the valance.

● Cut out the valance and the lining, piecing, if necessary, using ½" (1.3cm) seams.

● Place the valance and lining right sides together. Stitch a ½" (1.3cm) seam across the top. Turn right side out and press.

● Machine-baste the layers together close to the raw edges. (See illustration A on the following page.)

● Apply bias tape to the side and lower edges. (See illustration B on the following page.)

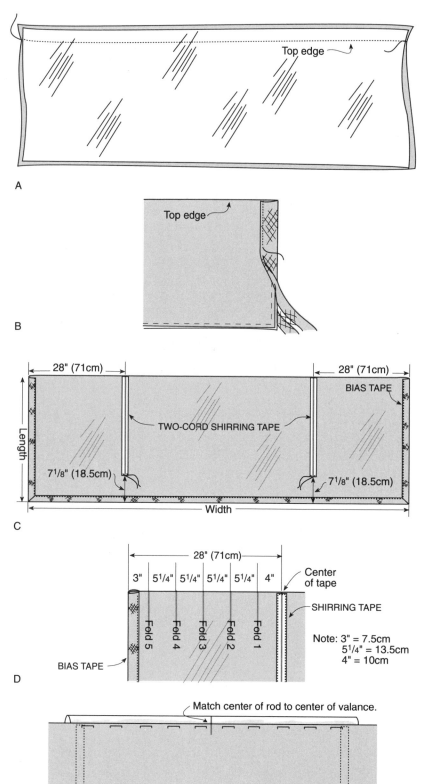

A

B

C

D

E

Top edge

Top edge

28" (71cm)

28" (71cm)

BIAS TAPE

TWO-CORD SHIRRING TAPE

Length

7¹/₈" (18.5cm)

7¹/₈" (18.5cm)

Width

28" (71cm)

3" 5¹/₄" 5¹/₄" 5¹/₄" 5¹/₄" 4"

Center of tape

SHIRRING TAPE

Note: 3" = 7.5cm
5¹/₄" = 13.5cm
4" = 10cm

Fold 5 Fold 4 Fold 3 Fold 2 Fold 1

BIAS TAPE

Match center of rod to center of valance.

● With lining side up, measure in 28″ (71cm) from each side edge; mark, ending the line 7¹/₈″ (18.5cm) from the lower edge. Cut two lengths of shirring tape equal to this line. Be sure there are a few inches of loose cord at one end of each tape. Center the tape over the marked line, with the loose cord at the lower edge; pin. Stitch along both edges of the tape and across the top. (See illustration C.)

● Mark the upper edge of the valance, between the side and the shirring cord, for foldlines. (See illustration D.)

Step 4: Mount the valance on the rod.

● Center the upper edge of the valance on the rod. Staple along the edge, in between the shirring tape. Note that there will be about 2″ (5cm) of "empty" rod at each end. (See illustration E.)

● Fold the valance along Fold 1 and bring it as far as possible across the rod; staple.

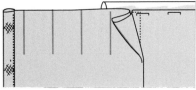

● Fold along Fold 2 and position it on the rod about ¹/₂″ (1.3cm) from Fold 1; staple. Continue folding and stapling, adjusting the space between the pleats so the edge of the

valance matches the end of the rod. Repeat for the other side.

Step 5: Install the valance.

● Mount the angle brackets onto the rod, as shown below, so that the upper edge of the valance is just above the angle bracket.

● Mount the angle bracket to the molding or wall, as previously determined.

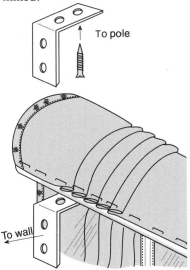

● Pull up the shirring cords until the swag is at the desired height. Tie the cords and cut off the excess.

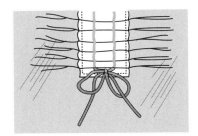

● Arrange the swag into soft, even folds. Then adjust the way the pleats fall.

● If desired, embellish the swag with bows, fabric flowers or tassels. See Chapter 10, DECORATIVE ACCESSORIES.

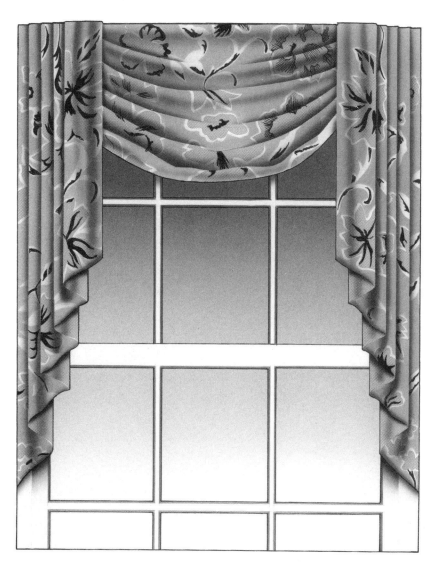

✤

FORMAL SWAGS AND JABOTS

Traditional swags and jabots are elegant, formal window treatments that can be enhanced by all manner of decorative braids, trims and tassels.

Swags are trapezoidal-shape sections of fabric that are pleated or draped to create scallop-like shapes that extend across the top of the window. *Jabots* are softly pleated or gathered side panels with an asymmetrical hemline.

The swag and jabot combination can be hung inside or outside the window frame—in the latter case, alone or over curtains or drapes. The swags and jabots are stapled to a 1″ (2.5cm) thick mounting board that is attached to the frame or wall with angle brackets. The board should be 2″–4″ (5cm–10cm) wide, depending on the amount of clearance that is necessary.

Refer to the measuring diagrams on page 86 as you determine the following:

● For an inside mount, cut the board equal to the measurements of the inner top window frame (CC), less ½″ (1.3cm).

● For an outside mount, the length of the board should be equal to width AA. Install it 2″–4″ (5cm–10cm) above the top of the molding.

● For an outside mount over curtains or drapes (a ceiling mount), the mounting board should extend at least 2″ (5cm) beyond the curtains at the front and the sides. Install it 2″–4″ (5cm–10cm) above the top of the curtains.

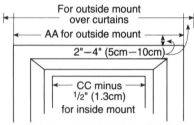

LOCATION OF MOUNTING BOARD

Cut the board to the exact width and length and mount in place. Now you're ready to determine the number and approximate size of your swags.

Make a muslin pattern for both the swag and the jabot. Use this pattern to determine how much fabric and lining you will need.

The Swag

Step 1: Measure.

You can change the look of this window treatment by varying the number of swags, the amount of overlap and how they are arranged in an over-/underlapping pattern. Sketch the arrangement that appeals to you. Then drape a series of strings or cloth tape measures at the edge of the mounting board to mimic the desired effect. As you do this, keep the following guidelines in mind:

● The width of the window and the desired drop will influence the number of swags.

● The width of any one swag should be no more than 40″ (102cm) across the top.

● The drop can range from 12″–20″ (30.5cm–51cm). Ceiling mounts should have the maximum drop.

● If the swags are hung in combination with curtains or drapes, be sure the swags overlap enough to conceal the curtain or drapery headings underneath.

Once the tape is adjusted to your satisfaction:

● Measure width A across the board between the tape or string.

● Use the B measurement for the total width of the swag.

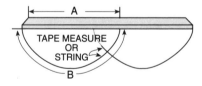

Step 2: Make the swag pattern.

The secret to a successful swag is a custom-made muslin pattern. With this method, the result is a swag with a completely finished outer edge. This makes it versatile enough to be used as either an over-lapping or an underlapping swag.

Cut a piece of muslin 36″ (91.5cm) long and 2″ (5cm) wider than the B measurement. Then:

● Fold the muslin lengthwise in half and mark the center.

● Open out the muslin. At the up-per edge, measure out and mark half the A measurement on each side of the center. Repeat for the lower edge, using half the B measurement.

● Draw two diagonal lines, connecting the corresponding top and bottom marks. Divide and mark these diagonal lines into six equal sections.

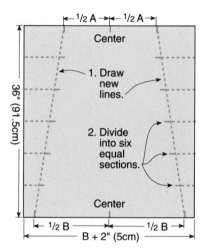

● Pin the upper edge of the muslin, between the markings, to the long, straight edge of your ironing board, with the raw edge overlapping the top of the ironing board by about ½″ (1.3cm).

● Working along one diagonal line, pinch the muslin at the first marking. Bring it up to meet the edge of the muslin; pin. Repeat for the corresponding mark on the other side. Smooth out the resulting fold. Repeat, alternating from side to side, for the remaining marks.

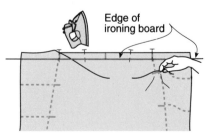

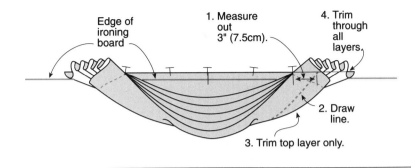

Edge of ironing board

1. Measure out 3" (7.5cm).

4. Trim through all layers.

2. Draw line.

3. Trim top layer only.

● Once all the pleats are formed, check the depth of the drop. If necessary, adjust the pleats.

Now, working on one side of the swag:

● Measure out along the edges of the ironing board about 3" (7.5cm) from the last fold; mark. Starting at this mark, draw the cutting line, gently curving it to meet the lower edge of the swag. Now cut off the excess fabric at the side of the swag.

First, trim only the top layer of fabric (see the illustration above).

Next, unpin this trimmed pleat and fold it toward the center of your swag so it is out of the way. Measure out along the edge of the ironing board about 1½" (3.8cm) from the pleats; trim, cutting through all the remaining layers.

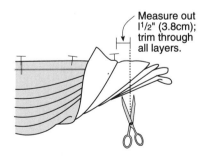

Measure out 1½" (3.8cm); trim through all layers.

To make your muslin pattern completely symmetrical:

● Unpin the swag and give it a good pressing.

● Place it on a flat surface, fold it lengthwise at the center marks and cut the other side to match.

Trim to match top layer.

Center

Step 3: Assemble the swag.

This method prevents the lower edge of the finished swag from curling to the outside, exposing the lining.

● Using the muslin pattern, cut out the lining.

● With right sides together, place the lining over a piece of decorator fabric that is slightly larger than the lining; pin.

● Stitch the lining to the fabric, ½" (1.3cm) from the lower edge of the lining, as shown.

● Trim both layers of fabric to ⅛" (3mm) from the stitching.

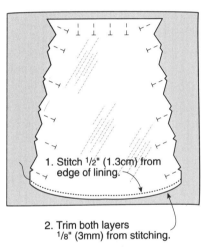

1. Stitch ½" (1.3cm) from edge of lining.

2. Trim both layers ⅛" (3mm) from stitching.

● Turn right side out. Working lining side up, gently roll the lower edge until ⅛"–¼" (3mm–6mm) of the decorator fabric is visible; press.

● Press, then pin the lining to the fabric. Trim the fabric to match the lining.

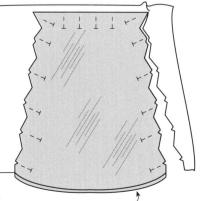

Roll lower edge; press.

● Zigzag or serge along the sides and upper edges.

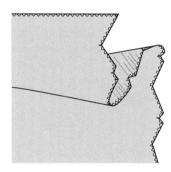

● Fold and pin the swag to form the pleats. Pin to the edge of the ironing board as before; adjust, if necessary.

● Machine-stitch across the upper edge, through all the layers, to hold the pleats in place.

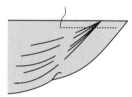

The Jabot

Step 1: Determine the dimensions of the jabot.

● Length:

The inside drop should be equal to, or just a few inches (centimeters) longer than, the swag drop. Measure, then add 1″ (2.5cm) for the inside cutting length.

The outside drop usually extends to one of three points: one-third of the window length, to the sill or to the floor. Measure, then add 1″ (2.5cm) for the outside cutting length.

● Width:

The finished width is a matter of personal preference, but a general

rule is from 9″–12″ (23cm–30.5cm) plus the depth of the return (2″–4″, or 5cm–10cm).

The cutting width is the finished width multiplied by 3 plus the return plus 1″ (2.5cm) for seam allowances.

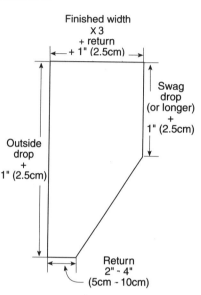

Finished width X 3 + return + 1″ (2.5cm)

Swag drop (or longer) + 1″ (2.5cm)

Outside drop + 1″ (2.5cm)

Return 2″ - 4″ (5cm - 10cm)

Step 2: Cut and construct the jabot.

● Using the cutting dimensions, make a paper or muslin pattern, as shown above.

● Cut two jabots from the lining and two from the decorator fabric. Remember to reverse the pattern for the other side of the window.

● Trim ¹/₂″ (1.3cm) off the diagonal edge of each lining section.

● Pin the lining and the fabric, right sides together, along the lower

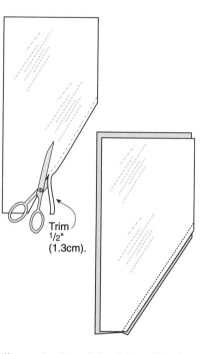

Trim ¹/₂″ (1.3cm).

diagonal edge of the jabot. Stitch a ¹/₂″ (1.3cm) seam. Press seam allowance toward lining.

● Working on a flat surface, with the lining side up, shift the lining up slightly so that ¹/₈″ (3mm) of the fabric is visible at the lower edge. Pin, then stitch the side seams and across the bottom return, using the raw edge of the decorator fabric as your reference point for the ¹/₂″ (1.3cm) seam allowances. Trim the corners.

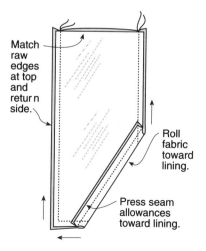

Match raw edges at top and return side.

Roll fabric toward lining.

Press seam allowances toward lining.

● Turn the jabot right side out; press.

Roll lower edge; press.

Step 3: Press the pleats.

● Place the jabot, lining side up, on a large, flat surface. Fold the outside edge over a distance equal to the return; press.

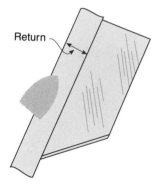

Return

● Turn the jabot right side up.

● Starting at the edge of the inside drop, fold the jabot into three evenly spaced, and parallel, pleats. Adjust until you've achieved the desired finished width (9″–12″, or 23cm–30.5cm). Steam-press to set the pleats.

● Stitch across the top of the jabot, ³/₈″ (1cm) from the raw edge.

Finished width

Step 4: Make the other jabot as a mirror image of the first one.

Step 5: Install the swag and jabot.

● Remove the mounting board from the window.

● Position the swag on the mounting board with the edge of the swag overlapping the board ¹/₂″ (1.3cm). Staple to the top of the board at the corners and approximately every 6″ (15cm) in between.

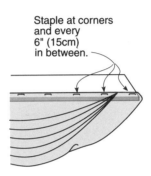

Staple at corners and every 6″ (15cm) in between.

● Position one jabot at one corner of the mounting board, upper edge overlapping by ¹/₂″ (1.3cm) and pressed fold at the corner. Staple as for the swags, folding the excess under at the corner. Repeat for the other jabot.

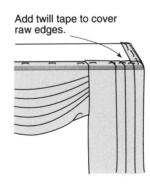

Add twill tape to cover raw edges.

● If desired, staple wide twill tape in place over the raw edges.

● Reinstall the mounting board.

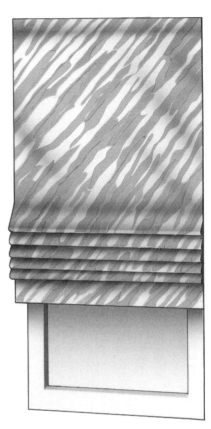

❈

ROMAN SHADE

This unlined shade is mounted on a board attached to the top of the window. A lattice strip inserted through a pocket at the lower edge of the shade provides the necessary weight.

In addition to decorator fabric, you'll need some special supplies:

● A 1″ × 2″ (2.5cm × 5cm) *mounting board*, cut to ¹/₂″ (1.3cm) less than the finished width of the shade.

● *Roman shade tape*. To determine the amount, multiply the finished length by the number of rows of tape. You'll need one row for each side of the shade, plus additional rows spaced 8″–12″ (20.5cm–30.5cm) apart across the shade.

- *Nylon cord*. You'll need enough cord to go up each row of ring tape, across the top of the shade and then down the side.

- *Screw eyes*—one for each row of ring tape.

- *Awning cleat*.

- *Weighted shade pull*.

- *Hook and loop tape*—a strip that is ¹/₂″ (1.3cm) less than the finished width of the shade.

The Roman shade can be mounted inside the window frame

TIP

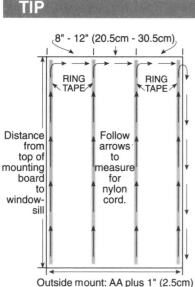

8" - 12" (20.5cm - 30.5cm)

RING TAPE   RING TAPE

Distance from top of mounting board to window-sill

Follow arrows to measure for nylon cord.

Outside mount: AA plus 1" (2.5cm)
Inside mount: CC minus ¹/₂" (2.5cm)

DIAGRAM FOR ROMAN SHADE
OR BALLOON SHADE

To accurately determine the amount of ring tape and cord for both the Roman shade and the balloon shade (see page 119), draw a small diagram of the shade, marking the finished dimensions of the shade as well as the spacing of the ring tape. Note that all the cords converge at one upper corner of the shade.

or on the wall above the window. Refer to the measuring diagrams on page 86 as you determine the following:

- For an inside mount, use the inside frame to inside frame measurement (CC), minus ¹/₂″ (1.3cm) for the finished width. Use angle irons to install the board.

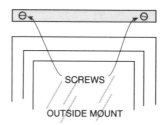

SCREWS

OUTSIDE MOUNT

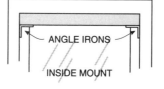

ANGLE IRONS

INSIDE MOUNT

- For an outside mount, use the outside frame to outside frame measurement (AA), plus 1″ (2.5cm) for the finished width. Use screws to install the board.

For the finished length, measure from the top of the mounting board to the windowsill.

Step 1: Determine the cutting dimensions.

- For the cutting width, add 5″ (12.5cm) to the finished width.

- For the cutting length, add 9″ (23cm) to the finished length.

Step 2: Prepare the shade.

- To determine the amount of fabric, see "Figuring Fabric" in Chapter 4, THE SEWING BASICS.

- Cut the fabric as determined by the cutting dimensions. If piecing is required, see the "Tip" on page 106.

TIP

For an outside mount, paint the mounting board to match the wall.

- Working on a large, padded surface, with fabric wrong side up, press in 1¹/₄″ (3.2cm) double side hems; pin.

- At the lower edge, press in a 2¹/₂″ (6.3cm) double hem; pin.

- At the upper edge, press in a 2″ (5cm) double hem; pin.

Step 3: Apply the ring tape.

- Pin the rows of ring tape in place over the side hems and evenly spaced (8″–12″, or 20.5cm–30.5cm, apart) across the shade.

- The bottom ring on each tape should be 3″ (7.5cm) above the top of the bottom hem allowance. Leave enough of a tail to tuck about 1″ (2.5cm) of the tape under the hem allowance at the top and bottom of the shade.

- Fold the top and bottom hem allowances out of the way and stitch each tape in place along both long edges.

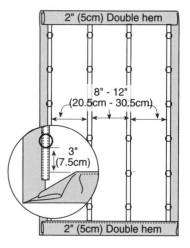

2" (5cm) Double hem

8" - 12"
(20.5cm - 30.5cm)

3"
(7.5cm)

2" (5cm) Double hem

- Refold the bottom hem; stitch.

- Open out the first fold of the top hem. Center and pin the loop side of the hook-and-loop fastener a scant ¼" (6mm) from the upper edge of the shade. Stitch along both sides of the tape, through the hem allowances only.

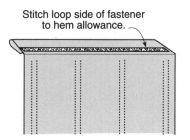

Stitch loop side of fastener to hem allowance.

- Refold the top hem; stitch.

- Insert the lattice strip into the bottom pocket of the shade.

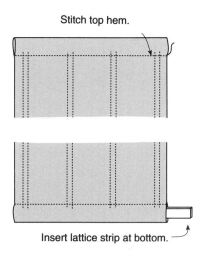

Stitch top hem.

Insert lattice strip at bottom.

Step 4: Rig the shade.

- Remove the mounting board from the window.

- Center the hook side of the hook-and-loop fastener along the upper edge of the 2" (5cm) face of the mounting board; staple to the board. Attach the shade to the board.

Staple hook section of fastener to board.

2" (5cm)

- Place the shade facedown on a large, flat surface. Attach the screw eyes to the underside of the board to correspond to the ring tape.

- For each row of ring tape:
Tie a cord to the bottom ring. Use a dab of glue to secure the knot.

Thread the cord up through the remaining rings, then across the board through the screw eyes to one corner. Trim the excess cord even with the lower edge of the shade.

Repeat for all the ring tapes, running all the cords through the screw eyes in the same direction.

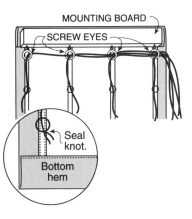

MOUNTING BOARD

SCREW EYES

Seal knot.

Bottom hem

Step 5: Install the shade.

- Reinstall the mounting board at the window.

- Adjust the cords so the tension on each cord is equal. Tie all the cords together in a knot at the upper corner, just below the last screw eye.

Apply glue to the center of the knot as you tie it. Trim off all but one cord, which will be used to raise and lower the shade. Attach a weighted pull to this remaining cord.

- Attach a cleat to the wall or side window frame, midway down the window.

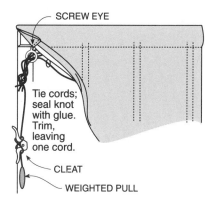

SCREW EYE

Tie cords; seal knot with glue. Trim, leaving one cord.

CLEAT

WEIGHTED PULL

- Pull the shade up, smoothing and straightening the folds. Loop the pull cord around the cleat to hold the shade in the "up" position. Steam to set the memory of the pleats and ring tape. Be sure the shade is thoroughly dry before releasing the pleats.

TIPS

If you want to line this shade, cut the lining to equal the finished length and finished width. Unpin all the hems. Center the lining on the wrong side of the shade, tuck the raw edges under the hem allowances and repin.

For easy installation, complete Step 4. Then pull up on the cords and tie the pleats together. After the board is mounted at the window, release the pleats and continue as in Step 5.

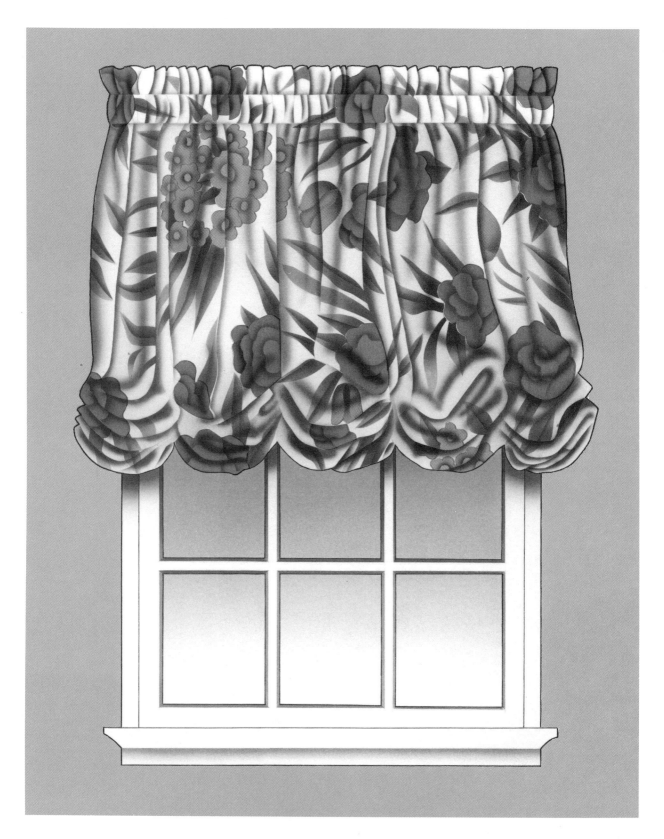

❀ BALLOON SHADE

This shade is a variation of the Roman shade. It provides a soft, gentle window covering that is easy to install.

In addition to *decorator fabric*, you'll need some special supplies:

- ³/₄″ (2cm) diameter *wooden dowel*, cut to the inside frame to inside frame (CC) measurement.
- 1¹/₂″ × ¹/₄″ (3.8cm × 6mm) *lattice strip*, cut to the inside frame to inside frame (CC) measurement.
- *Conventional curtain rod*.
- *Roman shade tape*. To determine the amount, multiply the finished length by the number of rows of tape. You'll need one row for each side of the shade, plus additional rows spaced 15″–30″ (38cm–76cm) apart across the shade.
- *Nylon cord*. You'll need enough cord to go up each row of ring tape, across the top of the shade and then down the side.
- *Screw eyes*—two for each row of ring tape.
- *Awning cleat*.
- *Weighted shade pull*.
- *Angle irons* to install lattice strip.

Mount the curtain rod so the top of the rod is even with the top of the window frame.

- To determine the finished length, measure from the top of the rod to the windowsill.
- To determine the finished width, measure the rod plus projections.

Step 1: Determine the cutting dimensions.

- For the cutting length, add 28″ (71cm) to the finished length.
- For the cutting width, multiply the finished width by 2, then add 6″ (15cm) for side hems.

Step 2: Prepare the shade.

- To determine the amount of fabric, see "Figuring Fabric" in Chapter 4, THE SEWING BASICS.
- Cut the fabric as determined by the cutting dimensions.
- Working on a large, flat surface, with fabric wrong side up, press in 1¹/₂″ (3.8cm) double side hems; pin.
- At the lower edge, press in a 3″ (7.5cm) double hem; pin.

Step 3: Apply the ring tape.

- Pin the rows of ring tape in place

TIP

To eliminate stitching lines on the outside of Roman or balloon shades, choose iron-on ring tape.

over the side hems and evenly spaced (15″–30″, or 38cm–76cm, apart) across the shade.

The bottom ring on each tape should be 3″ (7.5cm) above the top of the bottom hem allowance, and the tape itself should extend ¹/₂″ (1.3cm) into the hem allowance.

End each tape 7″ (18cm) from the upper edge of the shade.

- Unfold the bottom hem and stitch each tape in place along both long edges.
- Refold and stitch the bottom hem.

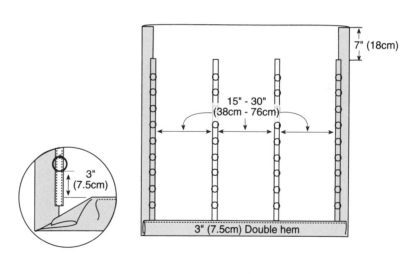

7″ (18cm)

15″ - 30″ (38cm - 76cm)

3″ (7.5cm)

3″ (7.5cm) Double hem

TIP

If piecing is required for the Roman shade or the balloon shade, refer to the shade diagram on page 116. Plan piecing seams so they will occur along a stitching line for the ring tape. Piece so there is one center panel, with two side panels. Press the seam allowances toward the side of the shade; trim them to ¹/₄″ (6mm).

Step 4: Make the header and rod pocket.

• At the upper edge, press a 4″ (10cm) double hem. Stitch close to the inner fold. Stitch again, 2″ (5cm) from the top, forming the header and rod pocket.

↕ 2″ (5cm) Header
↕ 2″ (5cm) Rod pocket

Step 5: Rig the shade.

• Insert the dowel into the bottom hem allowance so it rests against the hemline of the shade.

• Position one end of the dowel even with the side of the shade. Measure in ½″ (1.3cm) and insert a screw eye, through the fabric and into the dowel, at the hemline. Repeat at the other end of the dowel.

• Adjust the fullness across the dowel. Insert a screw eye to correspond to each row of tape.

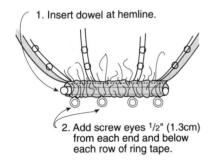

1. Insert dowel at hemline.

2. Add screw eyes ½″ (1.3cm) from each end and below each row of ring tape.

• For each row of ring tape:
Run the nylon cord through the screw eye and the first five rings; tie together, sealing the center of the knot with a dab of glue.

Thread the cord up through every other ring; then run it across the top of the shade, below the rod pocket, to one corner, and down the side of the shade. Trim the cord.

Use a safety pin to temporarily secure the cord at the top of the ring tape.

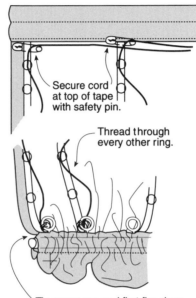

Secure cord at top of tape with safety pin.

Thread through every other ring.

Tie screw eye and first five rings together; seal knot with glue.

Step 6: Install the shade.

• Using the dowel as a template, mark the face of the lattice strip for the corresponding number of screw eyes. The marks should be aligned across the center, parallel to the lower edge of the strip. Insert a screw eye at each mark.

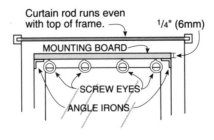

Curtain rod runs even with top of frame. ¼″ (6mm)

MOUNTING BOARD

SCREW EYES

ANGLE IRONS

• Using angle brackets, install the lattice board inside the window frame.

• Insert the curtain in the rod pocket. Hang the shade.

• Working on the wrong side of the shade, thread each cord across the lattice strip through the screw eyes to one corner. Remove the safety pins. Adjust the gathers evenly across the curtain rod.

• Adjust the cords so the tension on each cord is equal. Tie all the cords together in a knot at the upper corner, just below the last screw eye. Apply glue to the center of the knot as you tie it. Trim off all but one cord, which will be used to raise and lower the shade. Attach a weighted pull to this remaining cord.

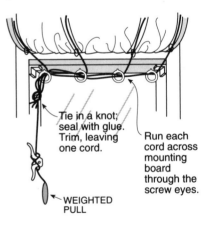

Tie in a knot; seal with glue. Trim, leaving one cord.

Run each cord across mounting board through the screw eyes.

WEIGHTED PULL

• Attach a cleat to the wall or side window frame, midway down the window.

• Loop the pull cord around the cleat to hold the shade in the desired position.

For additional ideas, including roller shades, cut-and-drape window treatments and cornice boards, see Chapter 11, TIMESAVERS.

LUXURIOUS LIVING ROOMS

Coordinated prints offer an easy, but effective, way to achieve a cozy, color-matched interior. Other solutions include a simplified color scheme that relies on textures to provide warmth (*left*) and one strong print that provides color inspiration and visual focus (*above*).

[*For more information about these color pages, see the GLOSSARY on page 227.*]

ELEGANT ENTERTAINING

Fabric touches almost every surface, adding high drama to a room with modest architectural details. Design alternatives include the upscale country look in soft garden tones (*left*) and a contemporary setting that can be achieved with minimal sewing (*above*).

BEAUTIFUL BEDROOMS

Because the master bedroom often reflects the personality of two occupants, it offers some special decorating challenges. A jewel-tone plaid, repeated throughout the room, has universal appeal. Multicolor stripes are an effective counterpoint to flora and fauna prints (*below, left*), while a sophisticated color scheme offsets what would otherwise have been an overly feminine room (*below, right*).

KIDS'/TEENS' BEDROOMS

Rooms that successfully follow the
occupant's transition from child to
young adult forsake juvenile themes
in favor of more grown-up looks.
Lavender florals and wicker furniture
create a romantic environment for a
young girl. A bold leaf print presents a
feminine, but tailored, alternative (*right*).
For her male counterpart, consider
the crisp, modern appeal of a room
dominated by graphic stripes (*above*).

LULLABY LAND

Engineered prints, designed specifically
with the nursery in mind, can be fashioned
into quilts and other items that coordinate
with the rest of the decor. Add a touch of
whimsy with soft sculpture pals outfitted in
the same fabrics. Check out the *Simplicity®
Pattern Catalog* for pattern ideas. For a
different look, consider gingham, reborn
for the newborn in three-color ways.

Sheers, as cafés or as undercurtains for floor-length treatments, filter the light, while providing daytime privacy (*right*). Roman shades partially block the light during the day but can be adjusted for total coverage at night (*above*). Add drama by framing the window with a coordinating wallpaper border (*top left*). When formality is the operative word, swag treatments are an appropriate choice (*bottom left*).

PILLOW PIZZAZZ

Printed or plain, smooth or textured, pillows add comfort and beauty to any room setting. And when it comes to opportunities for embellishment, nothing can outshine a pillow. Piping, lace edgings, tassels, fringe, appliqué work, ribbons, panel prints and machine embroidery are just a few of the ways to make them special.

AT THE TABLE

Whether it's a small occasional table or the main family dining area, beautiful table linens add a special ambience to any repast.

Sleeping
Beauty

Sleeping Beauty

Since the bed generally occupies the greatest amount of space in a bedroom, it tends to be the center of attention. And because it's the first thing one usually sees, it's the bed and all its trappings that set the mood for the entire room.

Bedcoverings can be tailored or romantic, functional or frilly, understated or elaborate. Like all your decorating decisions, the final choice is a matter of blending life-style with personal style.

SELECTING A BEDCOVERING

Almost all bedcoverings are variations on a few simple styles. It's the change of fabric and trim that alters their decorating personality. Even bed fashions for the nursery are nothing more than miniaturized versions of their adult counterparts.

A *bedspread* covers the bed, with enough extra length to tuck it under and wrap it over the pillows. Although it can be cut short and paired with a dust ruffle, it usually extends down to the floor. Of all the bedcoverings, the bedspread probably offers the most versatile use of fabric. Heavy- or lightweight fabrics are equally suitable. Bedspreads can be soft and flowing, lined for warmth and durability, or quilted to add both warmth and surface texture.

A *comforter*, or *coverlet*, is similar to a bedspread, but shorter. Rather than the full drop to the floor, the comforter extends only 4″ or 5″ (10cm or 12.5cm) below the bottom of the mattress. Use it in combination with a dust ruffle or on beds that have decorative foot- and sideboards. Because a comforter usually is not long enough to cover the bed pillows, coordinating pillow shams are a favorite accessory.

A *duvet cover* is like an oversize pillowcase. It protects the duvet itself, a high-quality, down-filled blanket that has long been popular in Europe. In homes without central heating, it was used on top of the bed linens to provide warmth without weight. Covers were necessary for two reasons. First, goose down is a luxurious filling that cannot be cleaned easily, and second, because these blankets were valuable, they were viewed as family heirlooms.

When high fuel costs forced everyone to turn down the thermostats, duvets had a resurgence in popularity on both sides of the Atlantic. Today's duvet is similar to a comforter and usually covers the top and sides of the mattress. Down-filled duvets are available in a variety of sizes, weights and thicknesses to satisfy personal tastes. Other fillings, such as wool or polyester battings, are also available.

The *dust ruffle*, sometimes called a *bed skirt*, adds the finishing touch to shorter bedcoverings, such as comforters and duvets. It hides the bottom half of the bed, including the box spring and the bed frame. It can be gathered or pleated, creating a soft or a tailored effect.

STYLE FOLLOWS FUNCTION

● If sprawling on the bed is your habit, or if your household includes a dog or cat that likes to cozy-up on the bed, then no-fuss, easy-maintenance bedcoverings are best.

● If the bedroom is strictly for sleeping or contains a sitting area other than the bed, then fragile fabrics, elaborate coverings, even antique linens, are possibilities.

● Children—and impatient bed makers of all ages—will welcome fuss-free, toss-'em-on comforters and duvets.

- A seldom-used guest room can be dressed for show.

- If the room doubles as an office or sewing room, a practical, pared-down look may be more suitable.

GENERAL DIRECTIONS

Measuring

Although mattresses come in standard sizes, there are variations in the thickness of the mattress and the height of the bed, which includes the depth of the box spring and frame. Antique or reproduction beds may be so high off the floor that you need a footstool to climb in and out. On the other hand, in order to ease the weight distribution, a waterbed may sit very close to the floor.

To be on the safe side, measure and record the dimensions of your bed. Because the thickness of your bed linens can affect the measurements, make up the bed with sheets and blankets before measuring.

- *Mattress width*. Measure across at the center of the bed, from edge to edge.

- *Mattress length*. Measure the length at the center of the bed, from edge to edge.

- *Depth of mattress*. Measure from the top edge to the bottom edge.

- *Full drop for bedspread and for studio-couch cover*. Measure from the top edge of the mattress to 1/2" (1.3cm) from the floor.

- *Comforter drop*. Measure from the top edge of the mattress to 4"–5" (10cm–12.5cm) below the bottom edge of the mattress.

- *Dust ruffle skirt drop*. Measure from the top edge of the box spring to 1/2" (1.3cm) from the floor.

Piecing the Cover

With 90" (229cm) or 120" (305cm) wide fabric, piecing *may not* be necessary. However, with narrower fabrics, you will need to piece the bedcover. To avoid an unattractive center seam, the bedcover should have one wide center section and two narrower side sections.

First, determine the finished width and length of the desired bed-covering; then:

- For double, queen- or king-size beds, use the full width of the fabric, minus 1" (2.5cm) for the piecing seams, for the center section. Subtract the center section from the finished width of the covering. Split the difference into two equal-width side sections.

- For a twin bed, make the center section approximately 40" (102cm) wide, plus 1" (2.5cm) for piecing seams. Subtract 40" (102cm) from the finished width of the covering. Split the difference into two equal-width side sections.

- Add the width of the side section plus 2" (5cm) hem allowance plus 1/2" (1.3cm) piecing seam allowance; then multiply by 2.

If this sum is equal to, or less than, the width of the fabric, you'll need two panels of fabric—one for the center and one for the sides.

If this sum is greater than the width of the fabric, you'll need three panels of fabric—one for the center and one for each side.

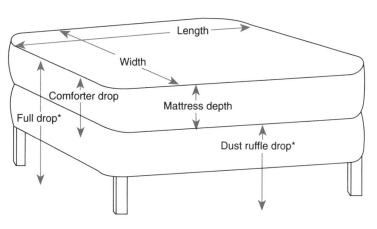

*These drop measurements end 1/2" (1.3cm) from the floor.

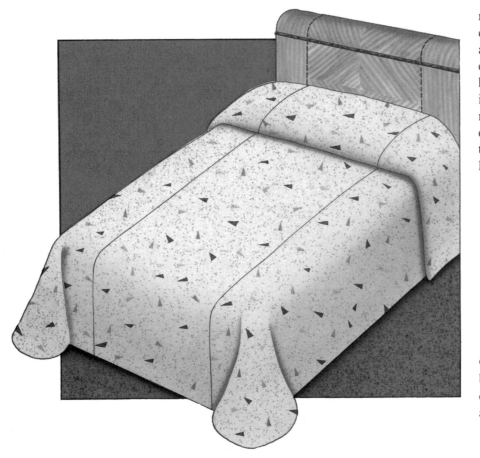

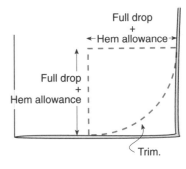

right sides together. At the lower corner, mark in from the side edge and the bottom edge a distance equal to the full drop plus 2″ (5cm) hem allowance. Connect the markings to form a square. Using a tape measure or yardstick as a compass, draw an arc, as shown, to round off the corner. Trim along the marked line.

- Hem the sides, then the top and bottom edges, using a 1″ (2.5cm) double hem, easing in the fullness around the corners.

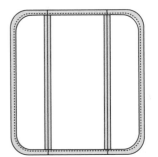

For additional information, including motifs that require matching, see "Fabric Basics" in Chapter 4, THE SEWING BASICS.

❁

BASIC BEDSPREAD

This bedspread is a full-size bed throw. Leave the lower corners square so they puddle on the floor or round them off so they clear the floor evenly with the sides of the spread.

Step 1: Determine the cutting dimension of the bedspread.

NOTE: Refer to the measuring information on page 123.

- Width = Mattress width + two full drops.

- Length = Mattress length + one full drop + 30″ (76cm) (to cover bed pillows).

- Add 4″ (10cm) to the length and the width. This provides for a 1″ (2.5cm) double hem all around.

Step 2: Determine the amount of fabric.

- Review "Piecing the Cover" on page 123 to determine the width of the center and side sections, as well as the number of panels of fabric.

- Multiply the length of the bedspread (including 4″, or 10cm, for hem allowances) by the number of panels. That's how much fabric you need for the bedspread.

Step 3: Assemble the bedspread.

- Cut and piece the three sections, using ¹⁄₂″ (1.3cm) seams.

OPTIONAL: To round off the corners, fold the spread lengthwise in half,

TIP

To add a design element to your bedcovering, include an insertion trim, such as piping or lace, in the piecing seam.

Design Options

● Add self-fabric or purchased ruffle trim to the sides and lower edge. When cutting out the sections, shorten the length and width the appropriate amounts so that, on the finished spread, the ruffles clear the floor by ¹/₂″ (1.3cm).

● Eliminate the hem allowances on the sides and lower edge, then finish with contrasting bias binding.

● Add a wide, contrasting band, using the clean-finish border technique. (See "Hems" in Chapter 4, THE SEWING BASICS.)

● For durability and decorating pizzazz, add a contrasting lining. Adjust the hem allowances on all the edges to ¹/₂″ (1.3cm), then round off the corners. Cut and piece the lining and the spread. Pin them wrong sides together and stitch a ¹/₂″ (1.3cm) seam, leaving an opening in the upper edge for turning. Turn right side out; slipstitch the opening closed. If desired, add piping to the outer seam before it is stitched, or apply bias binding to the outer edges of the finished spread.

✿

FLOUNCED BEDSPREAD

This bedspread has a fitted top and flounced, or gathered, sides. The entire spread can be made from one fabric, or a different fabric can be used for the top and sides.

Step 1: Determine the cutting dimensions of the top and the flounce.

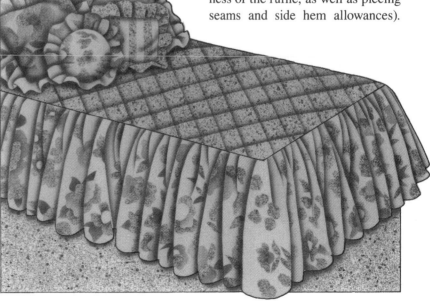

NOTE: Refer to the measuring information on page 123.

● Top width = Mattress width + 1″ (2.5cm) for seam allowances.

● Top length = Mattress length + 30″ (76cm) + 2¹/₂″ (6.3cm) for top hem and bottom seam allowance.

● Flounce depth = Full drop + 2¹/₂″ (6.3cm) for bottom hem and top seam allowance.

● Flounce length = Mattress width + two mattress lengths, all multiplied by 2¹/₂ (to allow for the fullness of the ruffle, as well as piecing seams and side hem allowances).

Step 2: Determine the amount of fabric.

FOR THE TOP. Review "Piecing the Cover" on page 123 to determine the width of the center and side sections of the top, as well as the number of panels it requires.

Multiply the length of the top (including hem and seam allowances) by the number of panels. This is how much fabric you need for the top.

FOR THE FLOUNCE.

NOTE: The flounce sections are cut crosswise on the fabric.

Divide the flounce length by the width of the fabric. This tells you how many crosswise panels you will need to cut.

Multiply the number of panels by the flounce depth (including seam and hem allowances). This is how much fabric you need for the flounce.

Step 3: Assemble the top of the bedspread.

• Cut and piece the top, using ½" (1.3cm) seams.

• Hem the upper edge, using a 1" (2.5cm) double hem.

• Divide and mark the sides and lower edge of the top into sixteenths.

Step 4: Assemble the flounce.

• Cut and piece the flounce, using ½" (1.3cm) seams.

• Hem the sides and the bottom edge, using 1" (2.5cm) double hems.

• Divide and mark the upper edge of the flounce into sixteenths.

• Machine-gather the upper edge.

Step 5: Complete the bedspread.

• With right sides together, pin the flounce to the top, matching the markings and the hemmed edges at the upper edge of the spread. Adjust the gathers, then stitch a ½" (1.3cm) seam.

Design Options

• To define the fitted shape, include piping, rickrack or other insertion trim in the seam that joins the flounce and the top.

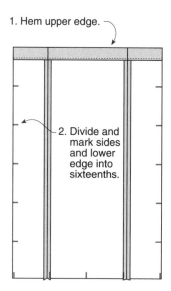

1. Hem upper edge.

2. Divide and mark sides and lower edge into sixteenths.

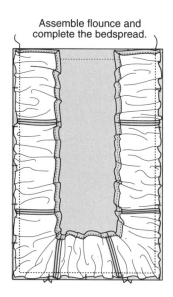

Assemble flounce and complete the bedspread.

• For a very feminine look, consider a double flounce, using a sheer to lightweight fabric. Cut a second flounce, approximately two-thirds the depth of the first one. Piece and hem separately, then baste them together along the upper edge. Gather and attach as one.

• Use a quilted fabric for the top and its unquilted coordinate for the flounce.

• Eliminate the hem allowance and finish the lower edge of the flounce with contrasting bias binding.

• Create a border on the flounce by adding bands of lace, braid, ribbon or other flat trim. Apply before the flounce is gathered.

✿ TUFTED COMFORTER WITH RUFFLED EDGES

On this comforter, two layers of fabric, with batting in between, are held together with tied threads—a quick and easy method of quilting. Choose coordinating fabrics for a reversible comforter.

Step 1: Determine the cutting dimensions of the comforter.

NOTE: Refer to the measuring information on page 123.

• Width = Mattress width + two mattress depths + 5″ (12.5cm) (for the mattress overlaps and seam allowances).

• Length = Mattress length + mattress depth + 3″ (7.5cm) (for seam allowances and mattress overlap).

NOTE: If you prefer to make the comforter without the ruffled border, add another 4″ (10cm) to the width and 2″ (5cm) to the length.

Step 2: Determine the amount of fabric and trim.

• Review "Piecing the Cover" on page 123 to determine the width of the center and side sections, as well as the number of panels of fabric.

• Multiply the length of the comforter (including the 3″, or 7.5cm, for seam allowances and overlap) by the number of panels. This is how much fabric you need for the top of the comforter. You will also need this same amount of fabric for the lining.

• For the ruffle, purchase an amount of 4″–8″ (10cm–20.5cm) wide pregathered eyelet trim. The

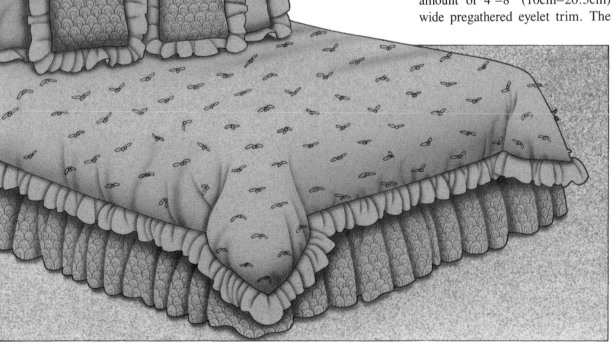

amount should equal one width and two lengths of the comforter . . . or make your own fabric ruffles. (See "Ruffles" in Chapter 4, THE SEWING BASICS.)

Step 3: Cut and prepare the comforter sections.

● Cut and piece the top sections, using $\frac{1}{2}''$ (1.3cm) seams. Repeat for the lining.

● Using a large dinner plate as a template, round off the lower corners of the top and the lining.

● Cut the batting to match the top section—piecing, if necessary.

● Pin, then baste the batting to the wrong side of the top.

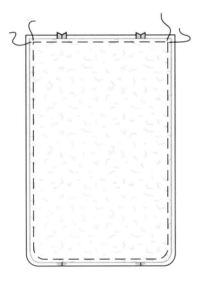

Step 4: Apply the trim.

● Finish one end of the ruffle trim with a $\frac{1}{2}''$ (1.3cm) double hem.

● With right sides together and raw edges even, place the hemmed end of the trim $\frac{1}{2}''$ (1.3cm) down from the upper edge. Pin the trim around the edge of the top and mark where the other end intersects the upper

edge seam allowance. Cut off the excess trim, leaving a 1″ (2.5cm) hem allowance.

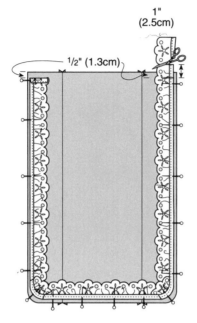

● Unpin the trim just enough so you can finish the raw end with a $\frac{1}{2}''$ (1.3cm) double hem. Repin the trim, then machine-baste it in place.

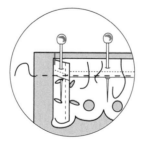

Step 5: Assemble the comforter.

● Pin the lining to the top, right sides together. Stitch a $\frac{1}{2}''$ (1.3cm) seam, leaving an opening in the upper edge for turning. Be careful—don't catch the ruffle in the upper seam allowance.

● Notch the curves. Turn the comforter right side out and slipstitch the opening closed.

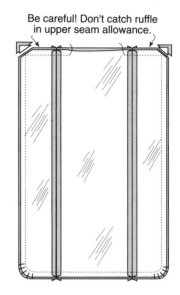

Step 6: Tuft the comforter.

● Thread a large-eye needle with heavy decorative thread, perle cotton, yarn or $\frac{1}{8}''$ or $\frac{1}{16}''$ (3mm or 1.5mm) wide ribbon. At random or at evenly spaced intervals, insert the needle from the top, through all layers and back up from the bottom. Tie the ends into a secure knot or bow and trim the tails to 3″ (7.5cm).

● Apply a drop of liquid seam sealant or white, clear-drying craft glue to the center of each knot or bow. (For ribbon, use seam sealant on the cut ends, too.)

TIP

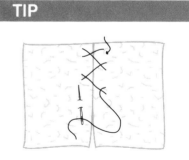

To piece batting, butt the cut edges together and secure with large cross-stitches.

A BIT ABOUT BATTING

The blanket of fibers that is sandwiched between two layers of fabric in a quilted item is called the *batting*.

When choosing a batting, consider end use, softness, warmth, care requirements and how densely it must be quilted. These properties are the result of both the fiber content and the chemical or physical treatments that have been applied to the batting.

Familiarize yourself with the following terms, then use the chart on the next page as a guide to selecting the best batting for your project.

● *Resilience* is the ability of the batting to return to its original shape, regardless of the amount of washing, wearing or crushing it has endured.

● *Loft* refers to the thickness, or fullness, of the batting. To maintain its fullness throughout the life of the quilt, a high-loft batting should also be resilient. A thicker-loft batting may not mean a warmer quilt.

● *Migration* describes the tendency of the fibers to move or shift to a different location. The result may be a lumpy quilt, with thick and thin spots.

● *Bearding* is the light fuzz that covers the surface of the fabric when migrating fibers push through the weave of the outer layer of fabric. To prevent bearding, choose specially treated battings and construct the outer layer of the quilt from firmly woven fabric. One or two manufacturers offer dark batting, which means that the bearding will be less noticeable on dark fabrics.

Several other terms describe the chemical or physical treatments whose purpose is to maintain stability and uniformity throughout the blanket of fibers.

● *Bonded batting* is created by feeding the batting through chemically treated or heated rollers. The result is a light glaze that holds the outer fibers together. This reduces the amount of bearding, often produces a higher loft and eliminates shifting fibers so the quilting stitches can be farther apart.

● *Needlepunch batting* is produced by passing the blanket of fibers through a machine with many small, hooked needles. These needles vibrate within the blanket, tangling the fibers to unify them, thus lessening the amount of bearding. This type of batting can have a high or low loft.

● *Resin-treated battings* are sprayed with a chemical that gently glues the fibers together. This treatment significantly reduces bearding but usually creates a stiffer batting that is suitable for structured projects, such as a padded window cornice.

TIPS

Make a template for your tufting design. Cut a piece of nonwoven pattern-duplicating material—the type with 1″ (2.5cm) grid markings—to the width of your comforter. The depth should be equal to at least one and a half repeats of your tufting design. Using the grid as a guide, plot out your tufting design. Make a small snip at each tufting mark with your scissors. Place the template over the quilt and mark at each hole, using a fabric marking pen, chalk or a soft lead pencil. Shift the template down and repeat until the whole comforter is marked.

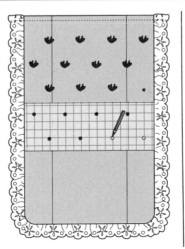

To make the comforter reversible, insert the needle from the top, tie a half knot on the lining side, then bring the needle back up and tie the ends in a knot or bow.

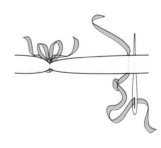

BATTING

FIBER	PROPERTIES AND ADVANTAGES	DISADVANTAGES	CARE	APPEARANCE	SUGGESTED USES
Polyester	Lightweight and resilient; inexpensive and readily available; resists moths and mildew; extensive quilting unnecessary.	Some migration of fibers if unbonded.	Machine-washable.	Available in many weights and thicknesses.	Quilts, tied quilts, crafts and baby quilts.
Cotton-polyester blend	Combines ease of handling found in a polyester, with natural moisture absorption and warmth of a cotton. When compared with 100% cotton, provides less matting and has better resistance to fiber migration.	Percentage of blend may determine degree of matting and bunching.	Hand- or machine-wash.	Low- to medium-loft appearance.	Quilts and clothing.
Cotton	Natural felting property holds fibers together, lessening migration.	May mat or bunch with repeated washings. Quilt no more than $1/2''$ apart to prevent shifting.	Hand-washable.	Traditional low-loft appearance of antique quilts.	Quilts, wearables, sleeve heads, shoulder pads, placemats.
Wool	Natural warmth.	Susceptible to insects and may cause allergies; some fiber migration; limited availability.	Hand-wash or dry-clean.	Somewhat heavier than other battings.	Warmer quilts, comforters. Lessen fiber migration by covering with a lightweight fabric cover.
Silk	Lightweight; does not pack down.	Quilt no more than $1/2''$ apart to prevent shifting; somewhat expensive; limited availability.	Hand-wash or dry-clean.	Drapes well.	Luxury garments.

✿

BASIC DUVET COVER

The duvet cover usually is coordinated with the dust ruffle and the pillow shams.

Traditionally, the cover bears a closer resemblance to a sheet than to a bedcovering. It's usually made from lightweight, easy-care fabric with minimal surface embellishment. Small tabs of snap tape concealed inside the cover prevent the duvet from shifting out of place.

Custom-made ruffles, pregathered trim, piping or welting can be incorporated into the outer seam of the cover. To add decorative dash, use contrasting fabrics for the top and lining.

Step 1: Determine the cutting dimensions of the duvet cover.

● Width = Width of the duvet + 1″ (2.5cm) for seam allowances.

● Length = Length of the duvet + 1″ (2.5cm) for seam allowances.

Step 2: Determine the amount of fabric.

● Review "Piecing the Cover" on page 123 to determine the width of the center and side sections, as well as the number of panels of fabric.

● Multiply the length of the duvet cover (including seam allowances) plus 2″ (5cm) by the number of panels. This is how much fabric you will need for the top of the cover. You will also need this same amount for the lining.

Step 3: Cut the cover sections.

● Cut and piece the top, using ½″ (1.3cm) seams.

● Cut the lining sections 2″ (5cm) longer than the top. Piece, if necessary, using ½″ (1.3cm) seams.

Step 4: Install the zipper.

NOTE: For a twin-size cover, use a 38″ (96.5cm) long zipper; for a double, queen- or king-size, use a 50″ (127cm) long zipper.

● Right sides together, fold the lower edge of the lining up 6″ (15cm) and press. For the zipper opening, center and mark, as shown on the following page, for a distance equal to the length of the zipper.

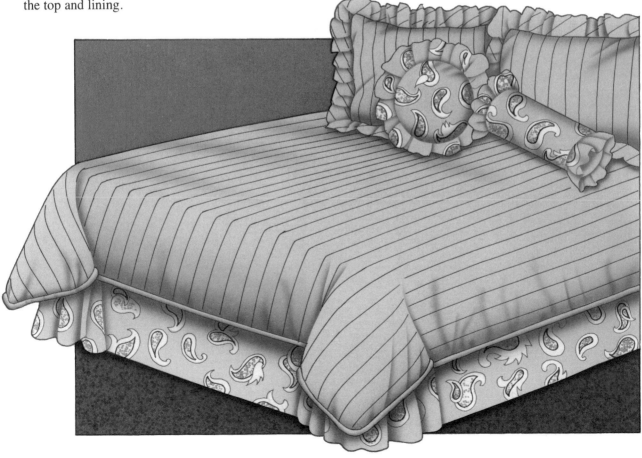

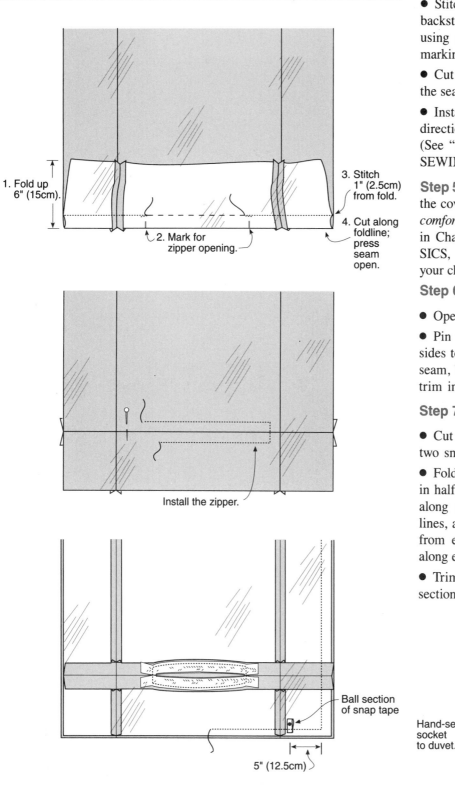

1. Fold up 6" (15cm).

2. Mark for zipper opening.

3. Stitch 1" (2.5cm) from fold.

4. Cut along foldline; press seam open.

Install the zipper.

Ball section of snap tape

5" (12.5cm)

- Stitch 1″ (2.5cm) from the fold, backstitching at each marking and using a basting stitch between the markings.

- Cut along the foldline, then press the seam open.

- Install the zipper, following the directions for the center application. (See "Zippers" in Chapter 4, THE SEWING BASICS.)

Step 5: Apply the trim to the top of the cover, as in Step 4 of the *tufted comforter*. (See "Special Touches" in Chapter 4, THE SEWING BASICS, for specific information on your chosen trim.)

Step 6: Assemble the cover.

- Open the zipper.

- Pin the lining to the top, right sides together. Stitch a ½″ (1.3cm) seam, being careful not to catch the trim in the upper seam allowance.

Step 7: Add snap tape.

- Cut four sections of snap tape, two snaps each. Separate the tape.

- Fold the ball sections crosswise in half, snap side out. Pin in place along the upper and lower seamlines, approximately 5″ (12.5cm) in from each corner. Stitch in place along each seamline.

- Trim one socket from each socket section. Fold the raw edges to the

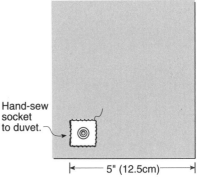

Hand-sew socket to duvet.

5" (12.5cm)

underside, then hand-sew in place on the upper and lower edges of the duvet, to correspond to the cover.

● Snap the duvet to the cover at the upper edge. Turn the cover right side out, encasing the duvet. Snap the tape together at the lower edge, then zip the opening closed.

―――― *Variation* ――――

Flanged Duvet Cover

For a pretty pairing, mate this duvet to flanged pillow shams (see Chapter 8, PILLOW PIZZAZZ).

Construct the flanged duvet as for the *basic duvet cover*, with the following adjustments:

Step 1: For the cutting dimensions, add 5″ (12.5cm) to the length and the width.

Steps 2–6: These steps are the same as for the *basic duvet cover*.

Step 7: Make the flange and add the snap tape.

● Turn the cover right side out. Mark 2½″ (6.3cm) from the outer edge.

● Cut four sections of snap tape, two snaps each. Separate the tape.

● Fold the ball sections crosswise in half, snap side out. Slip them in-side the duvet cover and pin in place along the upper and lower marked lines, approximately 5″ (12.5cm) in from each corner.

● Topstitch around the cover, along the marked lines, catching the snap tape in the stitching.

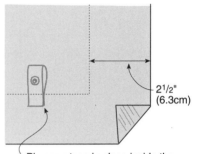

Pin snap tape in place inside the cover. Topstitch around the cover, along marked line, catching the tape in the stitching.

● Apply the socket section to the duvet and complete as for the *basic duvet cover*.

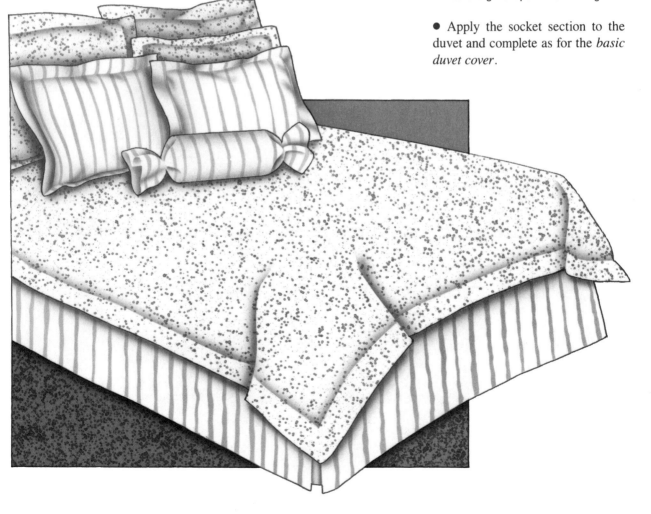

DUST RUFFLES: GENERAL DIRECTIONS

Dust ruffles are not only decorative, they're practical, too. Where storage space is at a premium, they not only conceal the box spring and bed frame, they also conceal everything else under the bed!

Measuring

For a secure fit, remove the mattress and take the following measurements:

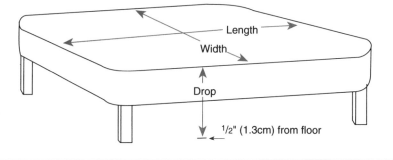

- *Box spring width*. Measure across at the center of the box spring, from edge to edge.

- *Box spring length*. Measure the length at the center of the box spring, from edge to edge.

- *Skirt drop*. Measure from the top edge of the box spring to 1/2" (1.3cm) from the floor.

The Deck

The dust ruffle skirt is usually sewn onto a platform of fabric, called a *deck*, which fits between the mattress and the box spring. The deck is commonly made from a sturdy, medium-weight, plain fabric, such as muslin, chintz or sheeting. Use these instructions to create the deck for all the dust ruffles in this book.

Step 1: Use the chart on the next page to determine how much fabric you need for the deck.

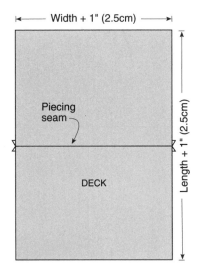

Step 2: To determine the cutting dimensions, add 1" (2.5cm) to the box spring width and 1" (2.5cm) to the length. Cut the deck, piecing it crosswise, if necessary, with 1/2" (1.3cm) seams.

TIPS

If your bed has an attached headboard, adjust the directions for all of the dust ruffles in this chapter so that the skirt ends at the corners of the head.

On a strict budget? Inquire at a mill end store about damaged, chintz-weight prints. Available for pennies, they are too flawed for most uses. However, no one but you sees the deck.

The easiest deck is the one you make from a fitted sheet. Cover the box spring with the sheet. Using chalk, a soft lead pencil or a fabric marking pen, mark the top edge of the mattress. Use this line as the seamline when attaching the skirt to the deck.

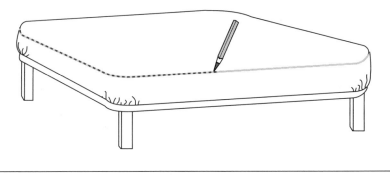

YARDAGE CHART: DUST RUFFLE DECK

Deck size (including seam allowances)	45″ (115cm) fabric	54″ (138cm) fabric	60″ (153cm) fabric	90″ (229cm) fabric
Twin (40″ × 76″) (102cm × 193cm)	2⅛ yd* (2m*)	2⅛ yd* (2m*)	2⅛ yd* (2m*)	1⅛ yd** (1.1m**)
Full (55″ × 76″) (140cm × 193cm)	3⅛ yd*** (2.9m***)	3⅛ yd*** (2.9m***)	3⅛ yd* (2.9m*)	1⅛ yd** (1.1m**)
Queen (61″ × 81″) 155cm × 206cm)	3½ yd*** (3.1m***)	3½ yd*** (3.1m***)	3½ yd*** (3.1m***)	2¼ yd** (2.1m**)
King (79″ × 81″) (201cm × 206cm)	4½ yd*** (4.1m***)	4½ yd*** (4.1m***)	4½ yd*** (4.1m***)	2¼ yd** (2.1m**)

* Cut lengthwise. ** Cut crosswise. *** Cut two lengthwise panels, then piece horizontally.

GATHERED DUST RUFFLE WITH CORNER OPENINGS

Because the skirt covers all four sides of the box spring and is open at each corner to accommodate protruding bed legs or posts, this version of the gathered dust ruffle is suitable for any style bed, including four-posters, and beds that are positioned away from the walls.

The Deck

Cut and assemble the deck as described previously. Mark the corners, then divide and mark each edge into fourths.

The Skirt

Step 1: Determine the cutting dimensions of the skirt sections.

● Skirt depth = Skirt drop + 2½″ (6.3cm) for bottom hem and top seam allowance.

● Side skirt length = Box spring length × 2½ (to allow for the fullness of the ruffles as well as piecing seams and side hem allowances).

● End (head/foot) skirt length = Box spring width × 2½.

Step 2: Determine the amount of decorator fabric.

NOTE: The skirt sections are cut crosswise on the fabric.

● Add two side skirt lengths plus two end skirt lengths. Divide this total by the width of the fabric. This tells you how many crosswise panels you will need to cut.

● Multiply the number of panels by the skirt depth. This is how much decorator fabric you need for the skirt.

Step 3: Assemble the skirt sections.

● Cut and piece one side skirt, using ½″ (1.3cm) seams.

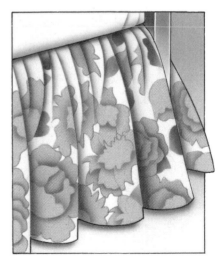

- Hem the sides and the bottom edge, using 1″ (2.5cm) double hems.

- Cut, piece and hem the other three skirt sections.

- Divide and mark the upper edge of each skirt into fourths; machine-gather the upper edge.

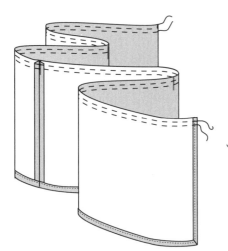

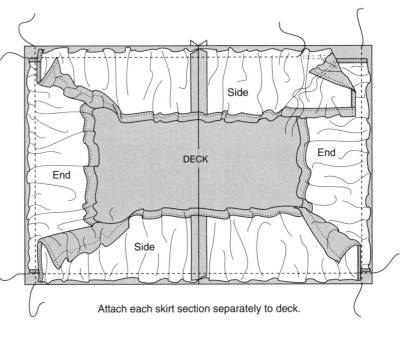

Attach each skirt section separately to deck.

Step 4: Attach the skirt.

- With right sides together, pin one side skirt to one side edge of the deck between the corners, matching the quarter markings. Adjust the gathers to fit, then stitch a ½″ (1.3cm) seam. Repeat for the other three skirt sections.

- Press the seam allowances toward the deck. Topstitch around the deck, through all layers.

TIP

If you're adding trim to this or any other dust ruffle, apply it after the skirt is hemmed but before it is pleated or gathered and attached to the deck.

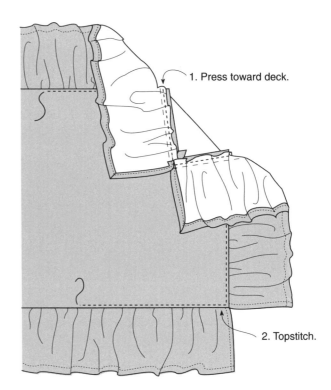

1. Press toward deck.

2. Topstitch.

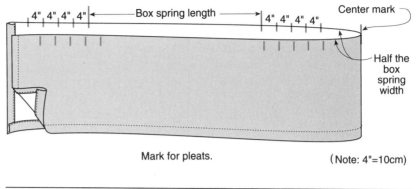

4" 4" 4" 4" — Box spring length — 4" 4" 4" 4"   Center mark

Half the box spring width

Mark for pleats.

(Note: 4"=10cm)

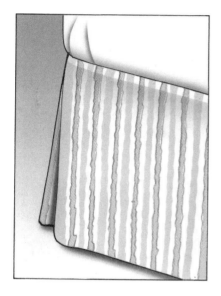

⚘

DUST RUFFLE WITH PLEATED CORNERS

This tailored dust ruffle has three flat sides with inverted box pleats at the corners of the bed.

The Deck

Cut and assemble the deck as described previously. Fold it lengthwise in half and mark.

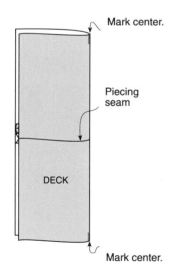

Mark center.

Piecing seam

DECK

Mark center.

The Skirt

Step 1: Determine the cutting dimensions of the skirt.

● Skirt depth = Skirt drop + $2\frac{1}{2}''$ (6.3cm) for bottom hem and top seam allowance.

● Skirt length = Box spring width + two box spring lengths + 80" (204cm) for the four box pleats, the side hems and the 6" (15cm) wraparound at each upper corner.

Step 2: Determine the amount of decorator fabric.

● Divide the skirt length by the usable width of the fabric (see "Fabric Basics" in Chapter 4, THE SEWING BASICS). This tells you how many crosswise panels you will need to cut.

● Multiply the number of panels by the skirt depth. This is how much decorator fabric you need for the skirt.

Step 3: Assemble the skirt.

● Cut and piece the skirt. If possible, plan the piecing seams so they are centered on the skirt and/or fall at the fold of a pleat (see Step 4).

● Hem the sides and bottom edge, using a 1" (2.5cm) double hem.

Step 4: Make the pleats.

● Fold the skirt lengthwise in half to locate the center; mark at raw edge.

● Working out from the center, along the raw edge, measure and mark for the four pleats, according to the illustration above.

● Place the skirt on the ironing board, right side up. Fold and match at one set of 4" (10cm) markings, as shown, to create an inverted pleat. Pin, press, then staystitch across the upper edge of the pleat. Clip to the stitching at the center of each pleat. Repeat for the other three pleats.

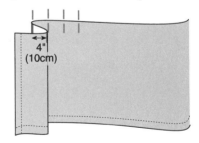

4" (10cm)

1. Staystitch across pleat.

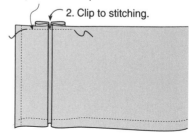

2. Clip to stitching.

For an easy way to make a box-pleated dust ruffle, see page 54 in Chapter 4, THE SEWING BASICS.

Step 5: Attach the skirt.

● With right sides together, pin the skirt to the deck, matching the center clips to the corners. With skirt side up, stitch a ½" (1.3cm) seam, pivoting at the corners.

● Press the seam allowances toward the deck, pressing the upper edge under ½" (1.3cm). Topstitch around the deck, through all layers.

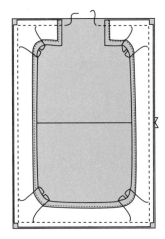

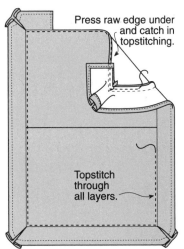

Press raw edge under and catch in topstitching.

Topstitch through all layers.

DUST RUFFLE WITH GATHERED CORNERS

This is a perfect solution when you want the softness of a gathered dust ruffle but need to economize on the amount of fabric.

The Deck

Cut and assemble the deck as described previously. Mark 8" (20.5cm) from each corner.

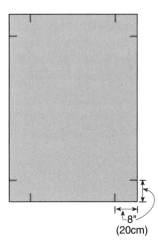

8"
(20cm)

The Skirt

Step 1: Determine the cutting dimensions of the skirt.

● Skirt depth = Skirt drop + 2½" (6.3cm) for bottom hem and top seam allowance.

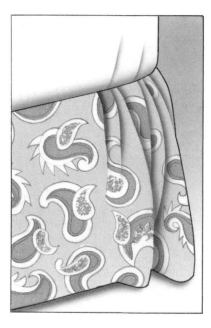

● Skirt length = Box spring width + two box spring lengths + 132" (335cm) for the four gathered corners and the side hems.

Step 2: Determine the amount of fabric. See Step 2, *dust ruffle with pleated corners*.

Step 3: Cut and assemble the skirt. See Step 3, *dust ruffle with pleated corners*.

Step 4: Gather the corners.

● Starting at one short end of the skirt, divide and mark the raw edge according to the diagram below.

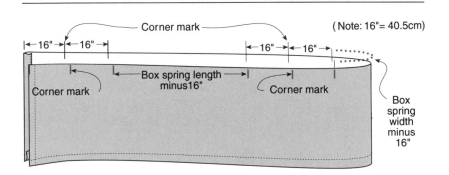

Corner mark · (Note: 16"= 40.5cm) · 16" · 16" · 16" · 16" · Box spring length minus16" · Corner mark · Corner mark · Box spring width minus 16"

SLEEPING BEAUTY

- Machine-gather between each set of 16″ (40.5cm) markings.

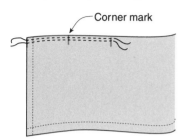

Corner mark

Step 5: Attach the skirt.

- With right sides together, pin the skirt to the deck, matching the corner marks to the deck corners and the remaining marks to the deck marks. Adjust the gathers to fit, then stitch a ½″ (1.3cm) seam. Clip the corners.

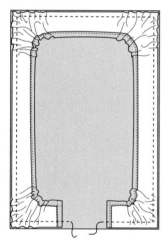

- Press the seam allowance toward the deck. Topstitch around the deck, through all the layers.

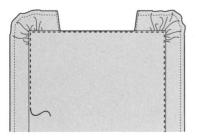

DAYBED

A daybed, commonly a twin-bed size, usually serves as a sofa by day and a bed by night. With a few simple adjustments, any bedcovering in this chapter, from a full-length bedspread to a comforter with dust ruffle, is suitable for a daybed. When measuring and determining the amount of fabric, keep in mind that all four sides of the daybed should be covered. This will give you greater flexibility when positioning the bed.

- If a bedspread is the desired covering, measure the drop on all four sides. Eliminate the extra "tuck-in" length for pillows. Instead, use throw pillows, bolsters or bed shams.

- Dust ruffles should cover all four sides of the bed frame.

- Comforters should be cut a little longer to cover the mattress drop at the head of the bed as well as on the sides and at the foot.

STUDIO COUCH WITH BOLSTER PILLOWS

This studio-couch cover goes over the mattress and conceals all four sides to the floor. Its smooth, tailored design features optional pleats at each corner. For an upholstered effect, the bolster pillows generally are covered to match the cover.

The Cover

Adapt the instructions for the *dust ruffle with pleated corners* as follows:

- Use decorator fabric for the deck, cutting it lengthwise so there is no piecing seam.

OPTIONAL: Add piping to the outer edge of the deck before attaching the skirt.

- Review the section on measuring at the beginning of this chapter, then determine the cutting dimensions of the skirt as follows:

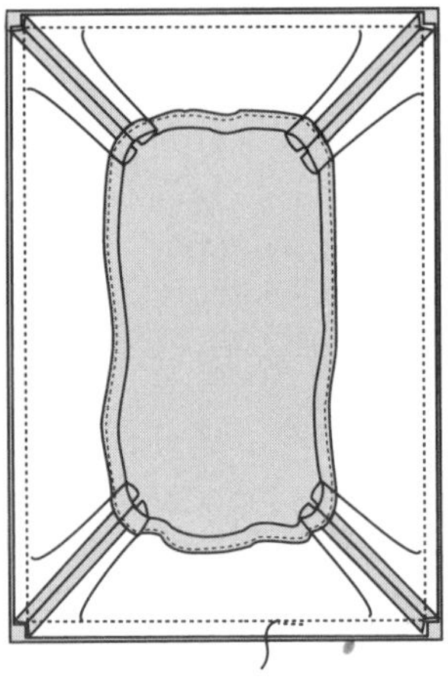

Skirt depth = Full drop + 2½″ (6.3cm) for bottom hem and top seam allowance.

Skirt length = Two mattress widths + two mattress lengths + 64″ (163cm) for four box pleats.

Cut and piece the skirt to make one continuous circle. Hem the bottom edge, using a 1″ (2.5cm) double hem. Mark and construct the pleats, then attach the skirt as for the *dust ruffle with pleated corners*, Steps 4 and 5. Eliminate the topstitching on the deck.

The Bolster Pillows

Bolsters for a studio couch generally are geometrically shaped, rather than round. To make a pattern for the end section, stand the pillow on its end, then trace the shape onto paper. Add a ½″ (1.3cm) seam allowance all around.

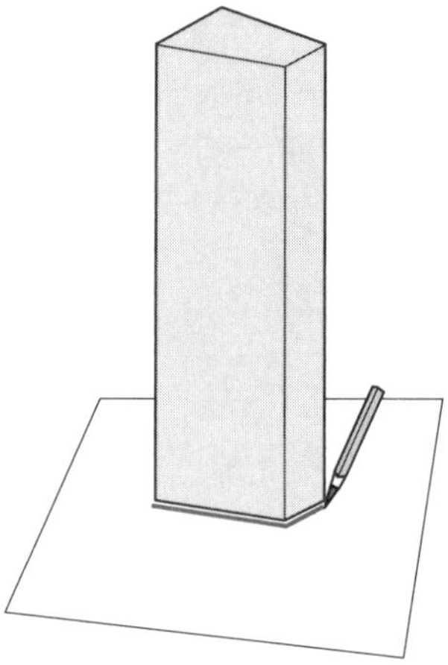

To cover the bolsters, follow the directions for the *plain bolster* in Chapter 8, PILLOW PIZZAZZ.

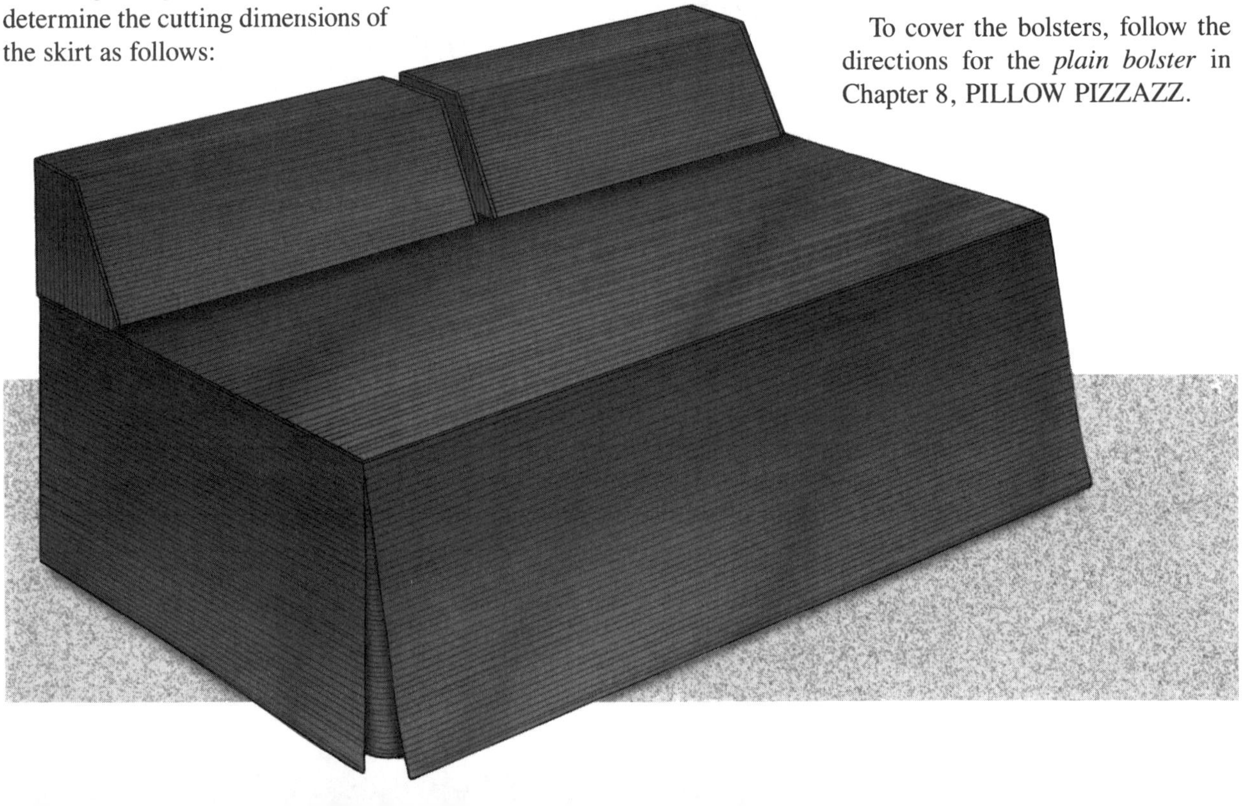

S L E E P I N G   B E A U T Y

NURSERY NICETIES

No decorating project could possibly be more rewarding than creating a warm, cozy environment for Baby! From lullabies to lollipops, from trucks to teddy bears, there's a motif to charm both parent and child.

Crib Quilt

Since there are no standard sizes for cribs and crib quilts, use the dimensions of the crib mattress as your starting point. Cut the quilt approximately 8″ (20.5cm) wider and shorter than the mattress's measurements. This size will cover the baby comfortably in the crib and will be large enough to double as a swaddling blanket out of the crib.

After establishing the cutting dimensions, follow the instructions for the *tufted comforter* on page 127. Use 3″ (7.5cm) wide ruffles to trim the edges. If you prefer, substitute machine quilting for the tufting. (See "Machine Quilting" in Chapter 4, THE SEWING BASICS.)

Dust Ruffle

The crib dust ruffle is merely a scaled-down version of the *gathered dust ruffle with corner openings.*

Since most cribs do not have a box spring, the dust ruffle's deck rests on a wooden platform inserted underneath the mattress. While the skirt can extend down to the floor, a more popular length is one that is equal to the bottom edge of the crib's side bars, when they are lowered.

Bumper Guards

Bumper guards provide both physical and emotional security for Baby. They absorb sound, protect Baby from accidental injury and transform that big crib into a snug little nest.

Because this bumper is made in four sections with ribbon ties, getting a good fit is easy. Mattress flaps at the lower edge of the side bumpers slip between the mattress and the crib bars, camouflaging the sheet and helping to hold the bumpers in place.

Step 1: Measuring.

● Measure the length, width and depth of the mattress as for any bed (see "Measuring" on page 123).

When stitching padded items, stitch with the batting side up. To prevent the sewing machine foot from getting caught in the batting, use strips of paper or nonwoven, tear-away stabilizer between the batting and the presser foot. When you're finished stitching, gently tear away the paper or stabilizer.

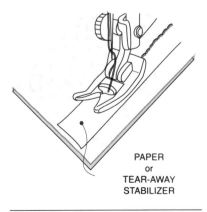

PAPER
or
TEAR-AWAY
STABILIZER

SLEEPING BEAUTY

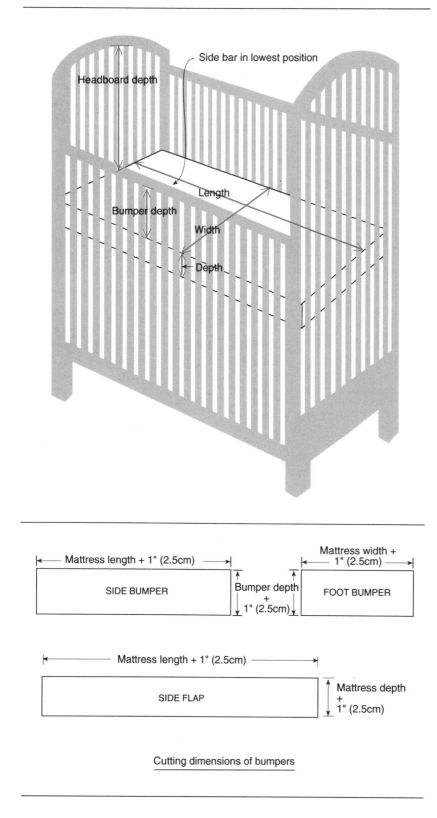

Cutting dimensions of bumpers

- Measure the bumper depth, from the top of the mattress to the bottom of the crib's side bar when it is dropped to its lowest position.

- Measure the headboard depth, from the top of the mattress to the top of the center railing.

Step 2: Determine the cutting dimensions of the bumpers and side flaps.

SIDE BUMPERS
- Length = Mattress length + 1" (2.5cm).
- Width = Bumper depth + 1" (2.5cm).

FOOT BUMPER
- Length = Mattress width + 1" (2.5cm).
- Width = Bumper depth + 1" (2.5cm).

SIDE FLAPS
- Length = Mattress length + 1" (2.5cm).
- Width = Mattress depth + 1" (2.5cm).

HEAD BUMPER
NOTE: The upper edge of the head bumper is usually curved, even if the upper edges of the side and foot bumpers are straight.

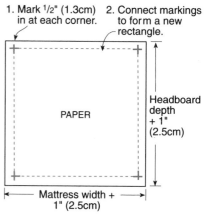

1. Mark 1/2" (1.3cm) in at each corner.
2. Connect markings to form a new rectangle.

SLEEPING BEAUTY

Start by cutting a paper rectangle. Its length should be 1″ (2.5cm) more than the headboard depth; its width should be 1″ (2.5cm) more than the mattress width. Mark ½″ (1.3cm) in at each corner. Connect these markings, drawing a smaller rectangle.

Fold the rectangle lengthwise in half. Working on the smaller rectangle, measure up and mark a distance equal to the bumper depth.

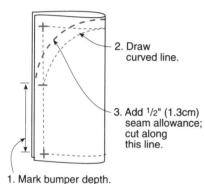

2. Draw curved line.

3. Add ½″ (1.3cm) seam allowance; cut along this line.

1. Mark bumper depth.

Draw a simple curved shape between the bumper mark and the line at the top of the fold. Add ½″ (1.3cm) to the curved edge, then cut along this new curved line. When unfolded, you have a paper pattern for the full headboard bumper, including seam allowances.

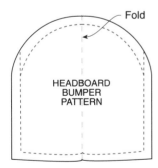

Fold

HEADBOARD BUMPER PATTERN

Step 3: Cut out the bumper sections.

The exact amount of fabric depends on the size of your crib, the depth of the bumpers and the width of your fabric. The fabric's motif may also affect whether you can cut the bumper sections lengthwise or crosswise. The best way to determine the right amount of fabric is to make the patterns for the bumper sections, then do a test layout in the store on the actual fabric.

● From decorator fabric, cut:
    four side bumpers
    two foot bumpers
    two head bumpers
    four side flaps

● From polyester batting, cut:
    two side bumpers
    one foot bumper
    one head bumper

● From a lightweight, fusible interfacing, cut:
    two side flaps

● From 17½ yards (17½m) of *ribbon*, cut twenty-six ties, each 24″ (61cm) long:
    seven for each side bumper.
    six for the foot bumper.
    six for the head bumper.

TIP

If you'd like your side and foot bumpers to have scalloped upper edges to match the headboard, draw a rectangular pattern equal to the bumper size, minus the seam allowances.

● **For the side bumpers, divide and mark one long edge into fourths. Then, at each corner, measure down 2″-4″ (5cm-10cm) and draw a line across the bumper. The deeper the measurement, the deeper the scallop. Extend the quarter markings to intersect with that line. Determine the center points along the upper edge of the bumper, between each set of markings. Draw an arc, connecting one center and two quarter marks, as shown. Use this arc as a pattern for three more scallops. After scallops are marked, add ½″ (1.3cm) seam allowances all around.**

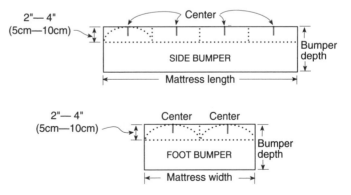

2″—4″ (5cm—10cm)

Center

SIDE BUMPER

Bumper depth

Mattress length

2″—4″ (5cm—10cm)

Center   Center

FOOT BUMPER

Bumper depth

Mattress width

Add ½″ (1.3cm) seam allowances to bumpers *after* scallops are drawn.

● **For the foot bumpers, divide and mark one long edge in half. Measure, mark and draw two scallops, in the same manner as for the side bumpers. Add ½″ (1.3cm) seam allowances all around.**

Step 4: Assemble one side bumper.

● Divide and mark the upper edge of the bumper into quarters. Mark the corners.

● Pin, then baste, the batting to the wrong side of one side bumper section.

● Fold each ribbon tie lengthwise in half. Pin, then baste one tie at each mark along the upper edge and at each corner mark, as shown.

OPTIONAL: With right sides together, baste ruffles, piping or other insertion trim to the upper edge of the batted bumper, between the corner markings.

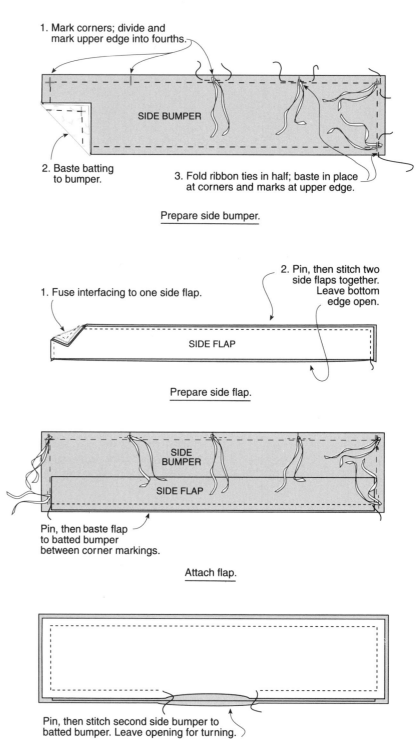

1. Mark corners; divide and mark upper edge into fourths.

SIDE BUMPER

2. Baste batting to bumper.

3. Fold ribbon ties in half; baste in place at corners and marks at upper edge.

Prepare side bumper.

1. Fuse interfacing to one side flap.

2. Pin, then stitch two side flaps together. Leave bottom edge open.

SIDE FLAP

Prepare side flap.

SIDE BUMPER

SIDE FLAP

Pin, then baste flap to batted bumper between corner markings.

Attach flap.

Pin, then stitch second side bumper to batted bumper. Leave opening for turning.

Finish bumper.

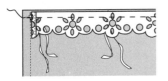

(OPTIONAL) Baste trim in place along upper edge between corner marks.

● Fuse the interfacing to the wrong side of one side flap. Pin to a second side flap, right sides together; stitch together, leaving one long edge open. Trim the seams, clip the corners, then turn right side out and press.

● With right sides together, pin, then baste the flap to the lower edge of the batted bumper section, between the corner markings.

TIPS

For extra-puffy bumpers, pad each bumper section with a second layer of polyester batting.

To avoid confusion once all the pieces are cut, separate the corresponding bumpers, batting, flaps and ribbon ties, creating a pile for each of the four crib sides.

• With right sides together, pin a second side bumper section to the batted bumper. Stitch, leaving an opening in the lower edge for turning, and being careful not to catch the ribbon ties in the stitching. Trim the seams, clip the corners, then turn right side out.

• Slipstitch the opening closed. Stitch through all the layers, from upper to lower edge of the bumper, just below the ribbon ties, as shown.

• Repeat for the other side bumper.

Step 5: Assemble the head bumper and the foot bumper.

• Divide the upper edge of one head and one foot bumper in half and mark the center. Mark the corners.

• Complete the foot bumper, following the instructions for the side bumpers in Step 4, omitting the references to the flap.

• Repeat for the head bumper, omitting the references to the flap and stitching through the layers.

Pillow

A matching pillow is a nice touch for the nursery. Although Baby won't use it, Mom and Dad will welcome it to support a tired back or forearm during feeding time.

Choose a relatively small pillow form (12″–14″, or 30.5cm–35.5cm). Coordinate the fabric and trim to the comforter. Select an easy-on/easy-off closure to accommodate frequent laundering. For additional information, see "The Basic Knife-Edge Pillow" in Chapter 8, PILLOW PIZZAZZ.

To make a coordinating nursery wall hanging, see Chapter 10, DECORATIVE ACCESSORIES.

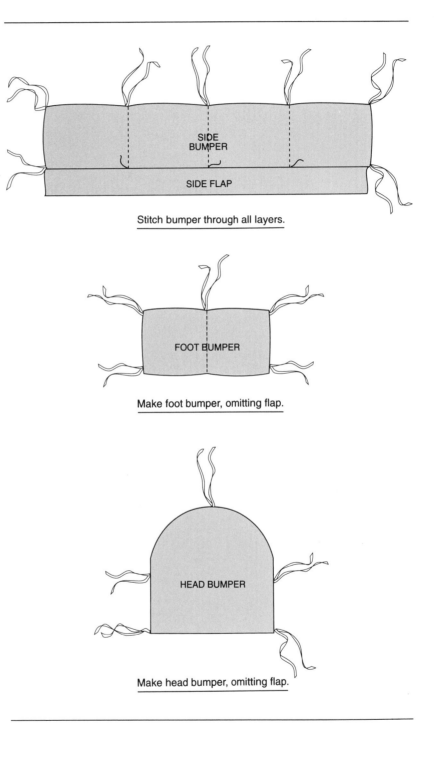

Stitch bumper through all layers.

Make foot bumper, omitting flap.

Make head bumper, omitting flap.

Pillow
Pizzazz

Pillow Pizzazz

Pillows are an easy way to accent an existing color palette or to introduce new tones to your design scheme. Without them, a beautifully decorated room is often not quite complete.

Pillows can be used to intensify the effects of a favorite color. They can be used to unify tones and textures that are scattered throughout the room. They can even be used to transform discord into harmony. For example, suppose you have an heirloom lamp, a gorgeous piece of artwork or an antique quilt that doesn't quite fit in. The solution to your decorating dilemma may be as simple as the introduction of a few color-matched throw pillows.

For a relatively minor investment of time and money, new throw pillows can lift the spirits of a ho-hum decor or change the entire atmosphere of a room. Bright florals can add a splash of summer; jewel-toned tartans bespeak cozy winters. Red and green pillows, accompanied by a few poinsettia plants, immediately create a festive holiday air.

❁
GETTING STARTED

You can make pillows in just about any size or shape your heart desires. You can make them durable enough to withstand childhood pillow fights or design them from fabrics so fragile that they are purely for show. You can make them plain or fancy, large or small, stuffed with foam, fibers or feathers, in almost any fabric you want. Who would guess that something so simple could offer so many decorating possibilities?

To make the most of your pillows' possibilities, here are a few things to consider:

USE. Are they mainly for display, or will they get a lot of day-to-day wear and tear? Pillows in a den or busy family room should be geared to comfort and practicality. This means durable (maybe even washable) fabrics, easy-on/easy-off closures and nap-in-front-of-the-television softness. Tassels and braids may be out of place there but elegantly at home in a formal living room. Antique lace and other high-maintenance details should be reserved for pillows that are strictly for show.

SIZE. Consider the size of its companion sofa, chair or bed. Don't create a pillow that's so large that it overpowers the chair or so small that it gets lost in the corner. Keep the scale of the desired fabric in mind, too. Small prints are appropriate for almost any shape or size pillow. Many large prints are not quite so adaptable. To avoid that chopped-up look, save the large prints for the bigger pillows.

SHAPE. Should you mix square, round, heart-shaped and bolster pillows . . . or stick with one shape, repeated in the same or different sizes? To help you decide, fold some fabric pieces into a variety of sizes and shapes. Arrange them on your bed or sofa; then stand back to analyze the effect.

TIP

For photography, professionally designed rooms are often accessorized with a profusion of pillows. Unless you never expect people to actually sit down in your house, resist the temptation to imitate this opulence. Otherwise, guests may find that every seat in the house is already occupied by a pillow!

STYLE. All pillows, regardless of their shape, are one of two basic styles:

A *knife-edge* pillow is constructed by sewing two panels together and then filling the shape with stuffing. This type of pillow is thicker in the center and flatter at the edges. Most throw pillows, all bed pillows and some cushions for occasional chairs are knife-edge pillows.

A *box-edge* pillow is constructed by covering a block of foam. The result is a pillow that has uniform thickness. Although sometimes used for throw pillows, this style is more commonly used as sofa or chair cushions. Because the foam can be cut into almost any shape, the cushions can conform to the angles and curves of the furniture.

PERSONAL TOUCHES. Beautiful prints and interesting textures may be best left unadorned. However, simpler fabrics can serve as canvases for some exciting decorative techniques. Appliqués, quilting, monograms, ribbon and trim collages, and fabric painting are just a few of the possibilities. Both plain and elaborate fabrics may benefit from edge treatments, such as piping, ruffles, fringe and tassels. These trims can enhance the fabric and emphasize the pillow shape.

FILLINGS

When you make your own pillows, you not only get to choose what's on the outside, but you also get to pick what's on the inside.

Down or Feather Filling

Goose down is probably the first—and still the most luxurious—substance ever used to stuff a pillow. It is prized for its resiliency and comfort. Because it is expensive, feathers are often mixed in with, or substituted for, goose down. Feathers are not as warm as down, but this is more of a concern for

comforters than for pillows. However, feathers, particularly coarse or large ones, have a tendency to migrate to the outside of the fabric. This can occur between the woven threads of the fabric or along the seamlines. Besides creating a bit of a mess, these feathers, with their sharp, pointed shafts, can be uncomfortably prickly. Another drawback is the fact that many people are allergic to feathers.

Fiber Filling

Fiber filling, which consists of feathery polyester fibers, is by far the most practical choice for home sewers. It is inexpensive and allergy-free, plus it has a suppleness that is comfortably resilient and attractive. You can purchase presewn, fiberfill pillow forms in basic shapes, or you can buy loose fiberfill by the ounce, and then make and stuff your own pillow forms.

Foam Filling

Polyurethane foam is the basis for several different types of pillow forms. All of these forms are easy to launder and air-dry.

● Foam blocks are the stuffing of choice for seat cushions. Because they are so resilient, they are comfortable to sit on, but spring back to their original smooth appearance when not in use. A block of foam can be cut to accommodate the most intricate curves and angles.

● Foam chips can be stuffed into a presewn pillow cover. These forms are usually inexpensive. However, because they have a great deal of bounce, they are also usually a bit

too resilient for comfort. This type of filling also tends to have a lumpy appearance, even when covered with heavy fabric.

● Sheets of foam, preshaped and sewn together, provide a much more attractive appearance than foam chips. However, since the sheets are also very resilient, they react somewhat like a springboard when touched. In fact, because the neck muscles have to work hard to compete with the force of the foam, some people feel even more tired after a night's rest on a foam bed pillow.

✿

THE BASIC KNIFE-EDGE PILLOW

Use these instructions to make a decorative cover for a presewn, knife-edge pillow form or to create your own pillow form. Use muslin, percale or other firmly woven cotton or cotton blends for the fabric shell, then stuff with the desired filling.

Step 1: Cut the cover.

Cut two fabric shapes equal to either the length and width or the diameter of the pillow form, plus ½" (1.3cm) seam allowances on all edges. These will be the front and back pillow covers.

NOTE: On this type of pillow, the opening is slipstitched closed. If you prefer to add a zipper, hook-and-loop tape or an envelope opening, first review "Easy-On/Easy-Off Closures" on pages 151–53 before cutting the cover.

Step 2: Assemble the cover.

Pin the front and back covers, right sides together, and stitch ½" (1.3cm) from the edge. Leave an opening, as shown, large enough to insert the pillow form or fiberfill stuffing. Trim the corners or notch out the fullness around the curves.

Trim corners.

Leave opening for turning.

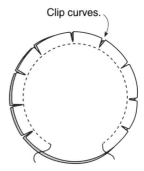

Clip curves.

Step 3: Finish the pillow.

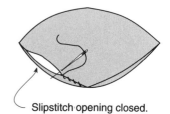

Slipstitch opening closed.

● Turn the cover right side out. Press, turning in the seam allowances along the opening.

● Stuff with fiberfill or insert the pillow form, then slipstitch the opening closed.

Variations

Easy-On/Easy-Off Closures

For easy sewing, the slipstitched opening is the simplest construction technique. However, when the pillow needs cleaning, you must either wash or dry-clean the entire pillow or remove the cover, clean it separately, then reinsert the form and slipstitch the opening closed.

This is fine for pillows stuffed with washable fiberfill or for those that seldom require cleaning. However, if easy maintenance is your goal, consider adding a zipper, a strip of hook-and-loop fastener or an envelope opening. All three are adaptable to any shape knife-edge pillow.

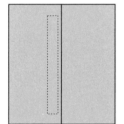

ZIPPER

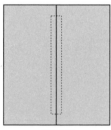

HOOK-AND-LOOP FASTENER

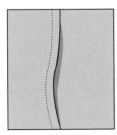

ENVELOPE OPENING

Zipper Opening

Choose a zipper that is approximately 2″ (5cm) shorter than the length of the opening (minus seam allowances). For example, a 14″ (35.5cm) square pillow would require a 12″ (30.5cm) zipper.

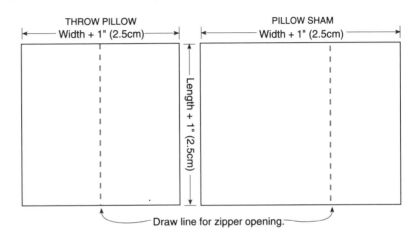

THROW PILLOW
Width + 1" (2.5cm)
Length + 1" (2.5cm)

PILLOW SHAM
Width + 1" (2.5cm)

Draw line for zipper opening.

Step 1: Using tissue paper, brown paper or nonwoven pattern duplicating material, make two pattern pieces, each equal to the length and width of the pillow form plus 1″ (2.5cm). Use one pattern to cut out the front pillow cover.

TIP

For a perfect fit, measure the length and width or the diameter of the pillow form across the center, from seam to seam. Many forms actually measure a little more or less than their labels indicate.

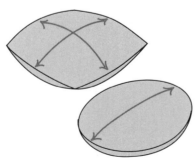

● To ensure sharp corners or a perfect circle, make a paper pattern from these measurements, adding ¹/₂″ (1.3cm) seam allowances.

● Use this technique anywhere you need a perfect circle: Take a large sheet of paper that is at least 1″ (2.5cm) larger than the diameter of the area. Fold it in quarters. Then, using a ruler as a compass, and a measurement equal to half the diameter plus ¹/₂″ (1.3cm) for seam allowances, draw a curved edge. Cut along the curve, then open out the paper pattern.

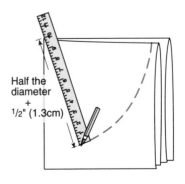

Half the diameter
+
¹/₂" (1.3cm)

Step 2: On the other pattern piece draw a straight line for the zipper opening. This line should be centered on the pattern or, for a pillow sham, placed approximately one-third of the way in from one edge. Cut the pattern apart along the marked line.

Step 3: Pin these back pattern sections to the fabric. Add 1″ (2.5cm) seam allowances along the zipper openings. Cut out the backs.

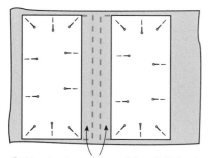

Cut two back sections, adding 1″ (2.5cm) seam allowances to opening edges.

Step 4: Pin the two back sections, right sides together, along the zipper openings. Mark 1½″ (3.8cm) in from the end of each seam. Machine-stitch along the 1″ (2.5cm) seamline to the first marking; then backstitch a few stitches. Lengthen to a basting stitch, stitch just past the next marking, shorten to a regular stitch, backstitch to the marking, then finish the seam. Press the seam open.

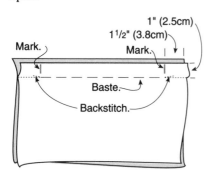

1″ (2.5cm)
1½″ (3.8cm)
Mark.
Mark.
Baste.
Backstitch.

Step 5: Install the zipper, following the directions for a center or a lapped application (see "Zippers" in Chapter 4, THE SEWING BASICS), then assemble the cover.

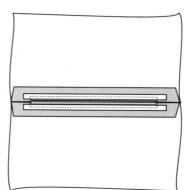

Self-Gripping Hook-and-Loop Fasteners

Use a strip of Velcro or another hook-and-loop fastener that is 1″ (2.5cm) shorter than the length of the opening (minus seam allowances).

Steps 1–4: Follow Steps 1–4 for "Zipper Opening" on pages 151–52.

Step 5: Trim one seam allowance to ½″ (1.3cm). Position the hook

Trim seam allowance to ½″ (1.3cm).

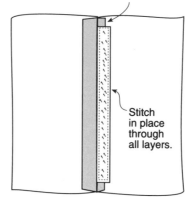

Stitch in place through all layers.

side of the tape over the seam allowance so that one long edge is just next to the seamline. The ends should extend ½″ (1.3cm) beyond the markings for the opening. Pin or glue-baste in place, then stitch around all four sides of the tape, through all the layers.

Step 6: Press the other seam allowance up ¼″ (6mm) to the right side. Position the loop side of the tape over the seam allowance so that one long edge of the tape meets the fold; pin or glue-baste in place. Stitch ⅛″ (3mm) from the folded edge, through the tape and seam allowance only. Then stitch ⅛″ (3mm) from the ends and other long edge of the loop tape.

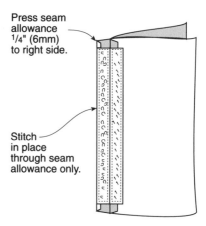

Press seam allowance ¼″ (6mm) to right side.

Stitch in place through seam allowance only.

Step 7: Remove the basting stitches along the opening and continue assembling the pillow cover.

Envelope Opening

This type of opening is particularly popular for pillow shams on bed pillows that receive regular nighttime use.

Steps 1–3: Follow Steps 1–3 for "Zipper Opening" on pages 151–52, centering the line for the opening and adding 5″ (12.5cm) extensions to the opening edges.

Step 4: Make a 1″ (2.5cm) double hem along the edge of each extension.

Step 5: To assemble the pillow cover, pin the cover backs to the cover front, right sides together, matching the cut edges and overlapping the hemmed edges. Stitch ½″ (1.3cm) from the cut edges.

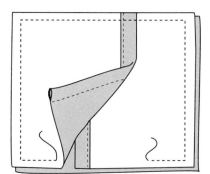

TIP

If you take a few minutes to taper the corners on a square or rectangular pillow cover before assembling it, you can eliminate that dog-eared effect.

● Fold the pillow top into quarters, carefully matching the raw edges. Pin to secure.

● Mark the midpoint along the two unfolded edges, then measure in ½″ (1.3cm) at the corner and mark.

● Draw new cutting lines, beginning at the corner and tapering back to the original lines at the midpoint marking. Trim along the marked lines, through all layers.

● Unfold the pillow top. Use it as a pattern to trim the pillow back to match.

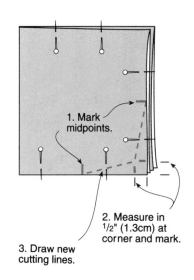

1. Mark midpoints.

2. Measure in ½″ (1.3cm) at corner and mark.

3. Draw new cutting lines.

NOTE: If you are planning on a zipper or hook-and-loop closure, construct the closure first, then trim the corners on the back.

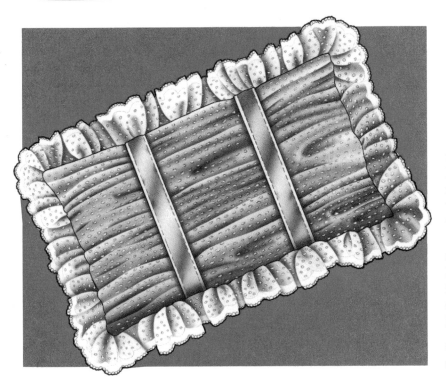

Variation

Shirred Pillow

For this top treatment, an overlay of fabric is gathered up to create an interesting texture. It is particularly suited to lightweight, "airy" fabrics, such as lace and dotted swiss. However, when heavier, light-reflecting fabrics, such as satin and velvet, are used, the effect can be very formal and dramatic.

For the sheer overlay, consider a contrasting color for the underlay. For a satin or velvet overlay, use a firm, medium-weight fabric such as chintz or broadcloth for the underlay.

● Measure and cut the front cover, as for the *basic knife-edge* (see page

150) or *fitted box-edge pillow* (see page 160). This will be the underlay. Mark the width into thirds.

● Cut the overlay equal to the width of the front cover and two times the length. Mark the width into thirds. Machine-baste along the markings and ½" (1.3cm) from each long edge, using two rows of gathering stitches, ¼" (6mm) apart. Pin the layers together, matching the markings. Adjust the gathers to fit; baste.

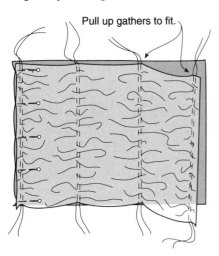

Pull up gathers to fit.

● Pin or baste ribbon or other flat trim over the two inner rows of gathers. Edgestitch in place through both layers.

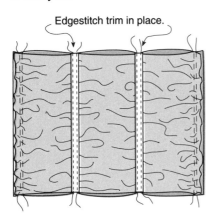

Edgestitch trim in place.

● Complete the pillow as for the *basic knife-edge* or *fitted box-edge pillow*.

TOP TREATMENTS

Quilting, appliqué, machine embroidery and fabric painting are just a few of the ways to embellish the top of a pillow. "Special Touches" in Chapter 4, THE SEWING BASICS, includes some basic information on several of these decorative arts. These personal touches should be done after cutting and before assembling the pillow.

Here are some other ideas to consider:

● Apply ribbons and/or flat trims in an interweaving pattern to form a mock plaid.

● Antique laces, including doilies and handkerchiefs, can be fashioned into interesting appliqués.

● Consider different fabrics for the front and back of the pillow. Try pairing lace with satin, tapestry with velvet, oversize prints with miniprints.

● Use ribbon to create a mitered border on a square or rectangular pillow. Use a flexible braid trim to create the same effect on a round pillow.

To determine trim yardage, cut a brown paper bag to the size and shape of your pillow. Lightly sketch in trim placement until you are pleased with the arrangement; measure.

_____ *Variation* _____

Basic Flange Pillow

This variation of the knife-edge pillow is simply an extra-large pillow cover, topstitched to create a self-fabric border.

Step 1: Cut the cover.

● Cut the front cover as for the *basic knife-edge pillow*, adding an additional amount all around for the flange. For a throw pillow, plan on a 2″ (5cm) wide flange; for a bed pillow, plan on a 3″ (7.5cm) wide flange.

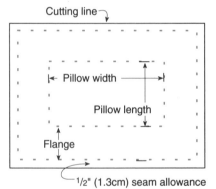

Cutting line

Pillow width

Pillow length

Flange

½″ (1.3cm) seam allowance

● Adjust the front cover pattern for a zipper, hook-and-loop or envelope

closure (see "Easy-On/Easy-Off Closures" on pages 151–53) and cut out the back sections.

Step 2: Assemble the cover.

● Install the closure in the back cover.

● Pin the front and back covers, right sides together, and stitch ½″ (1.3cm) from the edge.

Step 3: Finish the cover.

● Turn the cover right side out and press. Measuring in from the edge, mark the depth of the flange, then topstitch all around.

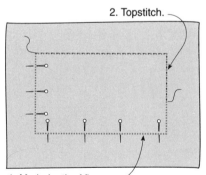

2. Topstitch.

1. Mark depth of flange.

Fancy up your flange by giving it a decorative edge:

● Serge-finish the outer edge with a narrow rolled hem and a decorative thread.

● Scalloped edges are very pretty but require some preplanning. Make a paper pattern first, planning the

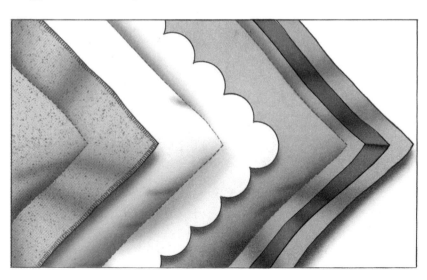

scallops so the repeat is centered at each of the four edges. Adjust the depth of the flange so that the scallops meet attractively at the corners.

● Add ribbon or other flat trim to the flange, carefully mitering it at the corners.

___ *Variation* ___
Custom Shapes

Pillows in unusual shapes, such as hearts, triangles, seashells, letters, numbers and Christmas trees, can add a touch of originality and whimsy to your decor.

Start by making a muslin-covered, fiberfill pillow form in the desired shape (see "The Basic Knife-Edge Pillow" on page 150). As a general rule, simple shapes produce the best results. To assure a good fit, use the same pattern pieces for the cover as for the form. Add edge treatments and top treatments as for the *basic knife-edge pillow*.

TIP

To make a heart-shaped pillow, use the grided pattern included with the directions for the *nursery wall hanging* in Chapter 10, DECORATIVE ACCESSORIES.

___ *Variation* ___
Flyaway Flange

This variation of the *basic flange pillow* uses two contrasting colors for the front and back, plus contrasting thread to serge-finish the edges.

Step 1: Cut the cover. Following the directions for the *basic flange pillow*, cut two front covers from fabric A. One will be the front lining.

● From fabric B, cut one front cover. This will be the back lining.

● Adjust the front-cover pattern for the desired closure (see "Easy-On/Easy-Off Closures" on pages 151–53) and cut out the back-cover sections from fabric B.

Step 2: Assemble the cover.

● Install the closure in the back cover.

● Pin the back cover and the back lining, wrong sides together. Serge-finish the edges with contrasting thread.

● On the back lining, measure in from the edge and mark the depth of the flange. Topstitch along the line, then cut away the center of the lining, leaving a 1″ (2.5cm) margin.

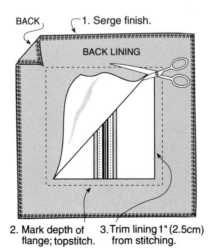

2. Mark depth of flange; topstitch.   3. Trim lining 1″ (2.5cm) from stitching.

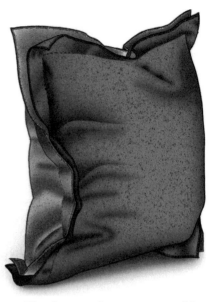

● Pin the two fronts, wrong sides together, and serge-finish the edges with contrasting thread.

● Pin the front to the back, lining sides together. Working zipper side up, topstitch over the previous stitching around the flange marking.

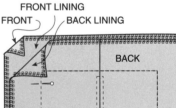

TIP

Chair pads are nothing more than flat, knife-edge pillows. They add warmth and comfort to hard-surface seating, such as Windsor chairs and rockers.

EDGE TREATMENTS

You can easily change the personality of any pillow by adding an edge treatment. Piping, gathered trims, self-fabric ruffles, rickrack and fringe, used alone or in combination, in matching or contrasting colors, are just a few of your decorative options.

On a knife-edge or a contemporary box-edge style, the edge treatment is basted in place along the seamline on the right side of the front section, before the cover is assembled. On a fitted box pillow, the edge treatment is basted in place along the front and back edges, before the boxing strip is attached.

To determine how much trim is required:

- For a *square* or *rectangular knife-edge* or *contemporary box pillow*, add the length and width of the pillow form, multiply by 2 and then add 1″ (2.5cm) for joining.
- For a *round knife-edge* or *con-temporary box pillow*, use a flexible tape measure to measure the circumference of the pillow form, then add 1″ (2.5cm) for joining.
- For a *fitted box pillow*, calculate as for the knife-edge style and then multiply by 2.

PIPING. When used alone, piping adds a tailored, custom touch to any basic pillow. Piping can also be used in combination with gathered trims and self-fabric ruffles. Baste the piping in place first, then baste the gathered trim or ruffle in place over the piping.

RICKRACK. Jumbo rickrack lends a casual, country air to the basic pillow. For extra "oomph," intertwine or layer two colors of rickrack. To apply the rickrack, center it over the seamline and baste in place. When the pillow is completed, the rickrack creates a sawtooth-edge finish.

FRINGE. Short, dense "caterpillar" fringe has a casual air. Longer "chainette" or "bullion" fringes, particularly those made from shiny fibers such as rayon or silk, lend touches of formality.

RUFFLES. To soften the shape of your pillows, consider purchased, pregathered ruffle trim or make your own from matching or contrasting fabric.

For a feminine bedroom or a Victorian decorating scheme, consider adding two or three layers of ruffles, in graduated widths, to the edges of a pillow.

To add emphasis to the ruffles, finish the edges with a narrow, contrasting binding or serge-finish the edges with a narrow rolled hem and a contrasting decorative thread.

Other trims, such as a narrow lace edging or a band of ribbon, can be applied to self-fabric ruffles. Apply these before the ruffle is gathered and basted to the pillow top.

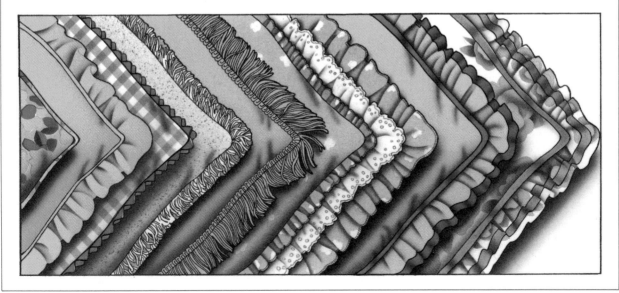

PILLOW SHAMS

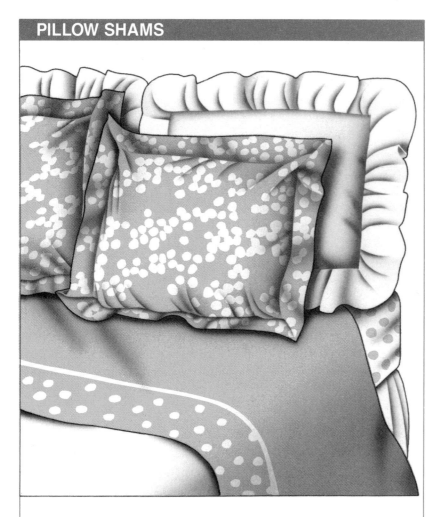

Variation

Turkish-Corner or Harem Pillow

Because it's plumped up, the Turkish-corner pillow is a square knife-edge pillow masquerading as a box-edge pillow. It makes a great throw pillow or a comfy floor pillow.

For this pillow, choose a feather or fiberfill form. These are squeezable forms that will conform to the shape of the cover. Also, select a pillow form that is at least 4″ (10cm) larger than the desired finished size of the pillow. The difference between the size of the pillow form and the desired finished size will be the thickness of your finished pillow. For example, a 20″ (51cm) square pillow form can be compressed to a 16″ (40.5cm) square Turkish-corner pillow that is 4″ (10cm) thick.

Step 1: Cut and assemble the cover according to the directions for the *basic knife-edge pillow*, Steps 1 and 2, on page 150. Use the slipstitch,

Pillow shams are no more than covers for extra-large, knife-edge bed pillows.

● Since many of these pillows are decorative during the day and utilitarian at night, the envelope closure (the easiest on/off choice!) is preferred. Position the closure one-third of the way in from one short edge.

● Any edge or top treatment that is suitable for a knife-edge pillow can also embellish a pillow sham. As a general rule, ruffles and flanges should be about 3″ (7.5cm) deep. Narrower ones tend to look skimpy; wider ones tend to flop over.

● To save you time, here are the measurements for the most common bed pillows.

	WIDTH		LENGTH	
STANDARD	20″ (51cm)	×	26″	(66cm)
QUEEN	20″ (51cm)	×	30″	(76cm)
KING	20″ (51cm)	×	38″	(96.5cm)

zipper or hook-and-loop tape closure. (The envelope back is not a suitable choice.)

Step 2: Turn the cover wrong side out. At each corner, and working along the seamline, measure and mark distances equal to half the desired thickness. For example, for a pillow that will be 4″ (10cm) thick, mark 2″ (5cm) in from each corner, along the seamline. Draw a line across each corner, connecting its two marks.

Step 3: Take long, hand-basting stitches along each line. Pull up on the thread to gather, then tie securely with strong string or heavy-duty thread.

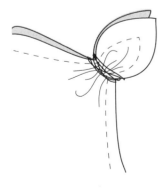

Step 4: Turn the cover right side out and insert the form.

Variation

Envelope Pillow

The envelope pillow is another easy variation on the square or rectangular knife-edge pillow. Consider contrasting colors for front and back.

Step 1: Cut the cover.

● Measure the pillow form.

● On a large piece of paper, draw a rectangle equal to the length and width of the form. Extend one side into a triangle for the envelope flap. (NOTE: The flap should be deep enough to cover one-third to one-half of the pillow front.) Add ½″ (1.3cm) seam allowances all around. Use as a pattern to cut the front cover. Transfer the markings for the base of the triangle.

● Cut the front and back sections.

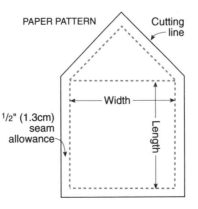

PAPER PATTERN

Cutting line

½″ (1.3cm) seam allowance

Width

Length

Step 2: Assemble the cover.

● Pin the front and back covers, right sides together, and stitch ½″ (1.3cm) from the edge, leaving an opening in the lower edge for turning and for inserting the pillow form. Trim the corners.

● Turn the cover right side out and press.

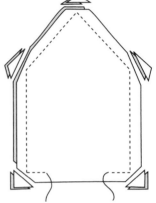

● Topstitch across the base of the triangle.

OPTIONAL: Add a large, machine-made buttonhole at the tip of the flap.

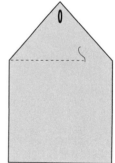

Step 3: Finish the cover.

● Insert the pillow form.

● Fold the flap down and mark the position of the button.

● Remove the pillow form. Sew a large button in place through the flap and the top cover.

● Insert the pillow form and slipstitch the opening closed.

❀

BOX-EDGE PILLOWS

Whether you are making a throw pillow or a seat cushion for a sofa or chair, the starting point is a block of foam cut to size.

● *Fitted box pillows or cushions* have defined edges. The cover is cut in three sections—front, back and side, called a boxing strip. Piping or some other type of edge treatment is incorporated into the seams to define the shape. When adding a top treatment to a seat cushion, remember that durability is an important consideration.

● *Contemporary box pillows or cushions* have mitered corners and soft edges. The cover is cut in two sections so that the front and back wrap over the edges and meet along the sides. This style is generally more suitable for casual furniture cushions than for throw pillows. Because the soft edges withstand abrasion better than the defined edges of a fitted cushion, the contemporary style is a particularly durable choice for areas such as family rooms and boys' rooms.

Fitted Box-Edge Pillow

Use these directions to make a square or rectangular box-edge pillow.

Step 1: Cut the cover.

● To determine the size of the front and back cover sections, measure across the top of the foam block from edge to edge. Measure both length and width.

● For the boxing strip:
Measure the depth of the foam block.

Measure the perimeter of the foam block *or* add the length plus the width of the foam block, then multiply by 2.

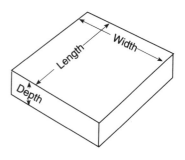

● Using these measurements, cut the front, back and boxing strip, adding ½" (1.3cm) all around for seam allowances. If the boxing strip requires piecing, add 1" (2.5cm) to the total length for each piecing seam.

NOTE: If you plan to add a zipper, see "Adding a Zipper" on page 162 before you cut out the boxing strip.

Step 2: Apply the edge treatment. Baste the edge treatment in place along the seamline on the right side of the front and back pillow sections. (For more information on edge treatments, see "Special Touches" in Chapter 4, THE SEWING BASICS.)

NOTE: Most fitted box pillows have some type of edge treatment. However, if you are making the *shirred box pillow* variation, you may want to omit an edge treatment.

Step 3: Assemble the cover.

● Pin the short ends of the boxing strip, right sides together, and stitch, using ½" (1.3cm) seams. Divide and mark the long edges of the boxing strip into four sections—length, width, length and width of

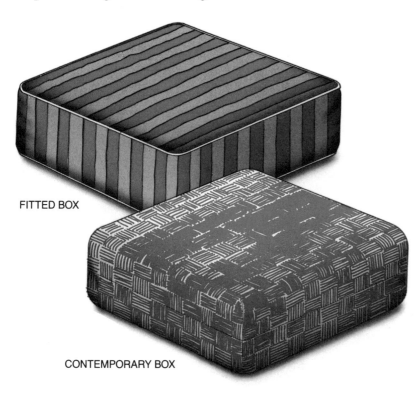

FITTED BOX

CONTEMPORARY BOX

the foam block—as shown. Plan the markings so that the joining seam falls at the center back of the pillow.

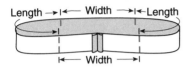

Staystitch at each marking, then clip to the stitching. If your fabric has a tendency to fray, seal the edges of the clips with seam sealant.

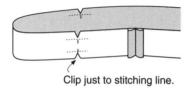

Clip just to stitching line.

● Pin the front and the boxing strip, right sides together, positioning the clips at the corners. Stitch, using a zipper foot and crowding the stitches next to the piping or trim.

● Repeat, stitching the back to the other edge of the boxing strip, leaving an opening, as shown, large enough to insert the foam block.

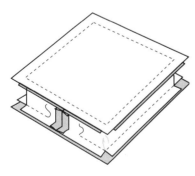

Step 4: Finish the pillow.

● Turn cover right side out.

● Insert the pillow form, then slipstitch the opening closed.

Round Fitted Box-Edge Pillow

The round fitted box-edge pillow is constructed similarly to the square or rectangular pillow. There are, however, a few differences:

● Measure the diameter of the foam block. Then make a paper pattern for the front and back covers, adding ½″ (1.3cm) seam allowances.

● To determine the length of the boxing strip, use your tape measure to measure the perimeter of the foam block.

● Use a zipper that is approximately 4″ (10cm) shorter than half the perimeter of the pillow.

● Before assembling the pillow, quarter-mark the edges of the front and back, as well as the boxing strip.

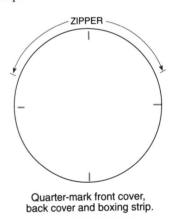

Quarter-mark front cover, back cover and boxing strip.

TIP

To give the finished pillow a fuller, more luxurious look, wrap the foam block with traditional, or low-loft, polyester batting. Slipstitch the cut edges together. Then wrap the pillow form in plastic (an old dry cleaner bag works fine!). Insert the pillow form into the cover, then gently remove the plastic.

Variation

Adding a Zipper

The longer the zipper, the easier it will be to get the cover on and off.

● For a throw pillow or cushion with three exposed sides, choose a

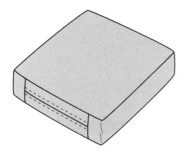

zipper that is a few inches (centimeters) shorter than the back of the pillow.

● If the sofa or chair is constructed so that the back and sides of the cushion are concealed, choose a zipper that is approximately 8″ (20.5cm) longer than the back of the cushion.

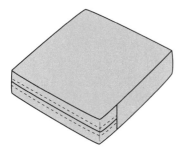

To cut the boxing strips:

● Cut one long strip of fabric. The length is equal to the perimeter of the foam block, minus the length of the zipper. The width is equal to the depth of the foam block. Add ½″ (1.3cm) all around for seam allowances.

● Cut two shorter strips of fabric. The length is equal to the zipper

SHIRRED BOX PILLOW

tape; the width is equal to half the depth of the foam block, plus 1½″ (3.8cm) for seam allowances.

● Pin the two shorter strips, right sides together, along one long edge. Baste a 1″ (2.5cm) seam. Press the seam open. Center the seam over the zipper. Baste, then stitch the zipper in place. (See "Zippers" in Chapter 4, THE SEWING BASICS.)

Press under ½″ (1.3cm).

● Press the ends of the long boxing strip under ½″ (1.3cm). Pin the zipper strip to the long strip, right sides

TIP

Can't find a zipper long enough? Use two zippers, installed so the tops of the zippers meet at the center back of the cushion.

together, so that the pressed lines and the ends of the zipper match. Stitch along each pressed line. To strengthen the seam, stitch back and forth several times at the top and bottom of the zipper.

● Press the seam allowances away from the zipper, then remove the center basting stitches.

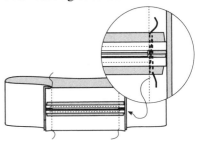

Complete the pillow cover according to the basic directions. Disregard references to the opening in Step 3 on page 161.

Variation

Shirred Box Pillow

For this pillow, cut the boxing strip two to three times longer than the perimeter of the foam block. Stitch the short ends together, then quarter-mark the strip. Using the *gathering over a cord* method (see Chapter 4, THE SEWING BASICS, page 39), gather both long edges of the strip.

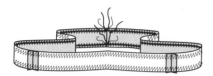

Construct the cover as for the *fitted box-edge pillow*, drawing the gathers up to fit and keeping them parallel as you attach the front and back covers. Before turning the assembled cover right side out (Step 3), hold the gathers in position along the opening by machine-stitching on the seamline of the boxing strip only. Then turn the cover right side out, insert the pillow and slipstitch the opening closed.

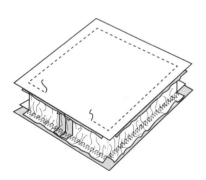

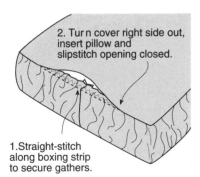

2. Turn cover right side out, insert pillow and slipstitch opening closed.

1. Straight-stitch along boxing strip to secure gathers.

Contemporary Box-Edge Pillow

This style of cover is suitable for square, rectangular or round pillows or cushions. It is not suitable for irregular shapes, including the T-shape.

Step 1: Cut the cover.

● Measure length and width, across the top of the foam block, from edge to edge.

● Measure the depth of the foam block, from edge to edge.

● Add the length and depth together. Add the width and the depth together. Then, to each of these measurements, add ½″ (1.3cm) for seam allowances.

● Using these two measurements, cut the front and back cover sections.

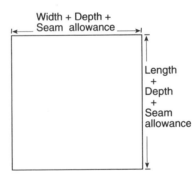

Width + Depth + Seam allowance

Length + Depth + Seam allowance

Step 2: Miter the corners.

● At each corner, measure in from each edge a distance equal to half the depth of the foam block plus ½″ (1.3cm). Draw two new intersecting lines.

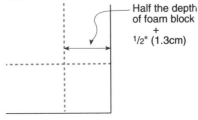

Half the depth of foam block + ½" (1.3cm)

● With right sides together, fold each corner diagonally so the raw edges are even and the drawn lines match. Stitch along the drawn lines, backstitching at the beginning and end.

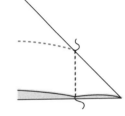

● Repeat, mitering all four corners on the front cover and all four corners on the back cover.

Step 3: *OPTIONAL*: Baste piping to the edge of the front cover. (See "Piping" in Chapter 4, THE SEWING BASICS.)

Step 4: Assemble the cover.

Pin the top cover to the bottom cover, right sides together, with corners matching. To reduce bulk at the

TIPS

● **If the pillow or cushion has an unusual shape, trace it onto paper, then add seam allowances.**

● **If you are re-covering a worn cushion, remember that old foam, like old covers, may disintegrate. If new foam is called for, remove the cushion, cover the seating area with paper and trace the shape. Take this paper pattern with you to the store so the foam can be cut to the exact size and shape.**

● **For multiple foam pillows or a very large cushion, consider this money-saver: Purchase bunk-bed or high-riser mattress foam. Use an electric knife to cut it to the desired shape.**

corners, fold the excess fabric in opposite directions. Stitch, leaving an opening for turning.

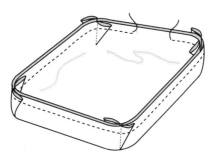

Step 5: Finish the cover.

Turn the cover right side out. Insert the pillow form, then slipstitch the opening closed.

Variation

Adding a Zipper

If you are planning on adding a zipper, follow Step 1 on page 163 but cut the cover with a 1″ (2.5cm) seam allowance all around. In Step 2, measure in and mark half the depth of the foam block plus 1″ (2.5cm). In Step 3, apply the piping so it falls at the 1″ (2.5cm) seamline. Then:

● Center and mark the zipper opening along the back edge of the back cover. Mark again, 3″ (7.5cm) out from each end of the opening.

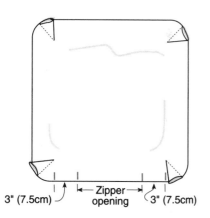

3″ (7.5cm) ← Zipper → 3″ (7.5cm)
opening

● Mark the front cover to correspond to the back cover.

● Install the zipper, following the directions for the _lapped application_ (see "Zippers" in Chapter 4, THE SEWING BASICS, page 43).

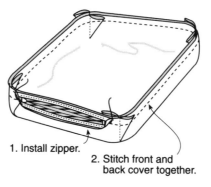

1. Install zipper.

2. Stitch front and
back cover together.

● Open the zipper and finish stitching the front and back covers together. Turn the finished cover right side out and insert the pillow form.

For more information on furniture cushions, see Chapter 9, SITTING PRETTY.

PLAIN BOLSTER

NECKROLL PILLOW

✽ BOLSTER PILLOWS

Here are two variations of the bolster pillow. Use a purchased bolster form or make your own form by rolling a sheet of polyester batting up into the desired size. Slipstitch the ends of the batting in place to secure. If desired, make a muslin cover, following the directions for the _plain bolster_. Omit the zipper and slipstitch the opening closed.

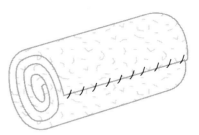

Plain Bolster

Step 1: Cut the cover.

● Measure the width of the form, from edge to edge, then add 1″ (2.5cm) for seam allowances.

● Measure the length around the form, then add 2″ (5cm) for seam allowances.

● Use these two measurements to cut the cover.

● Measure the diameter across one end of the form. Use this measurement to make a paper pattern for the circular end sections. (See "Tip," page 151.) Cut out two end sections.

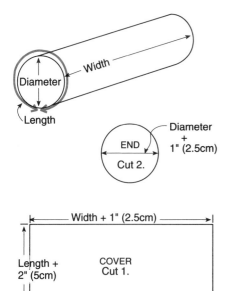

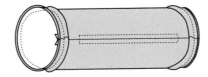

Step 2: Install the zipper.

Install the zipper, using a center application, in the long seam of the cover. Open the zipper.

Step 3: Assemble the cover.

OPTIONAL: If desired, baste piping, ruffles or other insertion trim in place along the seamline at the

ends of the cover. (See "Special Touches" in Chapter 4, THE SEWING BASICS, for additional information.)

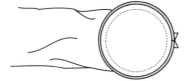

● Pin the cover and one end section, right sides together, raw edges matching. Working with the end section on top, stitch a ½″ (1.3cm) seam. Repeat for the other end section.

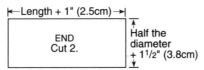

Step 4: Finish the cover.

Turn the cover right side out and insert the pillow form.

Neckroll Pillow

Step 1: Cut the cover.

● Measure and cut the cover section as for the *plain bolster*.

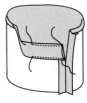

● Measure the diameter across one end of the form. Divide by 2, then add 1½″ (3.8cm) for seam allowance and casing. Use this measurement and the length measurement plus 1″ (2.5cm) to cut two rectangles for the end sections.

Step 2: Make the casings.

● Pin one end section, right sides together, short ends matching. Stitch a ½″ (1.3cm) seam, ending the stitching 2″ (5cm) from one long end. Press the seam open.

● At the open end of the seam, turn the raw edge under ¼″ (6mm) and press. Turn under again ¾″ (2cm) and press. Edgestitch close to each fold.

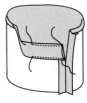

● Repeat for the other end section.

Step 3: Assemble the cover.

● Pin the cover, right sides together, long edges matching, and stitch a ½″ (1.3cm) seam. Press the seam open. Turn the cover right side out.

OPTIONAL: If desired, baste piping, ruffles or other insertion trim in place along the seamline at the ends of the cover. (See "Special Touches" in Chapter 4, THE SEWING BASICS, for additional information.)

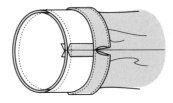

• Pin the cover and one end section, right sides together, raw edges and seams matching. Stitch a ½″ (1.3cm) seam. Repeat for the other end section.

Step 4: Finish the cover.

• Insert ribbon or cording into the casing. Insert the pillow form. Pull up the drawstrings and tie in a bow.

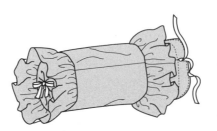

For more information on bolster pillows, see Chapter 7, SLEEPING BEAUTY.

For information on covering a cushion when you are slipcovering a sofa or chair, see Chapter 9, SITTING PRETTY.

For easy, no-sew pillow ideas, see Chapter 11, TIMESAVERS.

❈ ❈ ❈

Sitting Pretty

Sitting Pretty

As a decorating tool, slipcovers are a beautiful, yet inexpensive, way to extend the life of worn or faded upholstery. They are also a wonderful way to disguise those hand-me-downs and too-good-to-pass-ups that would otherwise be out of place with your decor. And they are the perfect way to impart seasonal interest and charm to even mint-condition furniture.

In this chapter, we offer you two ways to slipcover your furniture—the traditional fitted slipcover and the super-easy wrap-and-tie slipcover.

CHOOSING A FABRIC

There is a wide range of fabrics suitable for slipcovers. Among the choices are polished cotton, chintz, ticking, piqué, canvas, linen, corduroy, poplin, broadcloth or any medium-weight cotton with a slightly crisp hand.

For best results, keep the following in mind when selecting your fabric:

● The fabric should be closely woven so it will not ravel or stretch.

● Plain fabrics or fabrics with all-over designs are the easiest to use. Fabrics with a predominant design motif or a repeating pattern, including stripes, plaids and many floral bouquet designs, require extra time and work in planning, as well as extra yardage. The easiest fabric of all is a small print in a dense, random pattern. It doesn't have to be matched, plus the visual activity in the print will help camouflage any stitching imperfections.

● Coordinated fabric lines provide the wherewithal to transform basic slipcovers into ones with designer detail. Take advantage of them to create custom piping, contrasting bands or interesting skirt details.

● When it comes to slipcovers, there are no hard-and-fast rules regarding preshrinking the fabric. However, shrinkage is an important consideration if you plan to wash the finished product. Invest in an extra yard of fabric. Wash it, then check for shrinkage and observe whether laundering has changed the character of the fabric.

TRADITIONAL SLIPCOVERS

For traditional slipcovers, the amount of fabric will depend on the dimensions of the piece of furniture. However, the list of supplies is the same for almost every slipcover.

Supplies:

● *Fabric.*

● *Upholstery zipper, snap tape or hook-and-loop fastener tape*, such as Velcro®.

● *Piping or 1" (2.5cm) wide fringe.*

● *T-pins.*

● *Tape measure.*

● *Zipper foot* for the sewing machine.

● *Size 16 (100) sewing machine needle.*

● *Twill tape.*

TIP

To improve the look of a slipcover, study magazine advertisements for expensive upholstered furniture. Notice the placement of the print motif and the way the motif is matched.

How Much Fabric?

Use the Fabric Estimates chart to determine how much fabric you will need. Since this chart is on the generous side, it is possible that you will have some fabric left over. If you are planning to add other items, such as curtains or pillows, to your room's decor, make the slipcovers first. Any remaining fabric can be fashioned into piping cord, bands, ruffled trim or throw pillows, giving the whole room a totally coordinated, custom look.

NOTES:

● Estimates are based on 45″–54″ (115cm–140cm) wide fabric that does not require matching.

● Fabrics with motifs that must be matched require extra yardage. As a general rule, if the repeat is 3″–12″

FABRIC ESTIMATES				
YARDS OF 45″–54″ (115CM–140CM) WIDE FABRIC—PLAIN				
TYPE	NUMBER OF CUSHIONS	FACED FINISH	SKIRTED FINISH	ADDED YARDAGE PIPING	AMOUNT OF PIPING OR TRIM
ARM-, CLUB OR LOUNGE CHAIR	1	5³/₄ (5.3m)	11¹/₄ (10.3m)	1 (1.0m)	18 (16.5m)
WING CHAIR, LOW OR HIGH BACK	1	5³/₄–9 (5.3m–8.3m)	11¹/₄–15 (10.3m–13.8m)	1 (1.0m)	18–20 (16.5m–18.3m)
SOFA 6–7 FT (1.8m-2.1m)	2	16¹/₄ (14.9m)	26 (23.8m)	1³/₄ (1.7m)	36 (33.0m)
	3	17 (15.6m)	26³/₄ (24.5m)	1³/₄ (1.7m)	41 (37.6m)
LOVE SEAT	2	12 (11.0m)	19 (17.4m)	1¹/₂ (1.4m)	24 (22.0m)
EXTRA CUSHIONS		1¹/₂ (1.4m)	1¹/₂ (1.4m)	¹/₄ (0.2m)	5 (4.6m)

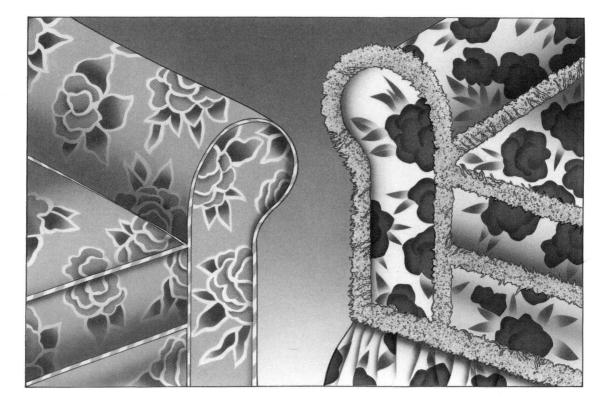

(7.5cm–30.5cm), add ³/₄ yard (.7m) for a chair, 1 yard (1m) for a love seat and 1¹/₂ yards (1.4m) for a sofa. If the repeat is more than 12″ (30.5cm), double these amounts.

● Consider purchasing extra yardage in case the slipcovers require some repair later on—¹/₂ yard (.5m) for a chair or 1 yard (1m) for a sofa is a good safety net.

● If you are covering more than the number of cushions indicated on the chart, add 1¹/₂ yards (1.4m) for each additional cushion.

Zippers and Other Closures

Upholstery zippers are strong zippers with metal teeth and a durable tape. They usually are available in a limited color range—white, beige and black. Fortunately, since the zipper is well concealed in the slipcover, color is of little importance.

● Upholstery zippers come in a range of lengths—from 12″–72″ (30.5cm–183cm). The most common lengths for slipcovers are 24″ (61cm), 27″ (68.5cm), 30″ (76cm) and 36″ (91.5cm).

● For a *sofa* or *armchair*, the zipper usually is installed on the back in the side seam that is on the right as you are facing the back of the chair. To determine the optimum length, measure along this side seam, starting 2″ (5cm) below the top of the chair down to the bottom edge of the slipcover.

● For *cushions*, the zipper should equal the length of the boxing strip along the back of the cushion, plus approximately 4″ (10cm).

Snap tape and *hook-and-loop tape* are fasteners that also can be used as closures on a slipcover. Measure as for a zipper.

For a slipcover without a skirt, both of these tapes are effective ways to anchor the slipcover to the chair. One half of the tape is sewn to a facing strip attached to the bottom edge of the slipcover. The other half is stapled to the wooden frame on the underside of the chair.

To determine how much tape is needed, measure the frame on the underside of the chair, between the legs.

Piping or Other Trim

Traditionally, piping is used to define the lines of the slipcover. Besides providing a decorative touch, it adds strength to the seams. For an added dimension, choose contrasting piping. For a subtle look, match the piping color to the slipcover fabric. For a whimsical touch, substitute 1″ (2.5cm) cotton or wool caterpillar fringe for the piping.

Use purchased piping or make custom piping by covering ¼″ (6mm) diameter piping cord in the fabric of your choice. Have the required amount of trim or piping on hand before you begin the fitting process.

To make custom piping, as well as to review how to apply piping, caterpillar trim and other insertion trims, see "Special Touches" in Chapter 4, THE SEWING BASICS.

In order to maintain the correct shape, a well-made slipcover should be planned so that the seams fall exactly on top of the seams of the original upholstery.

● To determine how much trim is needed, measure all the seams, add them together and then add one more yard (meter) for seam allowances and a margin of error.

● For a slipcover without a skirt, be sure to include the distance around the base of the sofa, chair or ottoman, above the legs.

● For a skirted slipcover, pin a piece of twill tape around the upholstered piece, parallel to the floor and at the level where you want the skirt to begin—usually around 8″–11″ (20.5cm–28cm) from the floor. Measure vertical seams down to the twill tape. Measure all other seams, including the distance around the chair, at the twill tape. Leave the twill tape in place as you pin and fit the cover.

General Directions

Because every piece of upholstered furniture has slightly different dimensions, the best-looking slipcovers are constructed by molding the fabric to the piece of furniture. This method is referred to as "pin fitting," or "blocking."

Fitting the slipcover is merely a matter of proceeding in order, from one section of the piece to another. The blocking order is always the same.

NOTE: Although we've illustrated a chair, the procedure is the same whether you are slipcovering a chair or a sofa. For additional information on covering a wing chair or ottoman, see pages 179–80.

General Tips

● All selvages should be trimmed off before you begin. Otherwise, they may pucker or distort the shape of the fabric.

● Work with the fabric right side out during the pinning and fitting process. This ensures a good fit, especially where the furniture may be slightly irregular. It also makes it easier to control the placement of fabric motifs and, where the fabric design demands it, makes precise matching easier.

● Each section of the slipcover should be pinned in position so that the lengthwise grain is perpendicular to the floor. Do this even if the section of the slipcover is on a slant.

● Unattached seat or back cushions should be removed and slipcovered separately.

Controlling Fullness

There are several ways to control fullness in curved areas:

GATHERS. Using a double thread, hand-gather along the seamline, then draw the gathered edge up to fit the other fabric edge.

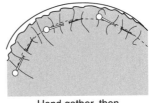

Hand-gather, then draw up and pin to fit.

TUCKS. Working from the center out, form small, equal folds until the larger edge fits the smaller edge of the fabric.

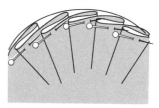

Form folds, then pin to fit.

DARTS. Working from the center out, fold the fabric into small, equal darts. Pin-baste the darts during fitting. When you're ready to permanently stitch that seam, first mark and stitch the darts on the wrong side of the fabric.

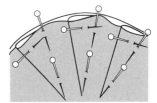

Pin-baste darts, then pin to fit.

Step 1: Pin-fit the inner chair.

The Inside Back

● Drape the uncut fabric over the inside back of the chair. The fabric should extend at least 1″ (2.5cm) over the outside back unless you will be pin-fitting a boxing strip. In that case, extend the fabric 4″ (10cm).

● Secure the fabric with a T-pin at the center of the inside back. Smooth the fabric out toward each side, then upward and downward.

● Keeping the lengthwise grainline perpendicular to the floor, pin down the center and then pin the sides. As you work, continue smoothing the fabric.

● If a boxing strip is not needed, pin the fabric along the top back edge of the chair.

The Boxing Strip

A boxing strip is a platform of fabric that runs along the top of the chair, connecting the inside back with the outside back. The easiest way to cover this area is to pin-fit it as an extension of the inside back.

● Pin a 1″ (2.5cm) deep tuck along the upper edge of the inside back.

● Smooth the fabric across the platform. Beginning at the center and working alternately out toward each side, pin along the top back edge of the chair.

The Seat Platform

● Where the fabric travels from the inside back to the seat platform, an extra 6″–12″ (15cm–30.5cm) of fabric is required for the "tuck-in." The exact amount of the tuck-in depends on the depth of the chair at that point. Use your hands to smooth the fabric in between the back and the seat.

● Check the lengthwise grainline, then smooth and pin-fit the seat platform as for the inside back. Pin the center grainline first, then the sides, the front and the back edge of the platform.

The Front Apron

● Bring the fabric down over the front of the chair. Smooth and pin at the center line, then at the sides.

Step 2: Trim the fabric.

● Trim the fabric 2″ (5cm) below the twill tape (for a skirted finish) or 2″ (5cm) below the lower edge of the chair (for a faced finish).

● Trim the fabric along the sides of the seat platform, leaving 6″ (15cm) extra for the tuck-in where the seat joins the inside arm.

● Trim all remaining seam allowances to 1″ (2.5cm). Clip the fabric where necessary to make it lie smooth.

NOTE: After stitching, these seam allowances will be trimmed to ¹⁄₂″ (1.3cm).

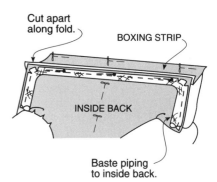

Cut apart along fold.

BOXING STRIP

INSIDE BACK

Baste piping to inside back.

Step 3: Add the piping cord.

● Pin the piping in place around the inside back, along any seamlines that are to be trimmed. Clip or notch the piping where necessary to fit curves or corners. If desired, piping can be hand-basted in place for more secure handling.

● If the slipcover has a boxing strip, slash the fabric along the fold, then pin the piping in place along the seamline of one of the sections.

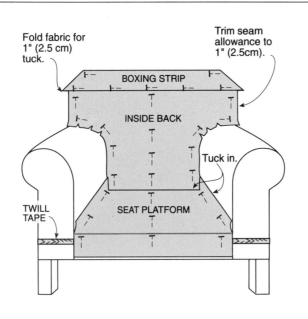

Fold fabric for 1″ (2.5 cm) tuck.

Trim seam allowance to 1″ (2.5cm).

BOXING STRIP

INSIDE BACK

Tuck in.

TWILL TAPE

SEAT PLATFORM

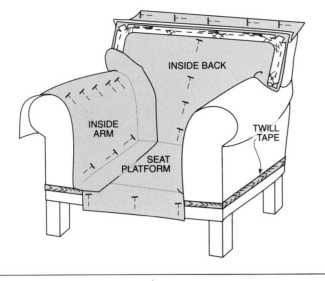

Step 5: Pin-fit the sides.

NOTE: If the arm does not protrude between the outside arm and the shoulder area, then the shoulder area can be fitted as an extension of the outside arm.

The Outside Arm

● Center and pin the fabric to the outside arm.

● Smoothing the fabric outward, then upward and downward, pin along the sides and upper edges, then along the twill tape.

● Trim the fabric 2″ (5cm) below the twill tape or the lower edge of the frame.

● Trim the seam allowances to 1″ (2.5cm).

The Shoulder Area

● Center and pin the fabric to the shoulder area.

● Smooth and pin the fabric along the side, top and bottom edges.

● Trim the seam allowances to 1″ (2.5cm).

Step 4: Pin-fit the arms.

The Inside Arm

● Center the fabric over the inside arm. Secure along the top of the arm with T-pins.

● Smooth the fabric down the inside of the arm to the seat. Pin along the side edge of the platform to secure.

● Trim away the excess fabric, allowing an extra 6″ (15cm) of fabric for tuck-ins at the seat platform and the inside arm.

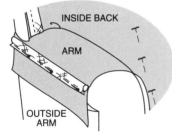

● If the chair has a curved or rolled arm, establish where the seam will be that joins the inside arm with the outside arm. It should be located along the fattest part of the outer roll. Pin horizontally to indicate the seamline. (NOTE: This seam does not have to be completely horizontal to

the floor. You may need to curve it up slightly in order to meet the seam where the back joins the arm.) Trim the fabric just below the pins so there is a 1″ (2.5cm) seam allowance. Pin the piping in place along the seamline.

● Repeat for the other arm.

The Front Arm

● Center and pin the fabric to the front of the arm.

● Trim the excess fabric so the seam allowances are 1″ (2.5cm).

● Pin the piping along the seamline, clipping, as necessary, along the curves.

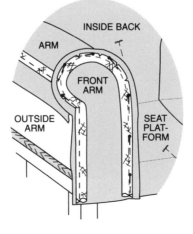

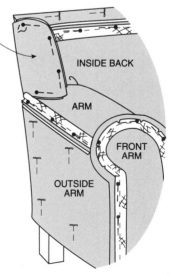

Step 6: Pin-baste.

Pin-baste all the sections together, working in the same order as for pin fitting.

● For seams that include piping, turn under 1″ (2.5cm) on the seam allowance without the piping. Pin, matching the seamlines, to the corresponding seam allowance with the piping.

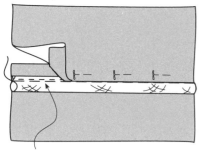

Piping is hand-basted to seamline.

● Pin the other seam allowances together, joining the front arm and the inside arm to the seat.

● Pin, then hand-baste the piping in place along the seamline where the inside back and the outside back will join.

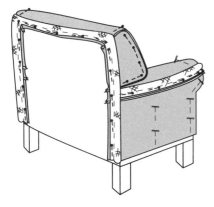

Step 7: Pin-fit the back.

● Center and pin the fabric to the outside back, the same as for the inside back, then pin along the twill tape.

● Trim the fabric 2″ (5cm) below the twill tape or the lower edge of the frame; trim the seam allowances to 1″ (2.5cm).

● Unpin the top edge of the outside back and pin-baste to the inside back. Repeat for the side seams.

Step 8: Assemble the cover.

To remove the cover from the chair:

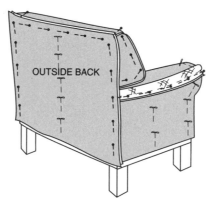

OUTSIDE BACK

● Remove all the T-pins that secure the fabric to the chair. To establish the zipper opening, unpin the side back seam (the one that is on the right as you face the back of the chair) to within 2″ (5cm) of the top.

● Carefully remove the slipcover from the chair.

All seams will be stitched in the same order as they were pinned. Before stitching across a piped seam, pull out and cut off 1″ (2.5cm) of the cording at the end of the piping. This will remove bulk from the seam. As each seam is stitched, trim the seam allowances to ½″ (1.3cm).

● Beginning with the inside back, stitch any darts, then stitch the boxing strip to the inside back.

Long, twisted fringe adds a formal touch to your slipcovers. To apply, topstitch the trim in place after the faced finish is attached in Step 10.

● Stitch the inside back to the inside arms, clipping curves as necessary and tapering the tuck-in allowance to meet the seamlines.

● Stitch the front arm section to the inside arm section, clipping the curves as necessary.

● Stitch the outside arm to the inside arm, then to the front arm section.

● Stitch the platform section to the inside arm section along the tuck-in allowances.

● Stitch the shoulder section to the inside arm, inside back and boxing strip.

● Stitch the outside back to the top and sides of the cover, leaving the right side seam open to within 2″ (5cm) of the top. At the zipper opening, turn the outside back seam allowance under and baste. *Do not* trim the seam allowances along the zipper opening—they should remain 1″ (2.5cm) wide.

Step 9: Pin-baste the piping or other trim to the lower edge.

● Once the slipcover is sewn together, put it back on the chair or sofa. Pin the zipper opening closed. Adjust the tuck-ins to their proper positions. Put the cushions on the chair.

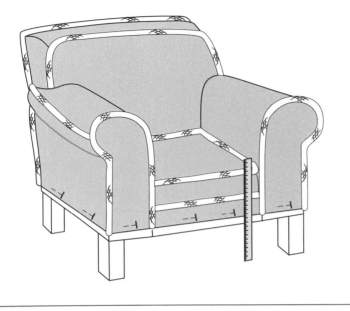

• Pin-mark the piping placement line.

For a *faced finish*, this seamline would fall at the lower edge of the chair.

For a *skirted finish*, this seamline would fall where the twill tape is pinned in place. Use a ruler to check that it is an even distance from the floor all around.

• With its raw edge toward the floor, pin the piping (or other trim) along the marked seamline. To reduce bulk at the zipper opening, pull out and cut off ³/₄″ (2cm) of the

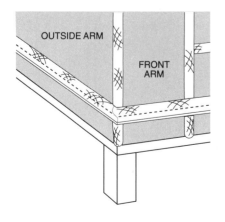

cording. On the outside back edge of the zipper opening, fold the end of the piping to the inside, over the seam allowance. Remove the slipcover and machine-baste the piping in place.

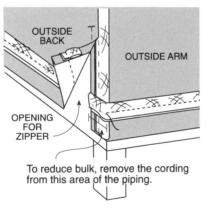

To reduce bulk, remove the cording from this area of the piping.

• Trim the seam allowance to ¹/₂″ (1.3cm).

Step 10: Finish the lower edge.

The Faced Finish

A faced finish leaves the legs of the chair exposed, giving the piece an upholstered look.

• On the lower edge of the slip-cover, mark the position of each leg. Remove the slipcover.

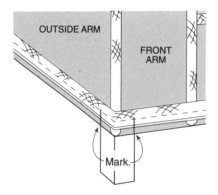

Mark.

• For each side of the slipcover, cut a facing piece 3¹/₂″ (9cm) wide by the length of the side between the legs, plus 1″ (2.5cm) for hem allowances.

FACED FINISH

• Hem one long and both short ends of each facing strip, using a ½″ (1.3cm) hem allowance.

• Pin the facings to the slipcover, right sides together, centering each facing strip between its corresponding leg markings. Stitch along the seamline, stitching all around the slipcover, even in the leg area where there is only piping. Press the facing down, then understitch.

• Clip the seam allowances at the leg markings. Turn the seam allowances in the unfaced areas to the inside and whipstitch them in place.

SKIRTED FINISH

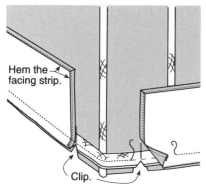

Hem the facing strip.

Clip.

Apply facings between markings.

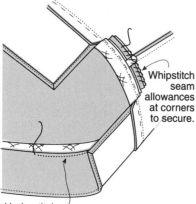

Whipstitch seam allowances at corners to secure.

Understitch.

The Skirted Finish

The skirted finish provides a softer look while concealing scratched or unattractive legs. Because it is self-lined, this skirt is easy to sew and will hang better on the finished slipcover.

• Measure and record the distance around the chair at the piping seamline. This distance will be used to determine the length of the skirt.

• Measure out 4″ (10cm) from each corner along the piping seam; mark. Measure and record the distance between each set of marks on the sides, front and back of the slipcover.

• Measure the distance from the piping seam to the floor. This measurement is the finished depth of the skirt. Remove the slipcover from the chair.

• Cut crosswise strips of fabric equal to the distance around the chair, plus 33″ (84cm), plus 1″ (2.5cm) for each piecing seam. The depth of the strip should be equal to twice the depth of the finished skirt, plus 1″ (2.5cm).

• Piece the strips as necessary and press seams open. Then fold in half,

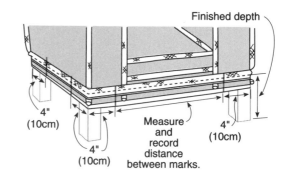

Finished depth

4″ (10cm)

4″ (10cm)

4″ (10cm)

Measure and record distance between marks.

right sides together and long sides matching. Stitch the ends. Turn right side out and press.

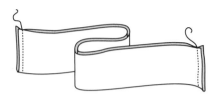

● Pin, then machine-baste the upper edges of the skirt together. Starting at one end, divide, then mark, as indicated. Machine-gather at the corners, between the markings.

● With right sides together, pin the skirt to the slipcover. On the right side of the zipper opening, match the finished edge of the skirt to the raw edge of the seam allowance; on the left side of the zipper opening, fold the seam allowance under and match it to the finished edge of the skirt. Match the remaining markings and draw the gathers up to fit at the corners.

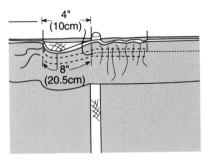

● Cut eight pieces of twill tape, each 20″ (51cm) long. Position the twill tape at the markings on the lower edge of the slipcover, as shown. Stitch. Press the seam allowances up, toward the slipcover.

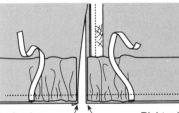

Left edge of opening: Seam allowance is folded under and matched to finished edge of skirt.

Right edge of opening: Finished edge of skirt is matched to raw edge of seam allowance.

BOX PLEATS

Step 11: Install the zipper.

● Position the open zipper, face-down, over the right side of the opening, so that the zipper teeth just cover the edge of the piping and the zipper tape is within the seam allowance. The tab end of the zipper should be ½″ (1.3cm) from the bottom edge of the skirt (or the bottom edge of the slipcover, if there is no skirt), and the tape end should be

TIPS

For an easy way to make a box-pleated skirt, see "Pleats" in Chapter 4, THE SEWING BASICS.

If you can't find a zipper the correct length, use one a little longer. To shorten it, refer to "Zippers" in Chapter 4, THE SEWING BASICS.

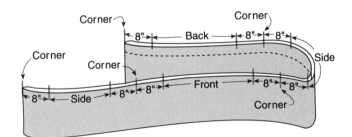

Note: 8" = 20.5cm

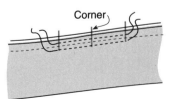

folded up. Pin, then baste the zipper in place to the piping and slipcover seam allowance only. Using the zipper attachment, stitch, crowding the stitches up against the piping.

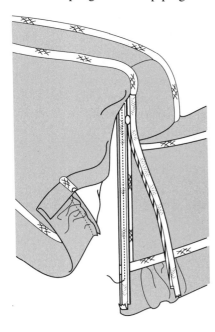

● Close the zipper. Lap the pressed edge of the opening over the zipper to meet the piping. Pin, then baste in place. Using the zipper foot at-

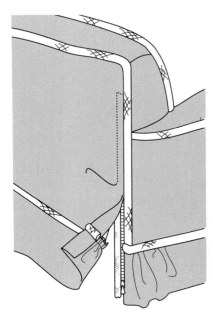

tachment, stitch across the bottom of the zipper, then down the side, 5/8″ (1.5cm) from the pressed edge.

Step 12: Secure the slipcover to the chair.

● For a *faced finish*, sew one half of a strip of hook-and-loop fastener to the wrong side of each facing strip. Staple the other half of each strip to a corresponding place on the frame on the underside of the chair.

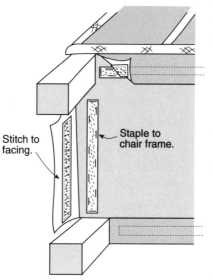

Stitch to facing.

Staple to chair frame.

● For a *skirted finish*, wrap the twill tape around the legs and tie.

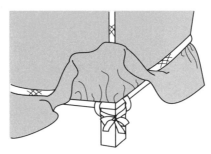

● To keep the finished slipcover from shifting during use, stuff the tuck-in areas around the seat platform with fabric remnants or tightly rolled-up magazines.

Covering the Cushion

Because the cushions on upholstered pieces often are not symmetrical, and because it's easier to match motifs if you work directly on the chair, the following method for covering a cushion is slightly different from the one in Chapter 8, PILLOW PIZZAZZ.

Step 1: Pin-fit the cover.

● Center and pin the fabric on the cushion top. Smooth the fabric and pin-fit the cushion. Trim the seam allowances to 1/2″ (1.3cm).

● Turn the cushion over and pin-fit the bottom exactly like the top.

● Pin-fit the boxing strip for the sides and front of the cushion, clipping the boxing strip at the corners.

● Pin-fit a strip of fabric for the back boxing strip that is long enough to go across the back of the cushion and wrap around each corner for 2″–4″ (5cm–10cm).

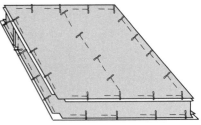

● Mark the corner locations on both edges of the boxing strip.

Step 2: Install the zipper.

● Unpin the back section of the boxing strip. Use it as a pattern to cut a second back boxing strip.

● Fold one back boxing strip in half lengthwise and press; open out the strip.

• Place the two boxing strips right sides together and baste along the foldline. Turn and press the back boxing strip so that the basted seam joins the two sections.

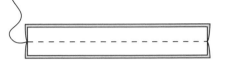

• Center the zipper facedown over the seam; baste. Stitch the zipper, using a centered application (see "Zippers" in Chapter 4, THE SEWING BASICS) and stitching several times across each end.

• With right sides together, stitch the back boxing strip to the side/front boxing strip. Press the seams away from the zipper. Remove the basting stitches and open the zipper.

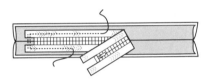

Step 3: Assemble the cover.

• Machine-baste the piping cord or other trim to the top and bottom of the cushion cover.

• With right sides together, pin the cover top to the boxing strip, matching the corner markings; stitch.

TIP

If the fabric has a motif that needs to be centered or matched, put the stitched-together slipcover back on the chair, then put the cushion in place on the chair and pin-fit.

• Repeat, stitching the cover bottom to the boxing strip.

• Turn the cover right side out and insert the cushion. Close the zipper.

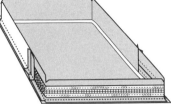

Covering a Wing Chair

To make a slipcover for a wing chair, use a faced finish at the lower edge.

Block and pin-fit the chair, as in "General Directions," Steps 1–5, on pages 172–73, until you get to the shoulder area. Then block and pin-fit the inside wing, clipping the seam allowances and easing the fullness as necessary. Leave at least a 3″

WING CHAIR

(7.5cm) tuck-in allowance between the wing and the inside back.

● Block and pin-fit the outside wing to the inside wing. Begin pin-fitting at the midpoint of the wing's outside edge and work downward. Then pin-fit across the top of the wing to the back.

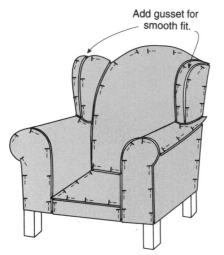

Add gusset for smooth fit.

NOTE: Some fabrics will not ease smoothly over the curve between the inside and the outside wing. If this is the case, add a gusset, as shown, to the front of the curved edge.

Continue with Steps 6–12. When you assemble the cover (Step 8), stitch the wing section before stitching the arm sections to the inside back.

Covering an Ottoman

Block and pin-fit an ottoman following the techniques in "General Directions" on pages 171.

● Pin-fit and assemble the platform cover first, then assemble and attach the skirt, omitting the zipper.

● Use twill tape ties to secure the slipcover to the frame.

WRAP-AND-TIE FURNITURE COVERS

Transform an old piece of furniture into something new and exciting with wrap-and-tie slipcovers. To accomplish this decorating wizardry, use sheets or the extra-wide 90″ (229cm) or 120″ (305cm) fabric. Although narrower fabric can be used, you may have to piece panels together before proceeding. This isn't difficult, but it will add a bit of time to this "timesaver."

TIP

For more information on decorating with sheets, see Chapter 11, TIMESAVERS.

Wrap-and-Tie Upholstered Sofa or Chair

NOTE: Although the illustrations are for a wrap-and-tie upholstered chair, the procedures are the same for a sofa.

Step 1: Prepare the fabric.

NOTE: Remove loose seat cushions before you measure.

● Measure the width of the chair (front to back), from the floor to the floor. Let the measuring tape conform to the contours of the piece.

● Measure the length of the chair (side to side), from the floor to the floor. Let the measuring tape conform to the contours of the piece.

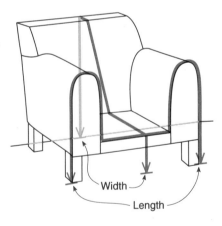

● To determine the amount of fabric or size sheets needed, add at least 10″ (25.5cm) to these two measurements. (To check sheet sizes, see the Sheet Conversions chart in Chapter 11, TIMESAVERS.)

Step 2: Assemble the cover.

● With the seat cushions still removed, "throw" the fabric, right side up, over your chair so that hemmed edges touch the floor at the front and back of the piece. Smooth the fabric up over the back of the chair, using T-pins to hold the hemmed edges temporarily in place.

● Working on the side of the chair, smooth the fabric up over the arms, tucking it in as you go and keeping the design or fabric grainline

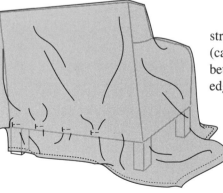

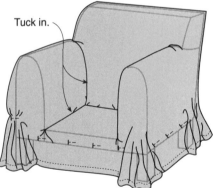

straight. Push the excess fabric (called the "tuck-in allowance") in between the padding along the inner edges of the frame.

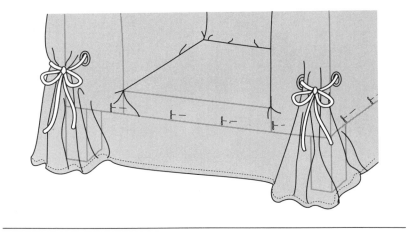

• Working at each corner of the piece, approximately 8″–10″ (20.5cm–25.5cm) up from the floor, gather up the excess fabric into folds with your hand. Hold it tight, so the fabric is taut across the back, sides and front. Mark the placement position for grommet or slashed buttonhole openings. They should be located just behind the gathered folds, one on each side of the corner.

• To make the openings, apply grommets according to the manufacturer's instructions, or cut a slash and seal the edges with seam sealant.

• Insert a heavy cord through each set of openings. Tie in a knot to secure the gathers. Fringe or seal the cord ends, as desired . . . or use drapery cord tiebacks with tassels. Remove the T-pins.

• To cover the seat cushions, use the *no-sew pillows/envelope fold* technique on page 210 in Chapter 11, TIMESAVERS, or use the following directions for the *drawstring cushion cover*.

TIPS

If your fabric is not wide enough to accommodate the width of the sofa or chair, you have two options:

   Option 1: Piece panels of fabric together with ¹/₂″ (1.3cm) seams.

   Option 2: Turn the hem allowance under and fuse along the selvage edges of the panels. Then, as you "construct" the cover, run the panels side by side, with the edges overlapping a few inches (centimeters).

Sheets will not need to be hemmed, but other fabrics will. Serge the edges on your overlock . . . or fuse hems in place.

As a guide, two king-size sheets are usually sufficient to cover an 84″ (214cm) wide sofa, plus one twin sheet to cover two average-size cushions. To check the needs for your furniture, make a "test" cover, using sheets from your linen closet.

Drawstring Cushion Cover

This cushion slipcover is super simple to measure and fit . . . and requires just a little bit of sewing.

To make it reversible, choose two compatible fabrics. Be sure they're opaque so there's no shadowthrough.

Step 1: Cut the cover.

Cut two rectangles of fabric large enough to cover the top and sides of the cushion, plus 5″–7″ (12.5cm–18cm) all around. Round off the corners.

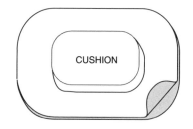

Step 2: Assemble the cover.

• With right sides together, stitch ¹/₂″ (1.3cm) from the edge, leaving an opening for turning along the center of one long side. Notch the corners.

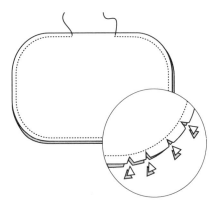

• Turn right side out and press, turning the seam allowance in at the opening. Topstitch along most of the opening, leaving about 1¹/₂″ (3.8cm) unstitched. Stitch again, 1″ (2.5cm) from the edge, forming a casing.

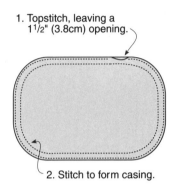

1. Topstitch, leaving a 1¹/₂″ (3.8cm) opening.

2. Stitch to form casing.

● Cut a piece of cord (or narrow elastic) that is a few inches (centimeters) longer than the perimeter of the cover. Use a safety pin to pull the cord through the casing.

● Center the cushion on the cover. Draw up the cord, covering the cushion. Adjust the fullness. Tie the cord in a knot and tuck the ends under the cover.

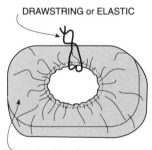

DRAWSTRING or ELASTIC

Underside of CUSHION

Wrap-and-Tie Straight-Back Chair Cover

● Start with a queen-size sheet or hemmed 90″ × 110″ (229cm ×

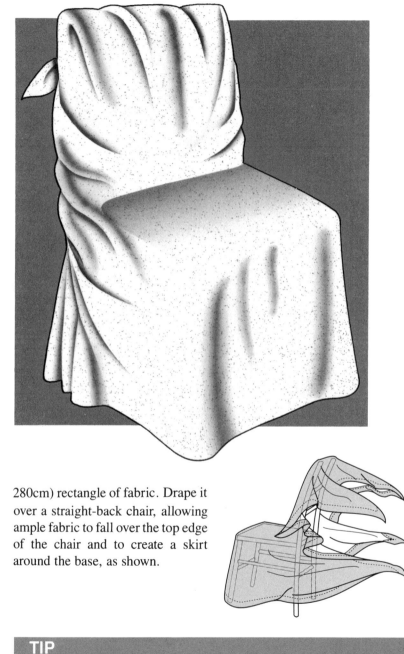

280cm) rectangle of fabric. Drape it over a straight-back chair, allowing ample fabric to fall over the top edge of the chair and to create a skirt around the base, as shown.

TIP

To help keep the finished cover in place, add some "stuffing" in the joint where the seat back and the seat platform meet—the area where you always find the loose change!

After the throw is adjusted, push the excess fabric into the joint, then stuff with any of the following: paper towel tubes stuffed with fabric scraps, fiberboard tubes cut to size or magazines rolled up tight and secured with tape or rubber bands. Don't use newspapers—the print might rub off on your cover.

● At the back, pull the sides to the center and knot halfway down.

● Pull the excess from the front of the skirt to the back and tie in a knot at center back, covering the legs.

As a general rule, wrap-and-tie covers look best in allover prints or solid fabrics. The wrap-and-tie process tends to distort high-contrast stripes and bold one-way designs.

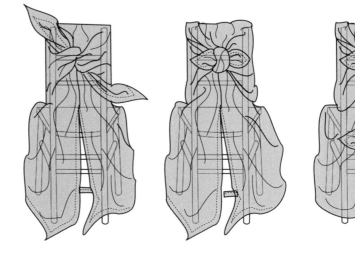

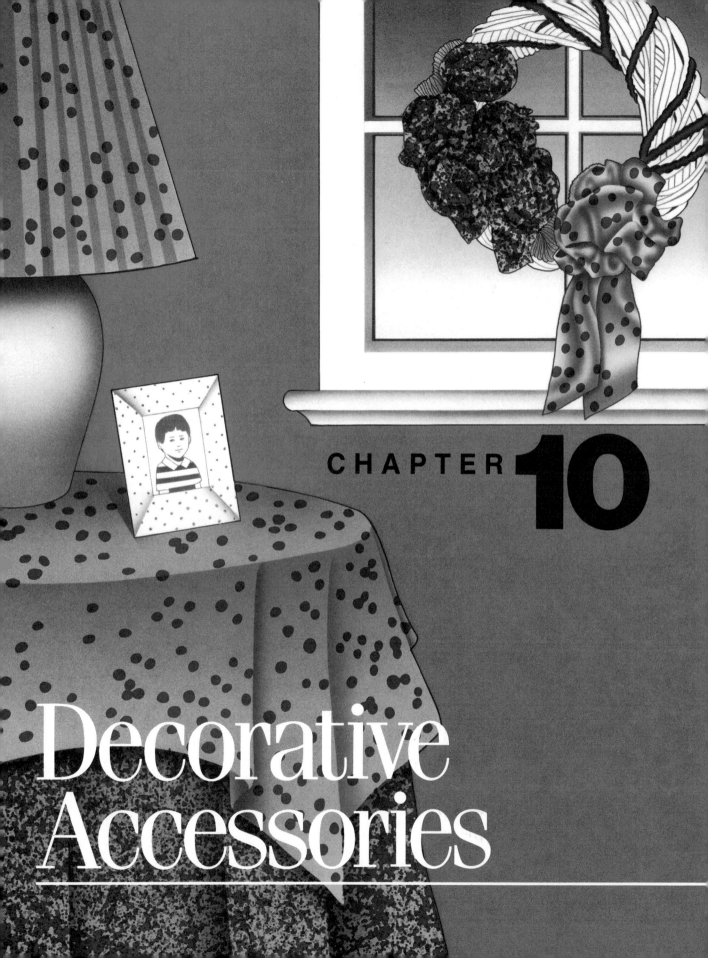

CHAPTER **10**

Decorative
Accessories

Decorative Accessories

From the welcoming wreath on your front door to the linens that grace your table, accessories are the little things that make a big difference.

In this chapter, you'll find ideas to spark your imagination . . . and your decor. For even more inspiration, check the "Home Decorating" and the "Crafts and Gifts" sections of the *Simplicity Pattern Catalog*.

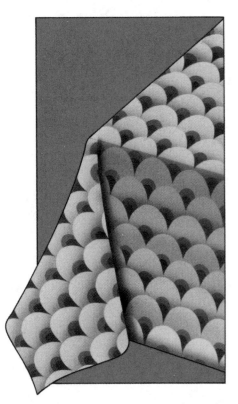

❀ TABLECLOTHS

Whether it's a tablecloth to enhance your dinner table or a floor-length covering for a more permanent effect, the measuring and sewing principles are the same.

Basic Tablecloth

Step 1: Determine the cutting dimensions.

● Measure the width and the length of the tabletop.

● Measure for the desired drop.

For a floor-length cloth, measure the height from the edge of the table to the floor.

For a dining table, measure from the table edge to within 1″–2″ (2.5cm–5cm) of the chair seats. This drop is usually 10″–12″ (25.5cm–30.5cm).

For a very formal dining room, the drop can be from 16″–24″ (40.5cm–61cm) and may drape on the chair seats.

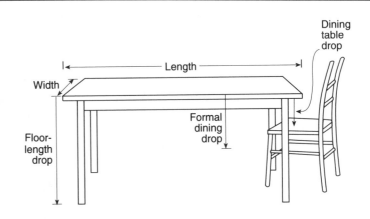

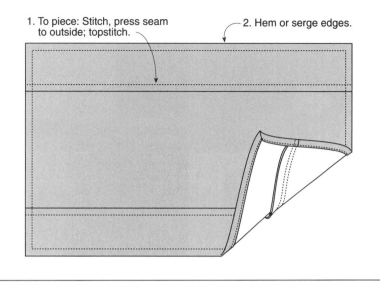

1. To piece: Stitch, press seam to outside; topstitch.

2. Hem or serge edges.

• For the cutting length, add:
Drop + length + drop + 1″ (2.5cm) for hem allowances.

• For the cutting width, add:
Drop + width + drop + 1″ (2.5cm) for hem allowances.

Step 2: To determine the amount of fabric, see "Figuring Fabric: Step by Step" in Chapter 4, THE SEWING BASICS.

Step 3: Assemble the cloth.

• If your cutting width is greater than your fabric's width, piecing will be necessary. Piece so there is one center panel and two side panels. To piece, stitch or serge a ¹/₂″ (1.3cm) seam, press the seam allowances toward the outside of the tablecloth and topstitch ¹/₄″ (6mm) from the seamline.

• Hem the edges, using a narrow

TIP

When adding a ruffle to the edge of the cloth, subtract the ruffle depth from the drop.

(¹/₄″, or 6mm) double hem or a serger rolled hem.

OPTIONAL: Apply ribbon, braid, fringe, double ruffle or other decorative trim to the lower edge. (See "Special Touches" in Chapter 4, THE SEWING BASICS.)

_____ *Variation* _____

Round Tablecloth

Follow the instructions for the *basic tablecloth*, but with these adjustments:

• In Step 1, for the cutting length and the cutting width, add:
Drop + diameter of the tabletop +

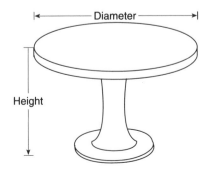

Diameter

Height

drop + 1″ (2.5cm) for hem allowances.

• In Step 3, after piecing but before hemming, fold the fabric in half, then in quarters, matching seams and edges; pin the layers together.

Pin a tape measure to the center point and use it as a compass to mark the radius (i.e., half the cutting width) with chalk or a marking pen.

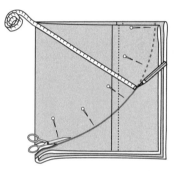

Cut along the marked line, then open out the cloth.

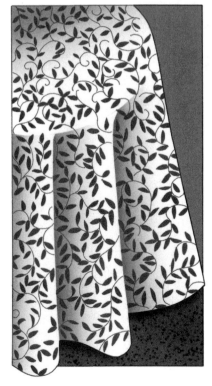

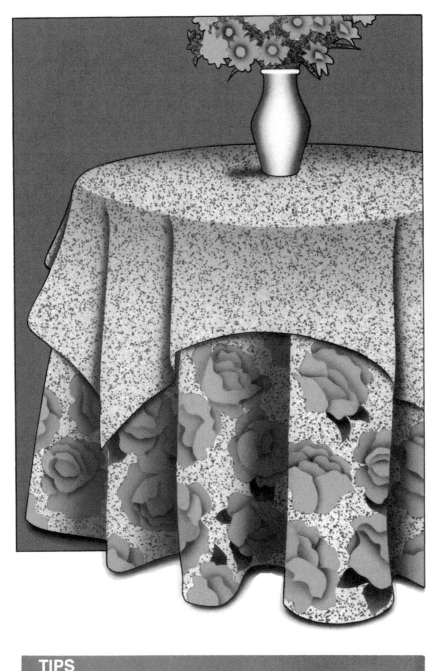

——— *Variation* ———

Oval Tablecloth

Follow the instructions for the *basic tablecloth*, but with the following adjustment in Step 3, after piecing, but before hemming:

● Place the panel on top of the table. Match the center of the cloth to

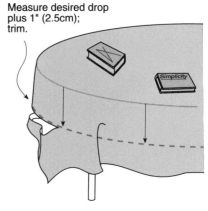

Measure desired drop plus 1″ (2.5cm); trim.

the center of the table and place the seams parallel to the length of the table and equidistant from the edges. To prevent shifting, weight the cloth with books. Then lightly chalk-mark at the edge of the table.

● Remove the cloth. Working on a large, flat surface, measure and mark from the edge marking a distance equal to the desired drop plus 1″ (2.5cm). Trim along this line.

——— *Variation* ———

Overskirt

To further coordinate your decor, consider adding an overskirt to a floor-length covering. Follow the instructions for the *basic tablecloth*, in whatever shape you desire, using one-third of the height as the drop measurement.

TIPS

On a round or oval cloth, if the fabric is too heavy for a narrow hem or a serger rolled hem, use ¹/₂″ (1.3cm) hem allowances. Serge or machine-finish the raw edge. Fold it under ¹/₂″ (1.3cm) and press; topstitch.

To divide and mark a round overskirt into even swags, use the fold-and-press method. For four equal divisions, fold in half and in half again. For six equal divisions, fold in half, then thirds.

TIP

If your floor-length cover ends up a bit too long (a frequent problem with thick pile carpets), add a sheet of thin quilt batting as a table pad to help raise the skirt.

_____ *Variation* _____

Swagged Overskirt

A round overskirt can be embellished with swags. This easy method uses two-cord shirring tape. Choose either the sew-on or iron-on type. For an opulent touch, add the tassels on page 194–95.

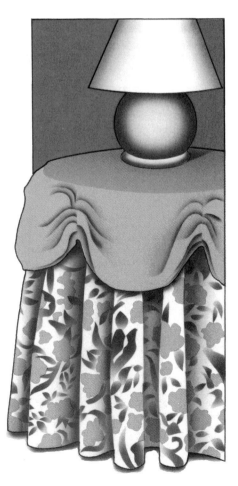

To determine how much tape is required, multiply the drop measurement by 6, then add 12″ (30.5cm).

Complete the round cloth, as in the *basic tablecloth*. Then:

● On the wrong side, divide and mark the edge of the overskirt into six equal parts. Mark the center.

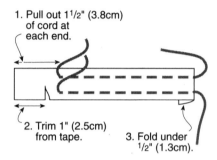

1. Pull out 1 1/2″ (3.8cm) of cord at each end.

2. Trim 1″ (2.5cm) from tape.

3. Fold under 1/2″ (1.3cm).

● Cut the shirring tape into six sections, each equal to the drop measurement plus 2″ (5cm). Use a pin to pull out 1 1/2″ (3.8cm) of draw cords at each end; trim off 1″ (2.5cm) of tape *only* and press the tape *only* under 1/2″ (1.3cm).

● Pin the tape to the wrong side of the cloth at the markings, so that one end is 1/2″ (1.3cm) above the hem allowance, and the tape itself points toward the center of the overskirt.

1/2″ (1.3cm)

1. Stitch tape in place.

2. Knot the cords.

(If necessary, use a yardstick as a placement guide.) Stitch along both edges of the tape, backstitching at the beginning and end.

● Tie the cords nearest the center into knots. Secure each with a drop of glue or seam sealant.

● Center the overskirt on the table. Weight it with a few books. Pull on one of the sets of cords, adjusting the swag to the desired depth. Tie the cord ends in a bow, then tuck the bow up inside the overskirt. Gather the remaining cords to match. Untie to launder.

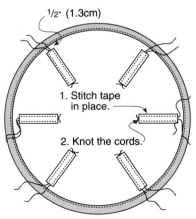

❦

PLACEMATS, NAPKINS AND TABLE RUNNERS

Placemats, napkins and table runners are quick ways to change the mood for any table setting.

The amount of fabric you need depends on the size of your project and how many items you are making. (See "Figuring Fabric: Step by Step" in Chapter 4, THE SEWING BASICS.)

Since *placemats* must be large enough to accommodate a place setting, a good standard size is 18″ × 12″ (45.5cm × 30.5cm).

TIP

To add a contrasting border and a clean-finished edge to square or rectangular placemats, tablecloths, runners and napkins, see "Special Touches" in Chapter 4, THE SEWING BASICS.

DECORATIVE ACCESSORIES

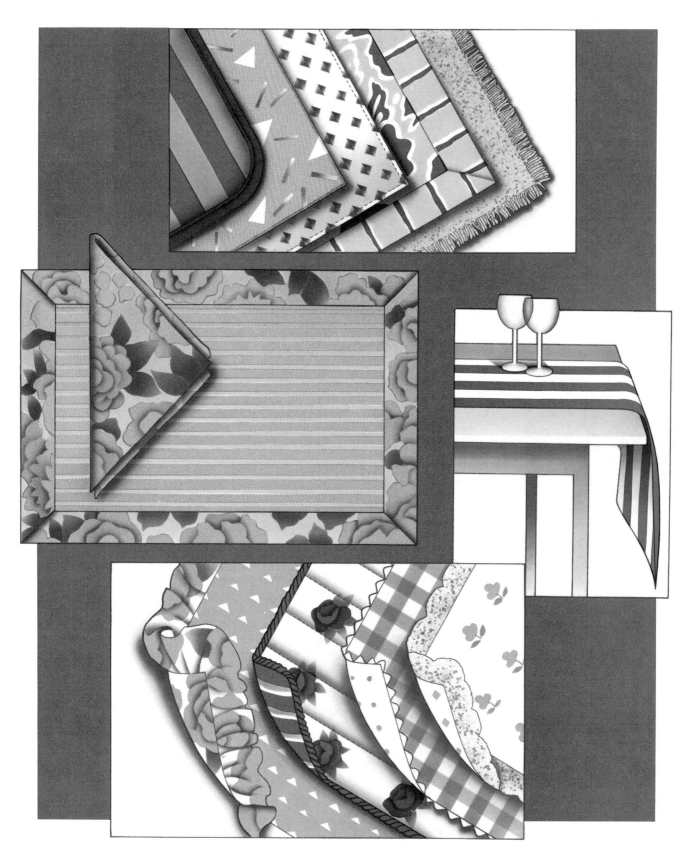

Napkins, generously sized to cover the lap, should be 18″–20″ (45.5cm–51cm) square. Cocktail napkins can be 10″ (25.5cm) square. Keep embellishments and edge finishes simple so they don't interfere with the purpose of a napkin!

Table runners should equal the length of the table (or the width, if you are placing them crosswise) plus a 10″–12″ (25.5cm–30.5cm) drop at each end. The average width for a decorative runner is 12″ (30.5cm). However, if you plan to use the ends for a place setting, the runner should be 18″ (45.5cm) wide.

The cutting dimensions for placemats, napkins and table runners depend on how you plan to finish them.

TIPS

While some edge finishes require it, adding a lining to placemats and table runners can also be a matter of durability, versatility and personal preference. For an easy lining, use prequilted fabric. Finish the edges with bias binding.

To curve the corners of placemats or table runners, use a drinking glass or a dessert plate as a template.

● For bias-bound edges, cut to the finished size.

● For serged edges, a narrow double hem, a clean-finished border or self-fringe, add a ½″ (1.3cm) hem allowance all around.

● To add ruffles or an insertion trim—such as cording, rickrack or lace edging—to placemats and table runners, add ½″ (1.3cm) seam allowances all around. Then cut one front and one lining for each placemat or table runner. Apply the trim to the front, right sides together. Pin the front to the lining, right sides together, and stitch, leaving an opening for turning. Trim, turn and press. Slipstitch the opening closed.

For more information on any of these finishing techniques, see "Special Touches" in Chapter 4, THE SEWING BASICS.

❀

PLEATED LAMPSHADE COVER

Fabric or wallpaper is cut to size and accordion-pleated. To hold the pleats in place, ribbon is woven through buttonhole-like slits and tied in a bow.

Choose a simple, cone-shaped shade with straight, not curved, sides. To avoid show-through when the light is on, the original covering should be a pale color with no patterning. If the original covering is damaged, you can remove it and put the new cover on over the frame. New, uncovered frames are also available.

Step 1: Determine the cutting dimensions.

● For the cutting length, measure the height of the lampshade, then add 2″ (5cm).

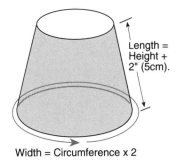

Length = Height + 2″ (5cm).

Width = Circumference x 2

● For the cutting width, measure the bottom circumference and multiply by 2.

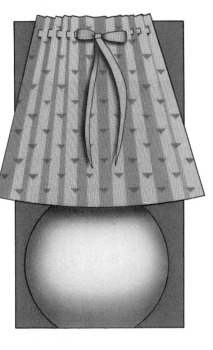

Step 2: Determine the amount of fabric and notions.

● *Fabric*—a rectangle equal to the cutting length and the cutting width.

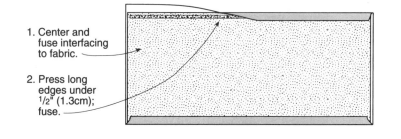

1. Center and fuse interfacing to fabric.

2. Press long edges under 1/2" (1.3cm); fuse.

• *Interfacing*—a rectangle of lightweight, fusible interfacing the same width and 2" (5cm) narrower than the fabric rectangle.

• *Ribbon*—a piece of 3/8" (1cm) wide satin ribbon approximately 27" (68.5cm) longer than the circumference measurement.

Step 3: Assemble the shade.

• Center and fuse the interfacing to the wrong side of the fabric.

• Press the long edges under 1/2" (1.3cm). Fuse in place, using strips of fusible web.

• Beginning at one end, and working on the wrong side, mark for the pleats by lightly drawing vertical lines spaced 1/2" (1.3cm) apart.

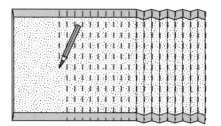

• Accordion-fold and press the pleats.

• Starting 3/4" (2cm) down from the top of the shade, cut 1/2" (1.3cm) long vertical slits in the center of each pleat. To get a clean cut, use small embroidery scissors or a razor knife and a mat board.

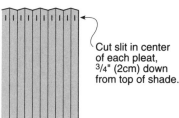

Cut slit in center of each pleat, 3/4" (2cm) down from top of shade.

• To join the ends of the shade, fold one pleat under on the overlap edge and glue to the underlap edge.

NOTE: In order to have the pleats continue in an accordion manner, it may be necessary to trim one pleat off the underlap.

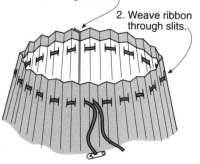

1. Overlap and glue end.

2. Weave ribbon through slits.

• Attach a safety pin to the end of the ribbon, then weave the ribbon in and out through the slits.

• Position this new shade over the frame or the existing shade. Distribute the pleats evenly, adjust the ribbon and tie a bow on the outside of the shade.

❁

BOW PICTURE HANGER

Tailored bows add a decorator touch to all your framed artwork. The completed hanger measures 35" (89cm) long × 8" (20.5cm) wide.

Each bow requires 1 1/8 yards (1.1m) of 36"–60" (91.5cm–153cm) wide fabric, plus 7" (18cm) of twill tape and one coat-weight hook and eye.

Step 1: Cut four strips, cutting the longer dimensions along the lengthwise grain of the fabric.

• For the bow, cut one strip 18" × 11" (45.5cm × 28cm).

• For the knot, cut one strip 7 1/2" × 7 1/2" (19cm × 19cm).

• For Tail 1, cut one strip 40" × 11" (102cm × 28cm).

• For Tail 2, cut one strip 32" × 11" (81.5cm × 28cm).

Step 2: Prepare the sections.

NOTE: All seam allowances are 1/2" (1.3cm).

• For the tail:

Pin the ends of the two tails, right sides together; stitch, forming one long tail. Press seam open.

Fold lengthwise in half, right sides together; pin. Diagonally trim the ends to slant in opposite directions. Stitch, leaving an opening for turning, as illustrated on the next page.

Turn right side out; press. Slipstitch the opening closed.

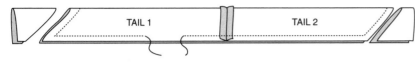

TAIL 1   TAIL 2

● For the bow:

Fold bow lengthwise in half, right sides together. Pin, then stitch the long edges together. Turn right side out and press.

Pin ends together, forming a loop; stitch. Press seam open.

● Make the knot, following the directions for the bow.

Step 3: Assemble the hanger.

● With the seams at the center back, slide the knot over the bow. Slipstitch them together on the back.

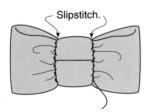

Slipstitch.

● Stitch the ends of the twill tape together.

● Fold the tail crosswise in half, pointed ends even. Slide the twill tape over the folded end and pin it in place at the seam. Sew the coat eye securely at the center back, through twill tape and tails.

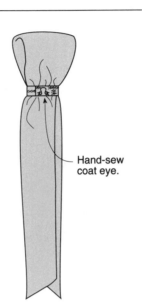

Hand-sew coat eye.

● Pin the bow to the front of the tails, centering the knot over the twill tape. Slipstitch in place.

● Check the position of the picture on the bow. Sew the coat hook in place securely through all the layers of the tails.

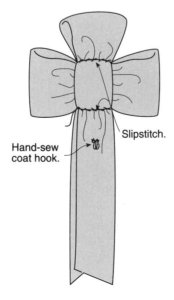

Hand-sew coat hook.

Slipstitch.

● For a rich, full look—and to keep the bow from drooping after several months on the wall—stuff the three loops with tissue paper.

TASSELS

Have you ever coveted those costly tassels that dangle from doorknobs, swoop down between swags or make gorgeous shade pulls? Here's how to achieve that truly luxurious touch at a bargain-basement price.

For each tassel, you'll need:

● One *large wood bead* with hole, approximately 28mm × 28mm.

● One *small wood bead* with hole, approximately 16mm × 16mm.

● One or two coordinating skeins of *perle cotton*.

● One yard (1m) of *twisted cord*, ¹⁄₈″ (3mm) wide *or* make twisted cord from perle cotton.

● ³⁄₈ yard (.4m) of ¹⁄₂″ (1.3cm) *gimp braid* or *tassel braid*.

● ¹⁄₄ yard (.3m) of 2″–3″ (5cm–7.5cm) wide *fringe*.

● *Hot glue and gun, darning needle and paper*.

Step 1: Cover the beads with perle cotton.

● Cut 6–8 yards (5.5m–7.4m) of perle cotton for the large bead.

● Using a toothpick or similar object, measure the length of the bead

hole. Cut a piece of paper equal to this length and 2″ (5cm) wide.

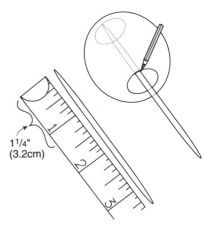

● Glue one end of the perle cotton to the paper, placing it parallel to the length. Thread the opposite end onto a darning needle.

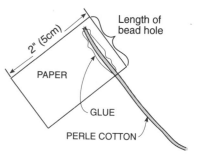

● Coil the paper and slip it into the bead hole. Wrap the bead with the perle cotton, dropping the needle through the hole and then bringing the thread up around the outside until the bead is covered.

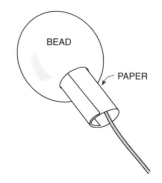

TIP

If the natural bead color is a sharp contrast to the selected perle cotton color, camouflage the bead first with acrylic paint that matches the perle cotton color.

● To secure the end of the perle cotton, apply glue to the thread for a distance approximately equal to the length of the bead hole. Drop the needle through the hole and hold the thread fast so it adheres to the inside of the bead. Trim off the excess thread.

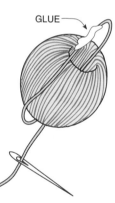

NOTE: Some very round beads may need to be wrapped again so they are completely covered.

● Cut 2–3 yards (1.9m–2.8m) of perle cotton for the small bead. Wrap in the same manner as the large bead.

Step 2: Assemble the tassel.

● To make the hanger, fold the twisted cord in half and tie several square knots in the cut ends.

● Glue the knotted end of the hanger to the top of the small bead, tucking the tails inside the hole.

● Glue the small bead to the large bead.

● Coil the fringe up and glue to the bottom of the large bead.

● Glue gimp or tassel braid between the large bead and the fringe.

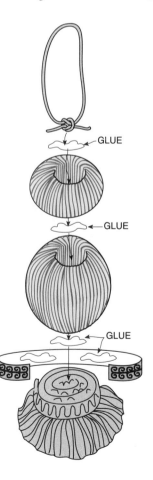

TIP

For perfectly matched twisted cord, make your own from three pieces of perle cotton, each 1 yard (1m) long. Using one, two or three colors, lay the threads parallel and tape them together at each end. Unthread your sewing machine. Tape one end of the perle cotton threads to the center of the hand wheel. Run the machine, twisting the threads until the cord begins to kink when relaxed.

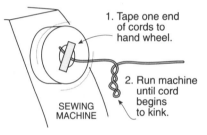

✿ SAY IT WITH FLOWERS

These two fabric flowers, with or without their leaves, can bloom anywhere you like, alone or in multiples. A few suggestions: at the corners of a throw pillow, as a garland across the top of a window treatment, to embellish a curtain tieback, on a straw or grapevine wreath or tucked into the folds of a swag.

Fast Flower

If you own a serger, this two-toned beauty can be made in a jiffy.

Because the strips are cut on the bias, 1 yard (1m) of 45″ (115cm) or

DECORATIVE ACCESSORIES

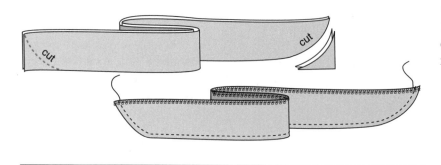

54″ (138cm) wide fabric in each of two coordinating fabrics will yield four flowers. The remaining fabric can be cut and pieced to make additional flowers.

Step 1: Make a tissue-paper pattern.

● Draw a rectangle 3¹/₂″ × 45″ (9cm × 115cm) for the petal pattern.

● Draw a 3″ (7.5cm) diameter circle for the base pattern.

Step 2: Cut and assemble the flower.

● Cut one petal from each coordinating fabric, following the bias grain of the fabric.

● Pin the petals wrong sides together. Round off the bottom corners at both ends.

● Serge the two fabrics together along the straight edge.

● Hand- or machine-gather along the curved edge. Draw up the gathers to shape the flower.

TIP

No serger? Pin the petals right sides together and stitch a ¹/₄″ (6mm) seam along the straight edge. Turn right side out and press. Hand- or machine-gather along the curved edge.

● Starting at one end of the strip, roll a few inches (centimeters) of the gathered edge; hand-stitch to secure. Continue rolling and stitching until the entire flower is formed.

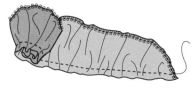

● Cut one base from the outside fabric. Turn the raw edges under and hand-stitch to the bottom of the flower. Add *leaves*, if desired.

Rose

This sculpted beauty can be fabricated in just about anything, from chiffon to chintz to velvet.

One rose requires ¹/₂ yard (.5m) of 45″ (115cm) wide fabric or ¹/₄ yard (.3m) of 54″ (138cm) wide fabric.

Step 1: Make a tissue-paper pattern.

● Draw a 10″ × 6″ (25.5cm × 15cm) rectangle. Mark the center of each edge. Connect these marks to round out the corners.

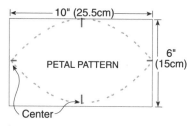

● Draw a 3″ (7.5cm) diameter circle for the base pattern.

Step 2: Cut and assemble the rose.

● Cut six petals, following the bias grain of the fabric. Cut one base.

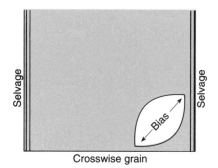

● Fold one petal lengthwise in half, wrong sides together. Hand- or machine-gather the raw edges. Repeat for all the petals.

● Roll the gathered edge of the first petal and hand-stitch to secure.

FIRST PETAL

FAST FLOWER

ROSE

● Wrap the gathered edge of the second petal around the first and hand-stitch together.

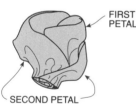

FIRST PETAL

SECOND PETAL

● Continue wrapping and stitching the remaining petals, alternating the placement of the petals.

● Turn the raw edges of the base under and hand-stitch to the bottom of the flower.

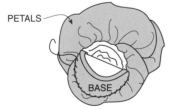

PETALS

BASE

Add *leaves*, if desired.

Leaves

These are the finishing touches to both fabric flowers.

Step 1: Cut and mark.

● Cut two 6¹/₂″ (16.5cm) squares of fabric for each flower.

● On the wrong side of one square, center and mark a 2″ (5cm) long diagonal line.

Step 2: Assemble.

● Pin the two squares right sides together. Stitch ¹/₄″ (6mm) from the raw edges. Trim the corners.

● Carefully cut along the marked diagonal line, through one layer only. Turn the leaves right side out through the opening. Press.

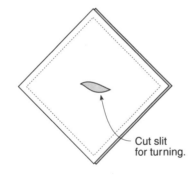

Cut slit for turning.

● Make two rows of hand gathers, placed parallel to, and on each side of, the opening. Draw up the gathers to shape the leaves.

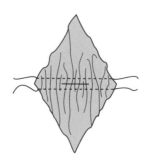

● Tuck the corners under at the end of the gathers. Hand-sew the leaf pair to the base of the flower.

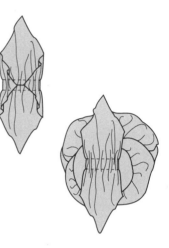

Flower Wreath

Perfect on a front door (one that's protected from the elements!), over a fireplace or adorning any wall in the house.

To make the wreath, you'll need:

● One *rattan wreath*, 18″ (45.5cm) in diameter.

● 2 yards (1.9m) each of *three colors of twisted cord*, ¹/₂″ (1.3cm) in diameter.

● 4 yards (3.7m) of *wire-edge taffeta ribbon*, 2¹/₄″ (5.7cm) wide.

● 1¹/₂ yards (1.4m) of *brush fringe*, 1¹/₂″ (3.8cm) wide.

● Fabric for five *fabric roses with leaves*.

● *Hot glue and glue gun, masking tape and heavy thread* or *wire*.

Step 1: Make five fabric roses with leaves, following the preceding instructions.

Step 2: Make six fringe flowers.

DECORATIVE ACCESSORIES

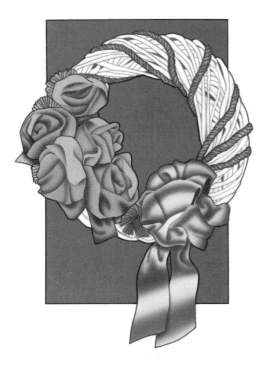

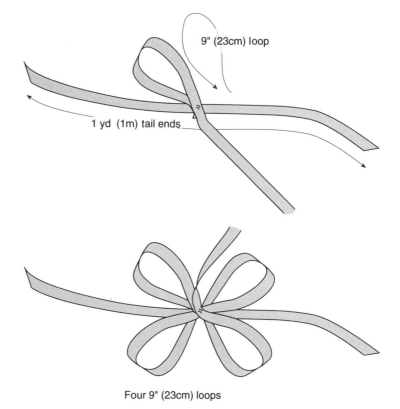

9" (23cm) loop

1 yd (1m) tail ends

Four 9" (23cm) loops

For each flower, cut 9″ (23cm) of fringe. Roll the fringe up tightly to form the flower. Use a dab of glue to seal the end.

Apply glue to end.

Step 3: Make the bow.

● Cut 1 yard (1m) of ribbon for the tails. Stitch the center of the tails to one end of the remaining ribbon.

● Starting at the stitched end, form approximately 9″ (23cm) of the remaining ribbon into a loop. Pinch together at the bottom of the loop and tack in place at the center of the tails. Repeat, making three more 9″ (23cm) loops.

● Following the same procedure as above, make four 8″ (20.5cm) loops.

● Following the same procedure as above, make four 7″ (18cm) loops.

● Form one 6″ (15cm) loop; tack in place at the center of the bow.

Four 9" (23cm) loops
Four 8" (20.5cm) loops
Four 7" (18cm) loops
One 6" (15cm) loop in center

Step 4: Assemble the wreath.

● To prevent the cords from raveling, wrap tape around one end of each color. Cut the cords through the center of the tape.

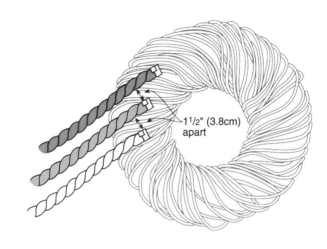

1½" (3.8cm) apart

2. Cut off ends.

1. Wrap with tape.

● Glue the wrapped ends of the cords to the back of the wreath. Space them 1½″ (3.8cm) apart.

● Wind the cords around the wreath four times, keeping them an even distance apart. Tape, cut and glue the unfinished ends to meet the wrapped ends.

● Glue the fabric flowers, fringe flowers and ribbon bow in place on the front of the wreath.

● To make a hanger, tie a loop of heavy thread or wire to the back of the wreath.

TIP

To vary the look of this wreath:

● **Use vines of artificial ivy instead of cords.**

● **Transform fringe flowers into daisies. Use white fringe. Color the centers with a yellow felt-tip pen.**

● **Use *fast flowers* as well as *roses*. Vary their sizes. For small roses, use four petals. For small fast flowers, cut bias strips 2″ × 40″ (5cm × 102cm).**

Key: **B**=Bow **R**=Rose **F**=Fringe flower

❀

NURSERY WALL HANGING

This is a festive way to enliven the walls in Baby's room.

To make the wall hanging, you'll need:

- ³/₈ yard (.4m) of *fabric* for each heart.

NOTE: There are three hearts—make them in the same or coordinating fabrics.

- ⁵/₈ yard (.6m) of *polyester fleece*.

- 2⁵/₈ yards (2.4m) of *pregathered eyelet trim*, 2¹/₂″ (6.3cm) wide.

- *Ribbon*, ³/₈″ (1cm) wide:
  4³/₈ yards (4m) of Color A.
  2⁵/₈ yards (2.4m) of Color B.
  ⁵/₈ yard (.6m) of Color C.

- Four ⁵/₈″ (1.5cm) *plastic rings*.

- ³/₈ yard (.4m) of 1″ (2.5cm) gridded *nonwoven pattern-duplicating material*.

Step 1: Cut out the wall hanging.

- Enlarge the heart pattern to size, using the pattern-duplicating material.

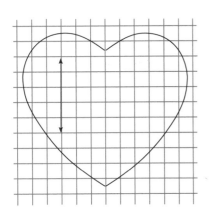

- Cut two hearts (front and back) from each fabric.

- Cut three hearts from the fleece.

Step 2: Assemble the wall hanging.

NOTE: All seam allowances are ¹/₂″ (1.3cm).

- Pin the fleece to the wrong side of one heart (heart front). Baste ¹/₂″ (1.3cm) from the raw edge. Trim the fleece close to the stitching.

FLEECE

- Pin the pregathered trim to the heart, right sides together, so the bound edge of the lace is inside the seam allowance. Allow some fullness at the point and taper the ends at the inner corners, as shown; baste. Stitch.

- Pin the heart front to the heart back, right sides together. Stitch, leaving an opening for turning. Trim the seam and the corners. Clip the curves.

- Turn right side out; press. Slip-stitch the opening closed.

- Repeat, making two more hearts.

Step 3: Finish the wall hanging.

- To form the streamers, cut two pieces of Color A ribbon, each 58″ (148cm) long. Fold each piece in half and sew folded end to the back point of two hearts.

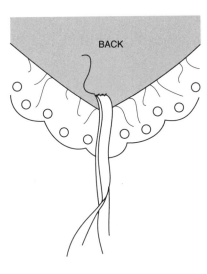

- Cut the remaining Color A in half. Tie each piece into a bow and tack to the front of the heart, above the point.

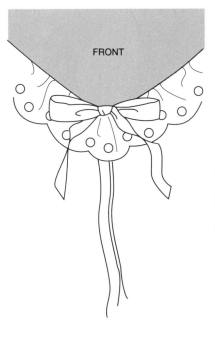

- Tack the four streamers together approximately 14″ (35.5cm) below the point of the heart. Do not twist the ribbons.

- Cut one piece of Color B ribbon, 72″ (183cm) long. Fold in half and sew the folded end to the back point of the remaining heart. Tie the rest of the Color B ribbon into a bow and tack to the front of the heart, above the point.

- Tack the two streamers together, approximately 23″ (58.5cm) below the point of the heart. Do not twist the ribbons. Using this as the center heart, tack all the streamers together at the previous tacking. Tie the Color C ribbon into a bow and tack on top.

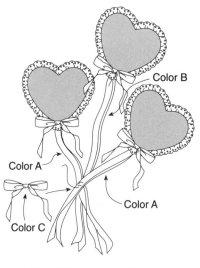

1. Tack "A" ribbons together.
2. Tack "B" ribbons to "A's."

- Sew rings for hanging to the back of the hearts at the top and to the back of the streamers at the tacking point.

CHAPTER 11

Timesavers

Timesavers

Pillow coverings that wrap and tie, sheets that save you the time and trouble of hemming and finishing, iron-on drapery tapes that turn fabric into fabulous window fashions with nary a sewing machine in sight—these are just a few of the exciting ideas you will encounter in this chapter.

These ideas are clever and fun to execute . . . and they are also practical. As "quick fix" decorating for a dorm room, a first apartment or a beach house, they can't be beat. And they are confidence boosters, too. Novice sewers and the "I-can't-sew-a-stitch" crowd will soon find themselves seduced by the possibilities of do-it-yourself decorating.

DECORATING WITH SHEETS

The linen department of your favorite specialty shop, department store or mail-order catalog offers lots of opportunities for creative home dec sewing. Decorating with sheets offers a multitude of beautiful coordinates and already-sewn-for-you features that add up to time saved shopping and time saved sewing. The economy-minded sewer can take advantage of seasonal white sales, making decorating with sheets a money-saving proposition, too!

W-i-d-e and Wonderful

Sheets are, of course, much wider than the average fabric. When covering a wall with fabric, one king-size sheet could cover a 9 foot (3m) span. Even your widest windows may only require one sheet per window.

These wider widths mean less matching and seaming, which can also mean less time at the sewing machine, plus fewer notions and less hardware to buy.

Making a Match

Sheets are cut into predetermined lengths at the mill. As a result, the matching motifs may not be in the same location from one sheet to the next. This means that, unlike working with by-the-yard fabric, it's not always easy to match motifs without a great deal of waste between the repeats. The red rose in the upper left corner of one sheet may, or may not, find its matching stem in the upper right corner of a second sheet. Although it will be there somewhere, the repeat may be down, or in, from the spot you could count on if buying continuous yardage.

If you have a large area to cover, and matching is an important factor, try to select a sheet design with a small repeat or a vertical stripe. You might also purchase extra sheeting so you have a pool of sheets to work from. Since dye lots can vary and patterns can be discontinued, buy all the sheets for your decorating scheme at one time. Create your large projects first, then use what remains for accessories. Remember, any sheets you don't use can always go on the bed!

TIP

Decorating with sheets started a trend. Many fabric houses are now marketing a wide variety of decorative fabrics in double widths—90″ (229cm) or 108″ (275cm) wide. They have many of the advantages of wide-width sheets.

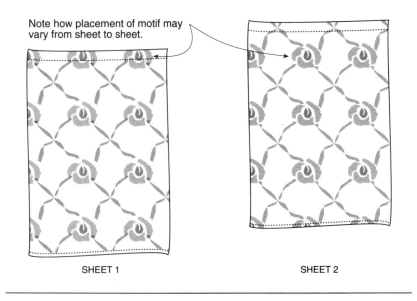

Note how placement of motif may vary from sheet to sheet.

SHEET 1   SHEET 2

When fabric-covered walls with high ceilings are in your decorating plans, it may be difficult to get the needed length from sheets, particularly when you have a motif that requires matching. Consider adding a detail, such as a chair rail or dropped ceiling moldings, to provide the extra wall coverage, to break up the span and add some fool-the-eye architectural interest.

Getting a Good Buy

Sheets can be an economical source of fabric, depending on the pattern and size you select. You must evaluate the cost of your intended use, along with the other aesthetic advantages, such as the availability of matching quilts and comforters, wide widths, a designer label, coordinating trims, etc.

Take a careful look at the Sheet Conversions chart on the following page. Your actual selection may differ slightly, depending on the headings (applied or self-fabric) and the

manufacturer's specifications. Note that the dimensions on European-size linens may differ from those listed here. Check the package description. Usually, the measurements stated are the dimensions *before* hemming. The only way to be absolutely sure what size you are

getting is to measure the sheets.

How do you know if $24 for a queen-size sheet is really a bargain? Study the Sheet Conversions chart. If you were to purchase a similar weight, over-the-counter fabric, 45″ (115cm) wide, you would need 5⅝ yards (5.1m) to equal the sheet. Divide that equivalent yardage into the price, and you'll find that you would be paying about $4.40 per yard (meter). If you were to select a twin size costing $10 and equivalent to 3¾ yards (3.4m), you would be paying $2.97 per yard (meter).

If, after you do your calculations, the price per yard seems high, consider whether you are paying for hem treatments and trimmings that could be put to good use. An attached border design might be very effective as a curtain or pillow trim. A few yards (meters) of crisp eyelet, purchased by the yard (meter), can often cost the same, or even more, than an eyelet-trimmed sheet.

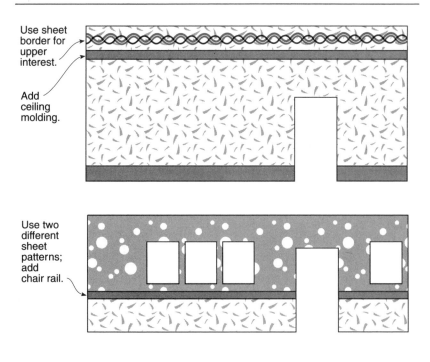

Use sheet border for upper interest.

Add ceiling molding.

Use two different sheet patterns; add chair rail.

SHEET CONVERSIONS

SHEET SIZE	YARDAGE/METRIC CONVERSION		
Flat sheet (W × L)	36″ (91.5cm) fabric	45″ (115cm) fabric	54″ (138cm) fabric
Twin (66″ × 96″) (168cm × 244cm)	4¾ yd (4.3m)	3¾ yd (3.4m)	3¼ yd (2.9m)
Full (81″ × 96″) (206cm × 244cm)	6 yd (5.5m)	4¾ yd (4.3m)	4 yd (3.7m)
Queen (90″ × 102″) (229cm × 259cm)	7 yd (6.5m)	5⅝ yd (5.1m)	4¾ yd (4.3m)
King (108″ × 102″) (275cm × 259cm)	8½ yd (7.8m)	6¾ yd (6.2m)	5¾ yd (5.3m)

The above measurements are a guide to the amount of fabric when hems are opened. Various hem treatments can change the yardage. Always check sheet packaging to note actual dimensions.

TIPS

Some linen manufacturers have joined forces with fabric houses to offer the same patterns in sheets and by-the-yard (-meter) decorator fabric. Ask, too, if your sheet choice can be ordered as continuous yardage direct from the manufacturer. Some sheet companies offer this service.

Look for a whole range of items coordinated with towels and bed linens. China and paper dinnerware, laminated wastebaskets and bathroom accessories, lamp bases and shades, rugs and artwork are all part of the cross-marketing concept.

Timesaving Features

NO SELVAGES / NO HEMMING. Sheet designs are printed to the very edge. There are no color codes, repeat markings or manufacturer's origins printed on the sheet selvage. You can often use the sheet "as is" for walls, curtains and drapes without hemming the sides and, if you're lucky, maybe even the bottom.

RUFFLED TRIMS. When recycling the ruffle, be sure to include a narrow margin cut from the body of the sheet. Otherwise, you might "lose" all that manufactured work.

BORDER BANDS. These headings have been folded in half and applied to the sheet with their edges turned under. With the help of your seam ripper, carefully remove the band. Now you can reapply it to the edge of any of your projects.

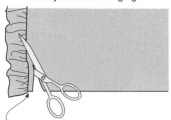

Recycle ruffled edging.

Leave margin for seam allowance.

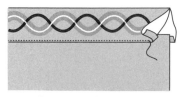

Recycle border bands.

SPECIAL FINISHES. Sheets often have a special "sizing," or finish, that helps retard dirt and dust. To preserve this finish, *do not* launder your sheets before creating a project. Later, when cleaning is necessary, care for the finished project as you would for the sheets. This usually means machine-wash and tumble-dry. If necessary, a bit of spray starch and touch-up ironing will restore the crisp hand. On wall and window projects, an occasional vacuuming will help keep the sheets looking fresh.

A Few Cautions

Sheets are firmly woven, with a high thread count. As a result, they stand up well under pressure and abrasion. However, some decorators feel that they don't wear as well as many other fabrics when used for slipcovers and upholstery. One way to increase their durability is to line and quilt the sheets . . . or to use the coordinating bedspread for soft furnishings.

In time, the sun can show its effects on sheets, particularly if they are placed near a window. To extend the life of your treatments, consider adding a protective lining.

Firmly woven sheets are a joy to stretch onto walls. There is little shrinking or sagging due to changes in the humidity. However, this same firm weave makes any sort of decorative hand stitching a tedious process. Glass-head pins, sharp needles and pushpins are a must when working with sheets.

Old Treasures into New

The sheets and linens you select need not all be fresh from the mill. Scour old hope chests, antique shops and tag sales for beautifully trimmed linens and laces. Treasures from the attic can add a valuable and traditional ambience to your decorating accents.

✿
NO-SEW PILLOWS

Pillows that wrap and tie are a quick and easy way to liven up a room. Items such as scarves, belts, buckles, safety pins and rubber bands can be used to create a refreshing change of pace.

Before you begin, review Chapter 8, PILLOW PIZZAZZ, for the basics of pillow selection, size, shape and filling.

Scarves and bandannas are available in beautiful colors and prints, in a variety of sizes and shapes. Because they are already hemmed, no finishing is required. One or two can be tied creatively and used as a pillow cover.

Four-Corner Tie

Scarf size: Two square scarves measuring 8″–10″ (20.5cm–25.5cm) larger than a square pillow form.

Place one scarf wrong side up. Center the pillow form on top and cover with the second scarf. Tie together at the corners. *Or* secure at the corners with rubber bands. Cover the bands with ribbon ties. If necessary, secure the scarves to the pillow form with safety pins concealed under the knots.

FOUR-CORNER TIE

SQUARE VERSION

This version can be done on the square or on the diagonal. With the latter, the pillow underneath provides a second color or texture.

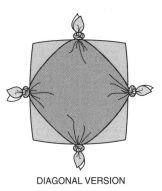

DIAGONAL VERSION

TIMESAVERS

SIMPLE AND QUICK DECORATING IDEAS

Since the edges are finished, just pin the two squares together and stitch $1/2''$ (1.3cm) from the edge, leaving a $3''$ (7.5cm) opening. Stuff with washable fiberfill, then machine-stitch the opening closed.

● Take advantage of finished edges and hems. Staple a sheet to a window or wall. Puddle the bottom for glamorous nonchalance.

● To add a soft touch to windows, shirr up a ruffled pillowcase or sheet, using one of the iron-on drapery/pleater tapes described later in this chapter.

● Take a pair of pillowcases or shams, add clip-on café rings across the upper edge and thread them onto a rod. In minutes, you'll have a nifty window covering.

● Use regular or king-size pillowcases as slipcovers for outdoor furniture cushions. To keep them all tidy, fold under any excess and secure underneath with safety pins.

● Utilize some of the new swag holders discussed later in this chapter to frame your window with dashing sheets. No hemming required, and the ruffled or banded edges make the view prettier.

● Make a round table cover using a queen- or king-size sheet. Your cloth can be as much as 100″ (254cm) in diameter with no piecing required. Cut as for the *round tablecloth* in Chapter 10, DECORATIVE ACCESSORIES.

● Make a washable crib pillow from soft, cuddly facecloths.

● For a fancy dressing table or sink skirt, turn a ruffled sheet upside down. Measure up from the bottom edge of the ruffle to the desired height, plus a 4″ (10cm) hem allowance. Fuse the top hem, then pleat or gather the fused edge. Apply one half of press-on hook-and-loop tape to the furniture rim. Stitch the other half to the sheet's upper edge, securing the gathers or pleats in the stitching. Attach the skirt to the dressing table or sink.

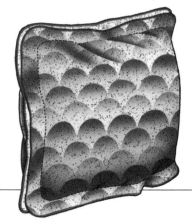

MOCK HAREM PILLOW

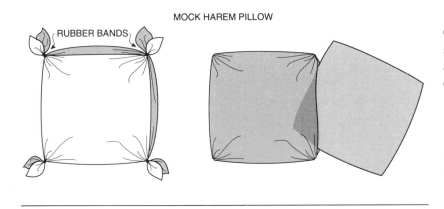

Place the scarf wrong side up. Center the form lengthwise on the scarf. Roll the bolster up in the scarf and tie the ends with a ribbon or decorative cord.

Gift Box Tie

Scarf or fabric: One square measuring approximately 2¹/₂ times the measurement of a square pillow form.

Center the form on the wrong side of the fabric, then fold two opposite sides up around the form. Fold the fabric ends as shown to form points. Then fold the two pointed ends to meet at the center. Secure with a small safety pin. Turn the wrapped pillow to the right side and complete the pillow package by wrapping and tying with a pretty ribbon bow.

Mock Harem Pillow

Scarf size: Same as for the *four-corner tie.*

Place the scarves right sides together and tie or rubber band them together at the corners. Turn right side out and carefully pull the tied scarves over the form. If necessary, secure the scarves to the pillow form with safety pins concealed under the knots.

Round Topknot

Scarf size: One square scarf measuring approximately 2¹/₂ times the diameter of a round pillow form. For example, a 12″ (30.5cm) pillow form requires a 30″ (76cm) scarf.

Place the scarf wrong side up on a flat surface. Place the form in the center and pull the straight edges up to the middle of the form. Secure with a rubber band. Twist the pointed ends, coiling them into a topknot. Tuck the ends into the rubber band.

Firecracker Bolster

Scarf size: One square or rectangular scarf. One side should equal the length of the bolster plus at least 16″ (40.5cm).

FIRECRACKER BOLSTER

GIFT BOX TIE

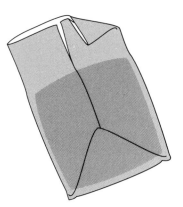

ROUND TOPKNOT

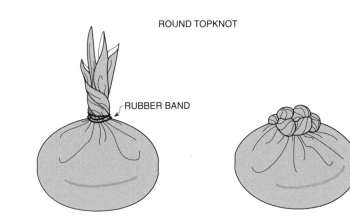

RUBBER BAND

Envelope Fold

Scarf or fabric: Two squares, each approximately 2½ times the measurement of a square pillow form. Coordinating or contrasting colors work well.

Place one fabric wrong side up. Fold two opposite sides in to form a rectangle equal in width to the pillow form. Center the form on the rectangle. Cover the form, folding the fabric ends up to the center, and secure with a safety pin. Repeat with the other square, covering the form in the opposite direction. Fold the corners under at one end to hide the raw edges and create the envelope point. Secure the point with a safety pin, then embellish the pillow with a ribbon tie or a pretty belt and buckle.

ENVELOPE FOLD

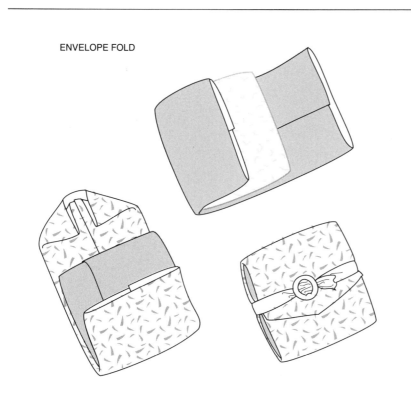

TIP

Fabric, too, works great for many of these no-sew pillows. Cut the fabric a little bit larger so the unhemmed edges can be hidden by folding them under as you wrap and tie. Or get out that overlock and quickly serge-finish all the raw edges.

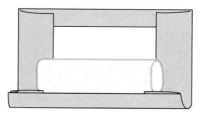

✥ DROP-IN SEAT COVERS

Many kitchen and dining room chairs, as well as some stools, have seats that are nothing more than fabric-covered wood bases or frames that fit into the chair frames. Re-covering these seats to match your new decor is a cinch. All it takes is a stapler—electric or hand-operated, open-flat variety—or tacks and a hammer.

Step 1: Measure and cut.

● Remove the seat cushion from the chair and put it on a table. Measure the length and the width, from table-top to tabletop, so that you include the depth of the cushion. To determine the cutting dimensions, add 8″ (20.5cm) to each of these measurements.

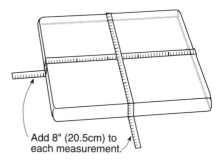

Add 8″ (20.5cm) to each measurement.

● Cut the cover from decorator fabric.

Step 2: Cover the seat.

● Remove the old fabric and the tacks. If necessary, replace the cushioning material.

● Place the new fabric on the table, wrong side up. Center the seat on the fabric, wrong side up.

TIMESAVERS

● Beginning at the center back, use pushpins or tacks to temporarily baste-tack the fabric along the edge of the base. Pull the fabric taut and "baste" the other side.

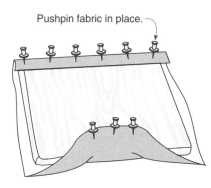

Pushpin fabric in place.

● Turn the seat over to check the alignment and tautness of the fabric, then "baste" the remaining two sides. Adjust the fabric and the tacks until the cover is smooth and taut.

● At each corner, pull the fabric firmly and hold with one tack, placed approximately 1″ (2.5cm) in from the corner. Fold the excess fabric in on either side to form a mitered corner. Using the foldlines as a guide, trim the excess fabric from inside the miter. Add additional tacks.

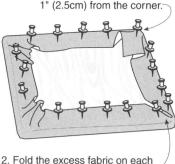

1. Hold fabric with one tack 1″ (2.5cm) from the corner.

2. Fold the excess fabric on each side to form a mitered corner.

● Permanently tack or staple the fabric to the seat.

Step 3: Finish.

For a professional finish, cover the bottom with muslin or other firmly woven fabric.

● Cut the undercover large enough to conceal all the staples and tacks, plus a ½″ (1.3cm) hem allowance all around.

● Fold the raw edges under ½″ (1.3cm), then permanently staple or tack in place on the underside of the drop-in seat.

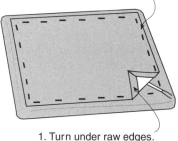

2. Staple to underside of seat.

1. Turn under raw edges.

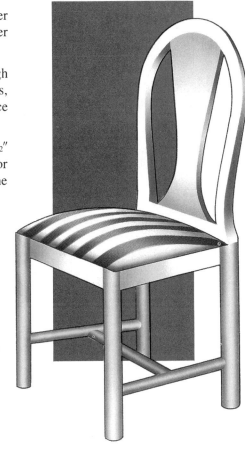

TIPS

For a round drop-in seat cover, put two rows of hand-basting stitches about 1″ (2.5cm) from the cut edge. Center the seat, face-down, on the wrong side of the cover. Draw up the gathers, then tack and permanently staple the cover to the seat.

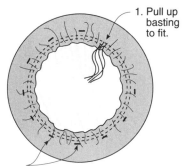

1. Pull up basting to fit.

2. Staple to frame.

To add decorative braid or other flexible trim to the cover, install the finished seat, then pin-mark the trim placement. Remove the cushion. Staple or hot-glue the trim in place, planning for the ends to meet at the back or at the least conspicuous location.

✿

FUSIBLES AND IRON-ONS

These days, you can accomplish a whole range of "sewing" tasks at your ironing board. Whether you use them as a substitute for machine work, or in combination with traditional sewing techniques, fusibles and iron-ons are wonderful additions to the decorator's toolbox. They can save you time and energy . . . and they can help you achieve more professional results.

Some products have fairly specific uses, while others fall into the category of "general helpers." Products to consider include fusible web (with or without paper backings and release sheets), fusible fleece, iron-on adhesives, iron-on backings, fusible thread, iron-on pleater tapes, hem tapes, smocking tapes and shirring tapes, fusible shade backings, craft-weight fusible backings . . . plus more. The accompanying Fuse-a-Log chart lists some of the more readily available iron-on and fusible products, along with some specific information. In Chapter 4, THE SEWING BASICS, you will find suggestions for using products such as fusible webs, transfer webs and fusible thread in conjunction with machine sewing.

Resins (glues, adhesives) are the magic ingredients in these products. During the manufacturing process, they are spread as a solid sheet (often through a screen), sprinkled randomly in granular form or applied in powder form as dots printed from a roller onto a woven, knitted or non-woven backing. When you apply heat, the resin melts, forming the bond.

As with any special tool, following the manufacturer's instructions is key to successful results. Pay particular attention to whether the product is described as an iron-on or a fusible—the application process is different.

● An *iron-on* is applied to your project using heat and pressure. While most iron-ons require a dry iron, a few recommend a steam setting.

● A *fusible* is applied to your project using a combination of heat, moisture and pressure. In order to achieve the desired combination of heat and moisture, the manufacturer may recommend a dry iron and a damp press cloth, a steam iron and a dry press cloth, or a steam iron and a damp press cloth.

One category of iron-on/fusibles is designed specifically to "glue" fabric to fabric or fabric to another porous surface, such as wood or cardboard.

● *Fusible web* is a network of adhesive fibers that melt when the prescribed combination of heat, moisture and pressure is applied, causing the two surfaces to adhere to each other.

FUSE-A-LOG

PRODUCT	WHAT IT IS	PURPOSE/USES	ADVANTAGES AND/OR NOTES	NAMES TO LOOK FOR
Fusible fleece/ padding	Polyester batting with resin applied to one surface; 44″–45″ (112cm–115cm) wide.	Padding for headboards, trapunto work, quilts, placemats, etc.	No pinning, less shifting.	Handler (HTC), Dritz®, Pellon®.
Craft-weight backing	Heavyweight backing, similar to interfacing but heavier; 20″–45″ (51cm–115cm) widths.	Stiffens fabrics, adds support.	Iron on.	Crafters' Choice™, Fuse-a-Craft™, Decor-Bond®, Craft-Bond®.

FUSE-A-LOG

PRODUCT	WHAT IT IS	PURPOSE/USES	ADVANTAGES AND/OR NOTES	NAMES TO LOOK FOR
Window shade backing	Nonwoven, very firm support backing; 36"–45" (91.5cm–115cm) wide range.	Window shades, lambrequins, where firm body is needed.	Directions vary for each product. Wonder-Shade® is a room-darkening version.	Fuse-a-Shade™, Shade Maker™, Wonder-Shade®.
Fusible web, release paper	Glue in sheet form; narrow-width rolls, 1/8"–3/4" (3mm–2cm) wide, or wide widths: 16"–18" (40.5cm–45.5cm).	Joins fabric to fabric, cardboard, etc.	Glue may look like a spun web, solid sheet or crosshatch.	Stitch Witchery®, Fine Fuse™.
Fusible web, with release paper	As above, except a backing sheet is provided.	As above.	Makes appliqué and design transfer easier; allows pressing to be done in stages.	Heat 'N Bond Lite, Heat 'N Bond Original, Hot Stitch Fusible Web, Trans-Web™, Magic Fuse, Wonder-Under®, Heavy-Duty Wonder-Under®, Hem-N-Trim.
Drapery tape	Shirring and gathering tapes with rows of glue on back side.	Decorative headings for drapes, curtains, table shirts, dust ruffles, etc.	Some varieties come with flocked surface, eliminating need for separate loop tape when using Velcro-type installation.	Dritz®, Conso, Thermo-Fuse™.
Fusible thread	Poly/nylon thread, covered with a glue that fuses when heated.	Fuse-baste ribbons, trims; matching aid.	Very fine line of glue possible.	Threadfuse™.

Other Fusible/Related Home Decorating Products

PRODUCT	WHAT IT IS	PURPOSE/USES	ADVANTAGES AND/OR NOTES	NAMES TO LOOK FOR
Release sheet	Nonstick, transparent, reusable pressing sheet.	Withstands extreme heat. Do not puncture or snip. Glue does not stick to it.		Easy Way Appliqué®.
Hovotex	One-side iron-on 4" (10cm) wide stiffening.	Drapery headings, etc. Dry-cleanable and washable.		Dritz®.
Glue remover	Liquid to clean hands, tools, glue guns and/or spray-on surfaces to help prevent sticking.	Read cautions on label.		Unstik™, Glue Gun Kleen.

● *Transfer webs* are fusible webs or iron-on adhesives affixed to a sheet of release paper. When heat is applied, the web is "transferred" from the backing to your fabric. With the paper backing, small and/or intricate shapes are easier to handle. Plus, you can iron the web in place on one surface, leaving the paper intact. When you are ready to fuse the two surfaces together, simply peel off the paper. For more information about using transfer webs for appliqués, see "Special Touches" in Chapter 4, THE SEWING BASICS.

Getting a Good Bond

Here are some guidelines to ensure that fusibles and iron-ons work their magic.

● *Always, always* read and follow the manufacturer's instructions.

● Test the application process on a scrap of your fabric before proceeding with the whole project. Special finishes, such as water-repellent and stain-resistant finishes, may inhibit the bonding process.

● Some metallics, vinyls, fake furs, leathers, laces, mesh and brocades,

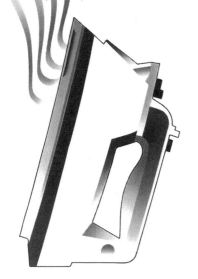

TIP

Separate, reusable, translucent, temperature-safe, nonstick pressing sheets can be purchased to use with fusible webs that do not have their own paper backing. Simply fold the pressing sheet in half, insert the fabric and the fusible web, and press. Peel the fabric off the pressing sheet and cut into the desired size and shape. Once the sheet is cool, gentle rubbing will remove any excess web from the sheet. Be careful with pins and scissors! Although very strong and tough, these sheets will tear easily if they are cut or snipped.

---

as well as sequined, heavily napped or textured fabrics, may be extremely difficult, or impossible, to bond. Testing is often the only way to be sure.

● Let your project cool completely before testing the bond. If necessary, repeat the fusing process.

● As a general rule, it's easier to handle large surfaces if you begin fusing in the center of the project and work out to the sides.

● Your work area can affect your results. Some products specifically recommend a well-padded surface; others, a firm surface. Check the directions!

● In some cases, a silicone ironing-board cover may inhibit a good bond. If you suspect this is a problem, try covering the ironing board with several layers of sheeting.

● Some products work better with a nonstick iron. With others, it doesn't matter.

DRAPERY/PLEATER TAPES

Many of the shirring, smocking and pleater heading tapes, as well as the ring tape for Roman shades and

balloon shades, referred to in Chapter 6, WINDOWS: A DIFFERENT VIEW, are also available in iron-on versions. Although iron-on tapes have been available in commercial workrooms for some time, recent developments have perfected an adhesive film that can be applied securely with a household steam iron. Like their sew-in counterparts, these tapes are applied while the window treatment is flat. Here are a few of the tapes you'll find in iron-on form:

● Two types of *pleater tape:*
Traditional pleater tape is a woven tape consisting of vertical pockets, which, with the help of four-pronged pleater hooks, make soft, almost 4" (10cm) deep pinch pleats.

Pinch pleat tape is a nonwoven, iron-on tape for crisp, 3½" (9cm) deep pinch pleats. Just form the pleats along the prescored lines and secure with pleat clips. This tape is especially effective on lightweight and sheer fabrics.

● Four types of *draw-cord tape:*
Pencil pleat tape comes in two versions. The narrower version has two draw cords for making small, precise, 1" (2.5cm) deep pleats. The wider one has four draw cords and a soft adhesive between the cords, for

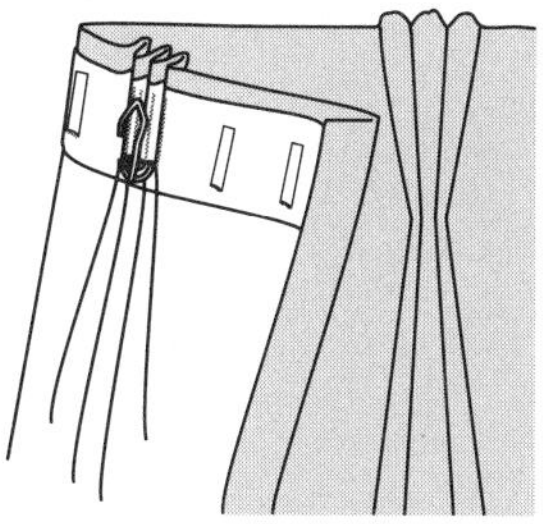

TRADITIONAL
PLEATER TAPE

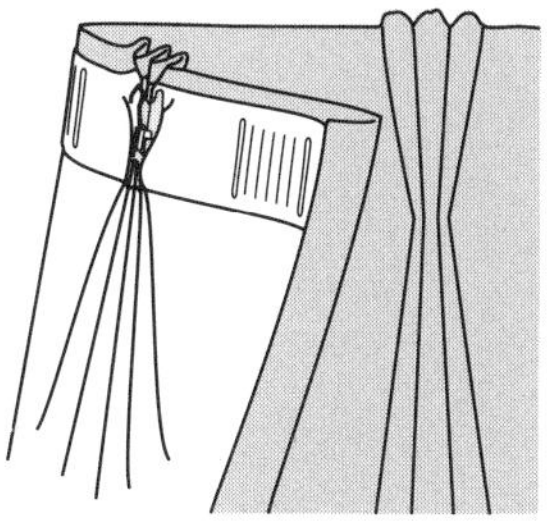

PINCH PLEAT
TAPE

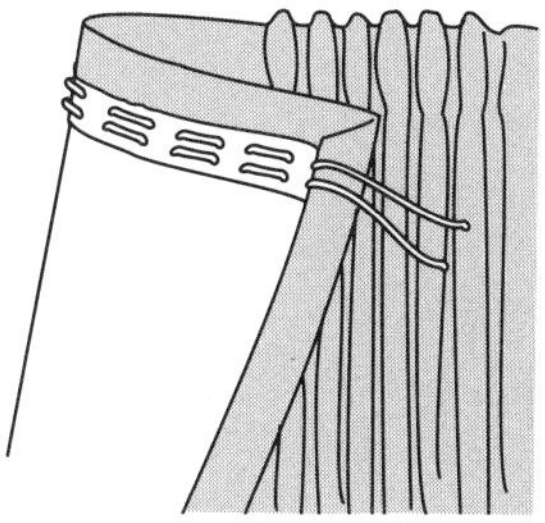

TWO-CORD
PENCIL PLEAT TAPE

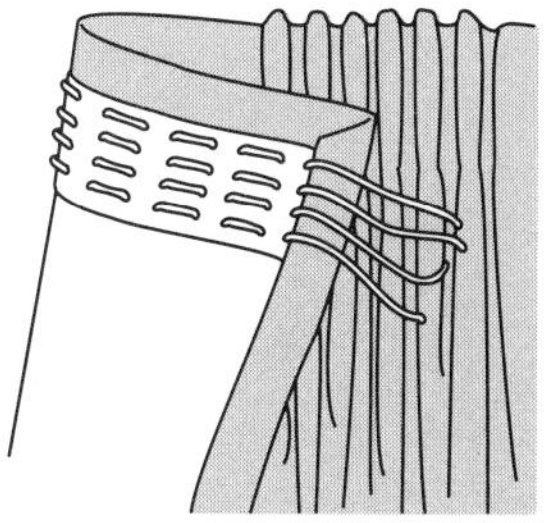

FOUR-CORD
PENCIL PLEAT TAPE

making slim, 4″ (10cm) deep pencil pleats.

Two-cord shirring tape makes a narrow row of soft gathers when you draw up the cords.

Four-cord shirring tape has four evenly spaced cords to make a wider gathered heading.

Smocking tape is 2¾″ (7cm) wide tape with two cords at the top and two at the bottom. When the cords are drawn, the finished effect is reminiscent of hand smocking.

- *Roman/balloon shade ring tape* has preattached plastic rings every 5″ (12.5cm) for creating Roman shades or balloon shades.

Some of these tapes are available with a flocked, or napped, finish on their exposed side. When the cords are drawn up, this napped surface will adhere to the hook portion of hook-and-loop tape, which makes installing the window treatment super easy. Just glue or staple the hook tape to the receiving surface (for example, the window frame, a cornice board, a flat curtain rod or the edge of a dressing table). When the window treatment is completed, draw the cords up until the treatment is the desired size. Press the napped surface in place against the hook tape. For easy cleaning, detach the window treatment and untie the cords.

Tips for Tapes

Here are a few special considerations to keep in mind when working with these iron-on tapes:

- When applying the tape, glide the iron over its surface with a continuous motion. Allow to cool.
- Before pulling up the gathering cords, warm the tape with your iron. The tape will be more pliable to work with and the finished gathers will be smoother.

CAUTION: Don't overwarm—a little heat is good, but a lot is *not* better!

- If you want to be able to flatten your project for cleaning, be sure you don't cut the cords. Instead, wrap them up, secure neatly with a rubber band and hide them in the folds of the project.
- If you prefer to cut the cords, be sure you leave enough lead cord for pulling. To avoid pulling the cord completely through its casing, tie a double knot or attach a button at each end.
- If you should accidentally pull a cord out of its casing, try using a large-eye needle to pull it back through the channel. If that doesn't work, lay the cord on top of the channel and zigzag over it.
- As wonderful as these no-sew tapes are, you might want the extra security of a few hand or machine stitches at the ends of the tapes. Then, if you accidentally tug too hard on the treatment, you won't cause pull-away strain.

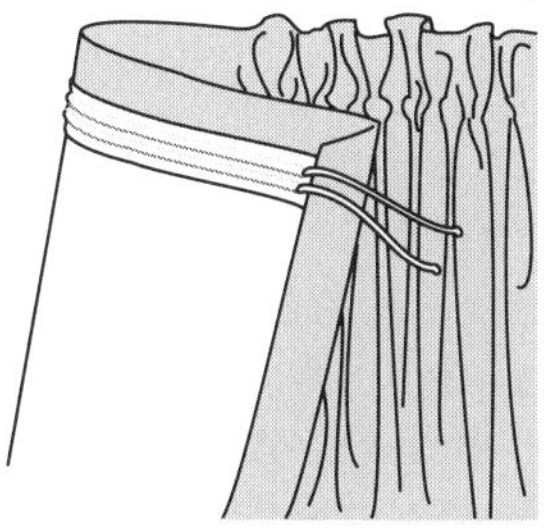

TWO-CORD
SHIRRING TAPE

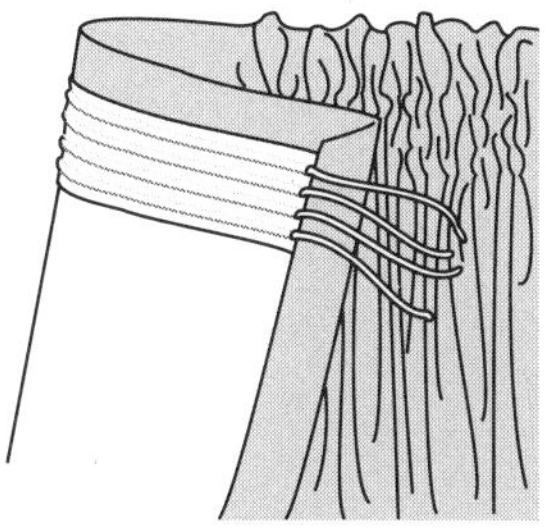

FOUR-CORD
SHIRRING TAPE

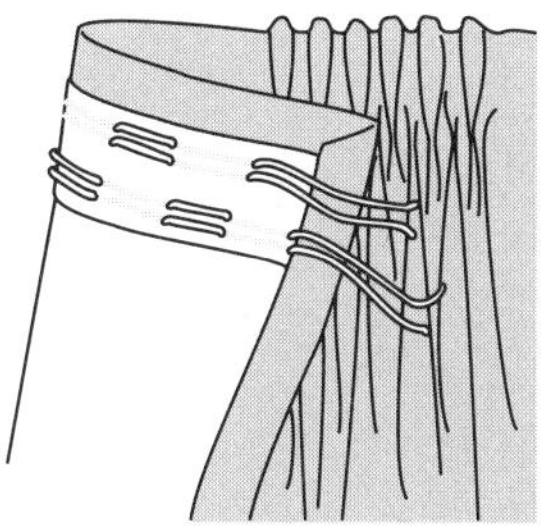

SMOCKING
TAPE

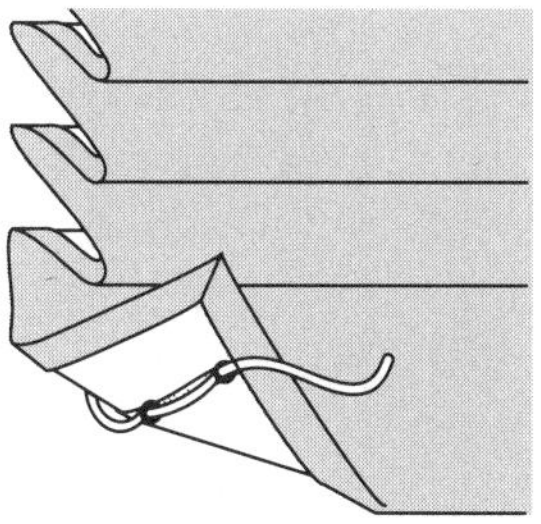

ROMAN/BALLOON SHADE
RING TAPE

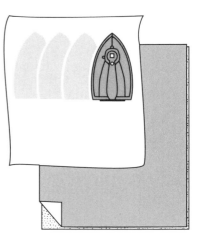

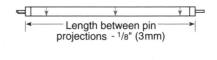

are special considerations when using this type of backing on sheets and dress-weight fabrics.

In addition to *decorator fabric* and *fusible shade backing material*, you'll need the following:

- *Brackets, roller mechanism and bottom slat* from an existing shade. Use either an old shade or a new, inexpensive one cut to the width of the window.

- *White glue* or *seam sealant* (optional).

- *Air-soluble marking pen*.

- *T-square* or *carpenter's L*.

- *Sharp shears*, plus a *rotary cutter* or *utility knife*.

Step 1: Measure and cut.

- Measure the window's length, then add 12″ (30.5cm).

- Measure the window's width, then add 4″–6″ (10cm–15cm).

- Cut the shade backing to these measurements.

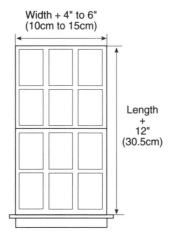

Width + 4" to 6"
(10cm to 15cm)

Length
+
12"
(30.5cm)

- Cut the fabric to these measurements. If the fabric has a motif that

should be centered, be sure to take this into account. Press to remove any wrinkles.

Step 2: Fuse.

Following the manufacturer's directions, fuse the shade backing to the fabric, wrong sides together.

Step 3: Trim.

- Remove the original shade from the roller. Before you do this, mark the roller to indicate the direction the shade falls.

- Install the empty roller at the window; check the fit. Remove the roller and measure the barrel, from end to end. Do not include the pin projec-

Length between pin projections - ¹/₈″ (3mm)

TIP

To achieve clean-cut edges, use a rotary cutter and mat or a sharp utility knife (and a protected surface). Use a metal ruler to ensure an even cut.

ROLLER SHADE: GENERAL DIRECTIONS

A professional-looking flat roller shade is one decorating project that would be practically impossible to create at home without the help of fusibles. Crisp, nonwoven backing materials have been especially designed with this end use in mind. Brand names include Shade Maker™, Fuse-a-Shade™ and Wonder-Shade®. The latter product has a special coated backing—white on the side that will be visible, gray on the fusible side—which gives it room-darkening abilities. Since ironing will harm the backing, the fabric is placed right side up on top of the gray side of Wonder-Shade. The fusing is done from the fabric side only. Read the manufacturer's directions carefully. There

tions. The finished width of your shade is this measurement, less ⅛″ (3mm).

● Using an air-soluble marking pen, mark the finished width of the shade. Use a T-square or carpenter's L for perfect right-angle corners. Cut the shade to the desired width. If the top and bottom of the shade require trimming, be careful to trim off no more than a total of 2″ (5cm).

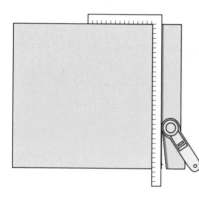

● If necessary, seal the cut edges of the shade with seam sealant or a thin bead of craft glue.

Step 4: Hem.

● Turn the lower edge of the shade up 1½″ (3.8cm). Stitch or fuse along the cut edge to form a 1¼″ (3.2cm) casing.

● Insert the wooden slat from the purchased shade.

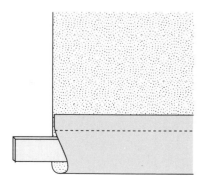

Step 5: Attach.

● Tape the upper edge of the shade to the roller, aligning the guideline on the roller with the upper edge of the shade.

● Use a staple gun and very short staples to permanently attach the shade. If you have a metal roller, use clear plastic tape.

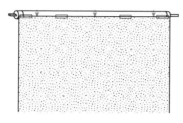

TIPS

If you are not planning on a top treatment, such as a cornice or a valance, to conceal the roller mechanism, the "reverse roll" installation has a nicer look.

● Be sure the brackets are installed so that the round pin will be on the left as you look out the window.

● Attach the shade, as illustrated, so it falls from the front, rather than from the back, of the roller.

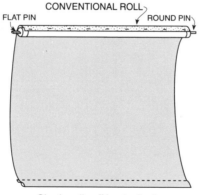 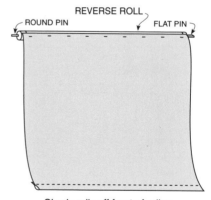

Shade rolls off back of roller. Shade rolls off front of roller. If necessary, reverse brackets at window.

Optional Edge Finish

If you prefer a shade with a scalloped or shaped lower edge, omit Step 4. Tape the shade to the roller, as in Step 5, but don't staple it yet. Then:

● Cut a strip of tissue paper at least 15″ (38cm) deep and equal to the

If your roller does not have a guideline, draw one on. Lay the roller on the table. Place a pencil flat against the table and slide the point along the length of the roller.

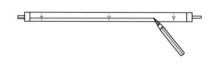

width of the shade. Fold the paper in half, thirds or quarters, depending on how many times you want the shape to repeat across the bottom of the shade. Draw the shape; then trim the tissue.

● Hang the shade in the window. Unfold the paper template. Hold it up against the lower edge of the shade to check the proportions. Then decide where you want to place the pleat for the wooden slat and mark the template. Generally, a pleasing proportion is from 8″–12″ (20.5cm–30.5cm) above the shaped lower edge.

● Remove the shade from the roller. Using the template, trace at the lower edge. Use scissors to cut the shape.

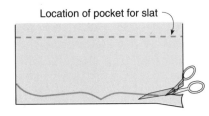

Location of pocket for slat

TIP

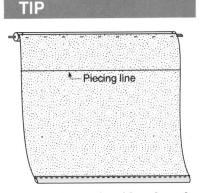

Piecing line

If your window is wider than the shade-backing material, cut and piece the backing horizontally. Position the piecing line so it is closer to the top of the shade, where, most of the time, it will be inconspicuous.

● Fold the shade wrong sides together along the pleat line; crease. Stitch or, to make this truly a no-sew project, staple across the shade, 1½″ (3.8cm) from the creased line. Insert the wood slat. Attach a shade pull at the center of the slat.

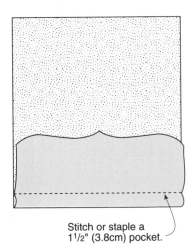

Stitch or staple a 1½″ (3.8cm) pocket.

● Seal the cut edge with seam sealant or a thin bead of craft glue. Glue or fuse a flexible trim along the lower edge and across the line of stitches or staples.

● Attach the shade to the roller as in Step 5.

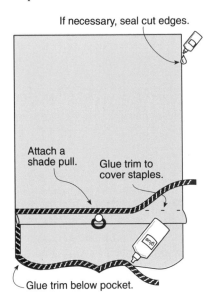

If necessary, seal cut edges.

Attach a shade pull.

Glue trim to cover staples.

Glue trim below pocket.

Cornice to Match

Use this easy cornice to repeat the shape and proportions of the lower decorative edge of the shade. To hang it, use a flat curtain rod with side projections.

● Add 3″–6″ (7.5cm–15cm) to the sides of the tissue template for the rod return. (Measure your curtain rod to determine the exact amount.) Add 3″ (7.5cm) to the upper edge for the rod pocket casing. This is your cornice pattern. (See the illustration on the following page.)

● Using the cornice pattern, cut and fuse fabric to shade backing.

● Fold the upper edge of the cornice down 3″ (7.5cm) to the wrong side. Fuse or stitch along the lower edge to form the casing.

● Fuse or glue trim to the lower edge of the cornice to match the shade.

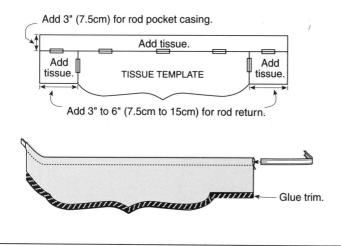

Add 3" (7.5cm) for rod pocket casing.

Add tissue.

Add tissue.

TISSUE TEMPLATE

Add tissue.

Add 3" to 6" (7.5cm to 15cm) for rod return.

Glue trim.

CUT-AND-DRAPE WINDOW TREATMENTS

The world of drapery hardware is full of a wonderful assortment of rods, specialty brackets and other helpers that can make beautiful window treatments a simple matter of push and pull, pinch and pin.

While they may seem like shortcuts, use them with pride. They are "secrets" of some of the finest professional drapery workrooms!

Most of the hardware items that follow can be used to create several different effects. We've collected some of our favorites, just to whet your appetite! All are available in fabric stores or in stores that specialize in drapery supplies.

U Swag and Festoon Holder

This shaped tulip, or U-bracket, holder is used to create rosettes, poufs and flounces. Used at the side

of the window, it can transform straight curtains into bishop curtains.

The bracket base is bolted or welded to an adjustable extension bar that is mounted to the wall. The movable arms of the U can be squeezed closer together to hold fabric in place.

To create a rosette pouf:

● Drape the fabric over the extension bar.

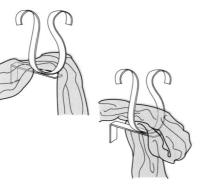

● Grasp the fabric that extends below the bar and gently pull about 18"–24" (45.5cm–61cm) of fabric up through the U opening to form a loop. Be careful—don't twist the fabric as you pull.

● Squeeze the bracket's arms together to hold the fabric.

● Spread the loop open. Pull the fabric up over the U arms to conceal the swag holder.

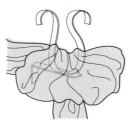

● Grasp the fabric in the middle, along the lower edge of the loop. Gently push it into the U, forming a rosette.

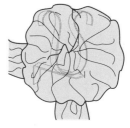

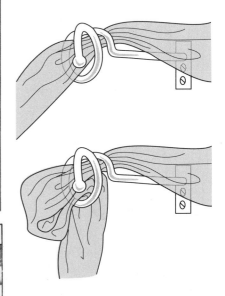

Spiral Swag Holder

These corkscrew-like brackets work similarly to the tulip, or U, bracket.

● Pull a length of fabric out through the spiral, then loop it under and pull it back through the first curve.

● Fan out the loop, then pull the fabric up over the bracket to conceal it.

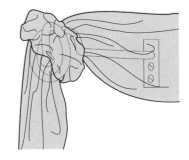

Prima™ Swag Holder

This swag holder and bracket is shaped like a donut with a removable button plug. It comes in plastic

Use simple hardware to create dramatic window treatments. Options include *(clockwise from top):* fabric artfully pulled through the spiral swag holder; a puffed rosette or a wrapped rosette fashioned from the same donut-like swag holder; and a bishop sleeve curtain created with an Infinity Ring.

or wood, so the plug can be painted, stained or covered with matching or contrasting fabric.

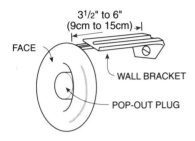

FACE
WALL BRACKET
POP-OUT PLUG
3½" to 6" (9cm to 15cm)

● For a wrapped effect, cover the donut section with a long, narrow strip of fabric, then insert the plug.

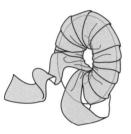

● For a button rosette, cut a 20" (51cm) circle of fabric. Center the fabric over the donut and insert the

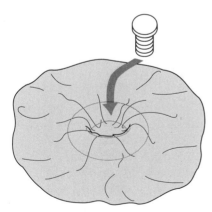

plug. Turn the swag holder over. Working around the circle, tuck the fabric into the channel. To secure, insert the accompanying plastic tubing into the channel, using a

screwdriver, if necessary. For a puffed rosette, cut a 24" (61cm) circle of fabric. Use fiberfill to puff out the rosette as you tuck the fabric into the channel.

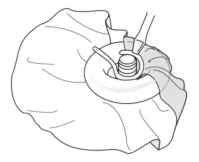

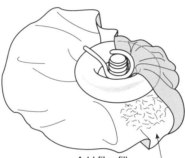

Add fiberfill for a puffy effect.

Infinity Ring

This versatile bracket is a continuous metal coil that spirals into two adjacent loops. It is available in a variety of sizes to accommodate different weights of fabric. To install it, just drop it over a cup hook that has been fastened to the wall or window molding.

For the optimum effect, plan on an extra yard of fabric for each bow, flounce or bishop sleeve.

● To make a simple bow, pull the fabric through the rings as in the following illustration. Then turn the ring so the ends are facing you; fluff out the bow.

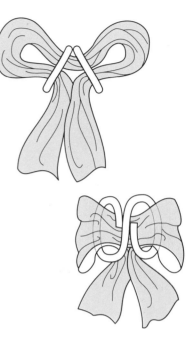

● To create a flounce, make the basic bow, then turn the ring sideways. Adjust the fabric loops so the upper one is shorter and the lower one is longer. Fluff out the fabric.

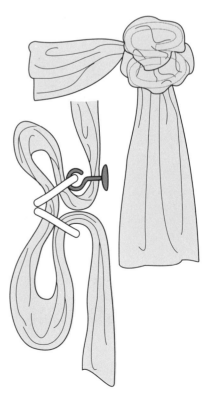

TIMESAVERS

• To make a bishop sleeve for your curtain, slip one spiral over the fabric and hook the other spiral to the cup hook. Pull the fabric up from the bottom through the unhooked spiral to form a generous loop. Fluff out the fabric.

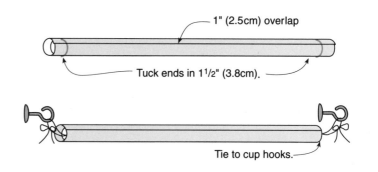

1" (2.5cm) overlap

Tuck ends in 1½" (3.8cm).

Tie to cup hooks.

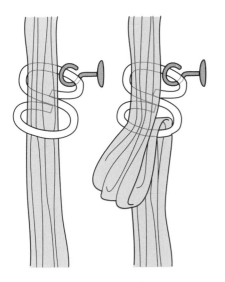

Covered Drapery Poles

Poles don't have to be wood or metal; they don't even have to be expensive. Fabric-covered poles are easy to make using PVC pipe, fiberboard tubes or existing wood rods.

• Cut a strip of fabric 3" (7.5cm) longer than the pole and wide enough to wrap around the pole and overlap 1" (2.5cm).

• Fold each end in 1½" (3.8cm). Using spray glue, and following the manufacturer's directions, adhere the fabric to the pole as in the following illustration.

• To install the wood rod, use the existing hardware. To install a tube rod, insert a thin round or flat curtain rod . . . or drop a string through

the tube and tie the ends of the string to rod brackets or cup hooks secured to the ceiling or wall.

Pinnacle® Rod and Globe™

Use this when a big, gutsy rod with an upholstered look is just what you need!

• Cut a strip of fabric 10½" (26.5cm) wide and slightly longer than the rod.

• Wrap the fabric around the rod. Snap it in place on the back with the accompanying flexible tubing.

• Cover the globes with a 25" (63.5cm) square or 21½" (54.5cm) circle of fabric, following the manufacturer's instructions.

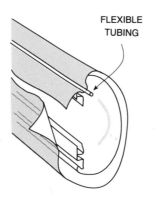

FLEXIBLE TUBING

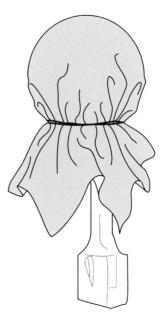

TIP

For a shirred pole cover, cut a strip of fabric wide enough to wrap around the pole, plus 1¾" (4.5cm) for easing and seam allowances. The strip should be two times the length of the pole. Press the short ends under ½" (1.3cm), then stitch the long ends, right sides together, with a ½" (1.3cm) seam. Turn the sleeve right side out, insert the pole and adjust the gathers.

T I M E S A V E R S

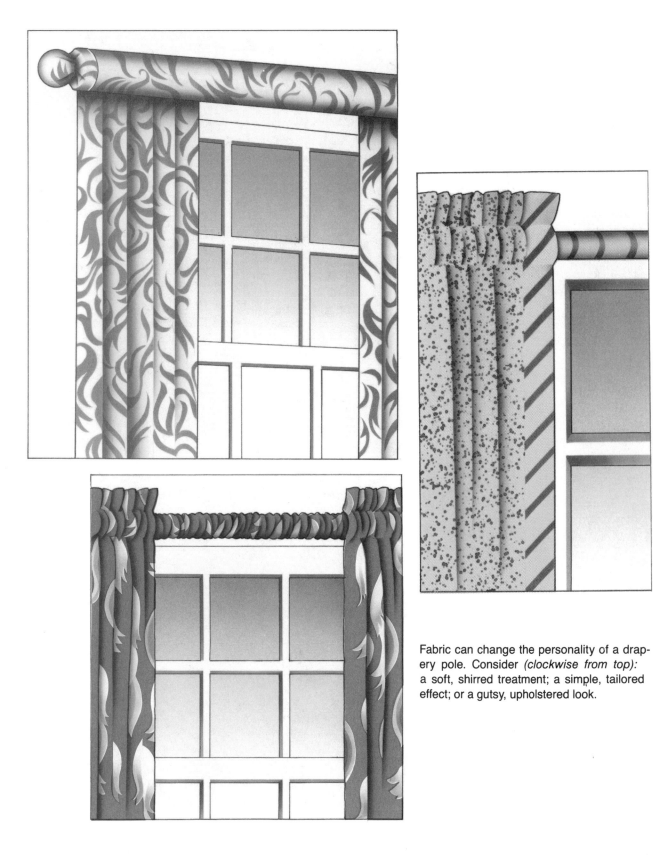

Fabric can change the personality of a drapery pole. Consider *(clockwise from top):* a soft, shirred treatment; a simple, tailored effect; or a gutsy, upholstered look.

DRAPING YOUR NO-SEW DRAPERIES

It's one thing to know how to make those fancy poufs and rosettes, but how do you get the rest of the fabric to hang attractively at the window? Here are a few tips:

● To determine the length of fabric:

Tack a tape measure across the top of the window to determine the length of the swag.

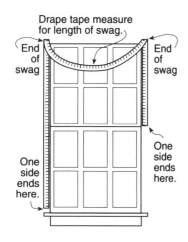

Decide how far down on each side of the window you want the treatment to extend. (Remember, they don't have to be the same!)

Add these three measurements together and then add 18"–24" (45.5cm–61cm) for *each* rosette, pouf or bow.

● Use the full width of the fabric. If possible, use the selvages for your side hems. If not, fuse, serge or machine-stitch the side hems.

● If the lower edge of the fabric will puddle on the floor, you can simply cut it off and seal with seam sealant. For shorter lengths, fuse, serge or machine-stitch the lower edge.

● Starting with the right side of the fabric on top, fold the fabric lengthwise into 4"–6" (10cm–15cm) deep accordion pleats. Use T-pins to temporarily secure the pleats and to mark the center and ends of the swag. When you do all this, work on the floor or on another flat surface that's large enough for the entire length of fabric.

● A curtain or drapery rod can be used to add support. With a decorative rod, the fabric can be draped so the swag dips below the center of the rod. If the rod is more utilitarian, lay the upper edge of the swag across the rod to conceal it.

● To "open out" the swag portion, gently pull the pleats apart.

● If necessary, use well-concealed, nonrusting straight pins to hold the fabric in place.

Understand that using many of these rings and swag holders is not an exact science. Therefore, it is sometimes difficult to achieve exact lengths.

● For floor-length treatments, solve the problem by planning to have the fabric puddle on the floor.

● For shorter lengths, temporarily tack the lower edge of the fabric to the window frame at the point where you want the treatment to end. Use pushpins or masking tape. Then pull up the fabric so the excess is evenly distributed in the rosettes, poufs, etc., and in the swag at the top of the window.

● Another way to solve the problem is to drape the fabric at the window, then use a separate piece of fabric for the rosette, pouf or other draped detail.

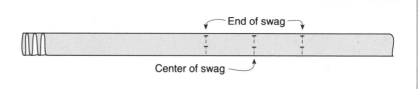

THE CORNICE

For years, cornice boards have graced windows, adding a formal, finished look to drapery treatments. They also conceal unsightly hard-ware, hide not-so-perfectly-formed pleats, provide a mounting place for indirect lighting and help deflect drafts from the outside. Aesthetically, they can unify a series of windows or magically change the proportions of a single window. But these heavy pine or plywood struc-tures have also been difficult to construct, too heavy for most do-it-yourselfers to handle and expensive to install professionally. But one clever interior designer has changed all that!

Cornice board kits, such as Window Crowns by Beverly®, contain

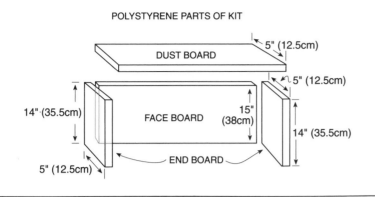

POLYSTYRENE PARTS OF KIT

DUST BOARD

5" (12.5cm)

5" (12.5cm)

14" (35.5cm)

FACE BOARD

15" (38cm)

14" (35.5cm)

5" (12.5cm)

END BOARD

face board and 1″ (2.5cm) less than the total width of the face board plus the two end boards.

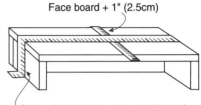

Face board + 1" (2.5cm)

Side + face board + side - 1" (2.5cm)

panels of extremely dense, but lightweight, polystyrene, plus nontoxic adhesive for gluing the "boards," special U-shaped pins to anchor your chosen fabric and clear acrylic brackets for mounting and hanging the four-sided cornice box. You provide the batting and the decorator fabric. Complete instructions are included with the kits, but here are some of the highlights:

● It's easy to customize the polystyrene panels to the desired dimensions using a craft knife and framing square. Simply trim to size, then glue the sections together. Let them cure overnight before applying batting and fabric. One kit makes a cornice board 44″ (112cm) wide by 15″ (38cm) high by 6″ (15cm) deep.

Join sections for double window size.

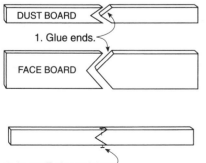

DUST BOARD

1. Glue ends.

FACE BOARD

2. Insert T-pins at joints.

If this isn't large enough, you can glue two kits together.

TO COVER THE CORNICE.

● Cut a rectangle of batting 1″ (2.5cm) more than the height of the

● Cut a rectangle of fabric 9″ (23cm) longer and wider than the batting. Piece, if necessary. Finish the raw edges on your serger *or* seal them with a thin application of seam sealant or white craft glue *or* press

NEWS ON GLUES

CATEGORY/BRAND	WHAT IT IS/DOES	USES/TIPS/HINTS
Liquid Fabric Glue Unique Stitch®, LIQUID STITCH™	Bonding agent for fabric to fabric; dries transparent.	Eliminates stitching; cannot be dry-cleaned; withstands machine washing and drying; do not use for hook-and-loop tape application or zippers.
Spray Glues/ **Adhesives** Scotch™ Spra-Ment™	Art and display adhesive; translucent; bonds fabric, cork, Styrofoam, upholstery foam.	Extremely flammable, so use in well-ventilated area, very quick bond; smooth results bonding fabric to plastic, cardboard, etc.
Super 77 Spray Adhesive	Bonds most lightweight materials, including metal, foil, fabrics, plastic films, felt, cork.	Adhesive lies on surface rather than soaking in; two spray tips provided for wide and small coverage.
White Craft Glues Sobo® ELMER'S® GLUE-ALL	Consistency of heavy cream in needle-nose plastic bottle; assorted-size containers.	Many uses; inexpensive seam sealant if project is not washed; dilute with water when covering pleated lampshade.
Aleene's Famous Original Tacky Glue™	Thick glue in needle-nose plastic bottle; dries clear.	Use with Styrofoam; wood, silk, paper, cloth, etc.; thin with water, thicken in freezer.
Glue Gun **Cartridge Sticks**	Glue in cylinder stick form; use with glue guns; available in various sizes.	Quick-setting; pinpoint accuracy possible; hot and low temperature varieties available.
Foam Fabric **Adhesive** Sprayway No. 55	Quick tack; nondimpling; bonds urethane- and latex-type foams to themselves or to metal, rigid plastic, fabric or wood.	Use in well-ventilated area; see cautions on label.
Vinyl Glue Instant Vinyl®	Transparent but not invisible; flexible; repairs cuts and tears in vinyl, leather, nylon foul-weather gear.	Extremely flammable; squeeze on to aluminum foil, then use toothpick to apply.

them under ¹/₂″ (1.3cm) and fuse or machine-stitch in place.

● Pin the batting flush with the top edge of the cornice and ¹/₂″ (1.3cm) in from the back edges of the side boards. The extra batting will roll to the inside at the bottom to soften that edge.

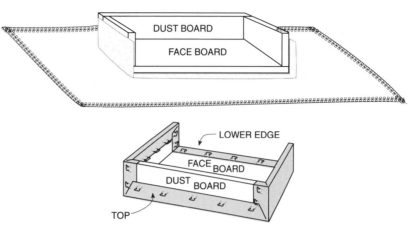

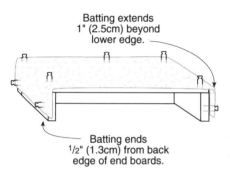

Batting extends 1″ (2.5cm) beyond lower edge.

Batting ends ¹/₂″ (1.3cm) from back edge of end boards.

● Place the cornice facedown on the wrong side of the fabric so that there is an equal margin of fabric on each side and 3″–4″ (7.5cm–10cm) margin at the dust board edge. As you wrap and pin the fabric to the cornice, always place the pins at a 45° angle, opposite to the direction you are pulling the fabric.

Starting at the end boards, wrap the fabric to the inside and pin at the center.

Working on the top, pull the fabric up and pin at the center of the dust board.

Working at the lower edge, wrap the fabric to the inside and pin at the center.

Turn the cornice over and check the alignment and tautness of the fabric. Readjust, if necessary. Then turn the cornice facedown and continue pulling and pinning the fabric, placing the pins approximately 4″ (10cm) apart. Handle the corners on the dust board as shown, just as you would if you were wrapping a package.

● Attach the brackets to the wall and install the cornice according to the manufacturer's instructions.

DESIGN OPTIONS. Feel free to adorn your cornice by gluing on additional trims, braids, appliqués or ribbons. Since you can pin into the boards, it's also easy to add cascades and swags to the cornice. Directions are included with the kit.

❁

NEWS ON GLUES

The chart on the opposite page lists a few glues that we think deserve a place in your no-sew decorator's toolbox. After all, sometimes only a glue will do!

For more timesaving projects, see "Wrap-and-Tie Furniture Covers," Chapter 9, SITTING PRETTY.

❁ ❁ ❁

Glossary

FURNITURE TEMPLATES

In Chapter 2, DECORATING THEORY, we discussed the importance of making a plan. As part of that process, we recommended creating a maquette by plotting out the room on 1/4″ (6mm) graph paper.

The maquette can do more than help you come to terms with the architectural details of the room. Use it to help you examine everything about the room from a new perspective.

Take the time to analyze your current furniture arrangement. Do it now—before you finalize your plans for new wall coverings, window treatments, slipcovers, etc.

On the next few pages, you will find templates, drawn to 1/4″ (6mm) scale, of many common pieces of furniture. We suggest you reproduce these pages on a copy machine, cut out the appropriate shapes and experiment on your maquette with various arrangements. A bit of glue stick or double-faced tape will secure the shapes to the graph paper.

If some of your furniture does not match the sizes and shapes supplied here, you can easily draw your own. Use 1/4″ (6mm) graph paper and remember that 12″ (30.5cm) on the furniture equals 1/4″ (6mm) on paper.

Note that this method will not be as accurate as a floor plan executed by a professional interior designer. It is merely a guide. When you have an arrangement that you think will work, then it's time to exert the (wo)man power necessary to reposition the actual furniture.

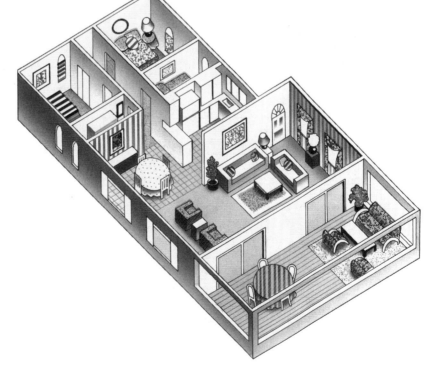

DINING TABLES

42" (107cm)
18" x 18"
(45.5cm x 45.5cm)

48" (122cm)
18" x 18"
(45.5cm x 45.5cm)

54" (138cm)
18" x 18"
(45.5cm x 45.5cm)

42" x 60"
(107cm
x
153cm)
18" x 18"
(45.5cm x 45.5cm)

36" x 60"
(91.5cm
x
153cm)--
extends to
86" (219cm)
18" x 18"
(45.5cm x 45.5cm)

42" x 64"
(107cm
x
163cm)
18" x 18"
(45.5cm x 45.5cm)

54" x 74"
(138cm
x
188cm)
18" x 18"
(45.5cm x 45.5cm)

STORAGE UNITS
(Dressers, chests, entertainment centers, armoires, etc.)

| 17" x 25" (43cm x 63.5cm) | 17" x 30" (43cm x 76cm) | 17" x 36" (43cm x 91.5cm) | 17" x 38" (43cm x 96.5cm) | 17" x 42" (43cm x 107cm) | 17" x 48" (43cm x 122cm) | 17" x 52" (43cm x 132cm) |

17" x 60" (43cm x 153cm)
17" x 66" (43cm x 168cm)
17" x 72" (43cm x 183cm)

| 19" x 30" (48.5cm x 76cm) | 19" x 33" (48.5cm x 84cm) | 19" x 36" (48.5cm x 91.5cm) | 19" x 42" (48.5cm x 107cm) | 19" x 45" (48.5cm x 115cm) | 19" x 48" (48.5cm x 122cm) |

19" x 52" (48.5cm x 132cm)
19" x 60" (48.5cm x 153cm)
19" x 66" (48.5cm x 168cm)
19" x 72" (48.5cm x 183cm)

| 21" x 30" (53.5cm x 76cm) | 21" x 36" (53.5cm x 91.5cm) | 21" x 40" (53.5cm x 102cm) | 21" x 44" (53.5cm x 112cm) | 21" x 48" (53.5cm x 122cm) |

21" x 60" (53.5cm x 153cm)
21" x 64" (53.5cm x 163cm)
21" x 68" (53.5cm x 173cm)

21" x 78" (53.5cm x 199cm)
21" x 84" (53.5cm x 214cm)

Corner Cabinets
34" (86.5cm)
34" (86.5cm)
34" (86.5cm)
34" (86.5cm)

BEDDING

King Size
78" x 80"
(199cm x 204cm)

Queen Size
60" x 80"
(153cm x 204cm)

Double
54" x 75"
(138cm x 191cm)

Twin
or
Studio
39" x 75"
(99cm x 191cm)

Bunk Bed
36" x 76"
(91.5cm x 193cm)

Crib
30" x 54"
(76cm x 138cm)

SEATING

Wing Chair

33" x 34"
(84cm x 86.5cm)

Lounge Chairs

32" x 32"
(81.5cm x 81.5cm)

30" x 30"
(76cm x 76cm)

28" x 32"
(71cm x 81.5cm)

Barrel Chairs

30" x 30"
(76cm x 76cm)

33" x 31"
(84cm x 78.5cm)

Sectional Sofa

Side Section
36" x 50"
(91.5cm x 127cm)

Amchairs

29" x 27"
(73.5cm x 68.5cm)

27" x 27"
(68.5cm x 68.5cm)

Loveseats

32" x 50", 55 or 60"
(81.5cm x 127cm, 140cm or 153cm)

Sofas

34" x 72", 78", 84", 90", 96" or 102"
(86.5cm x 183cm, 199cm, 214cm, 229cm, 244cm or 259cm)

Side Chairs

18" x 18"
(45.5cm x 45.5cm)

23" x 19"
(58.5cm x 48.5cm)

Side Section
36" x 50"
(91.5cm x 127cm)

Center Section
36" x 70"
(91.5cm x 178cm)

TABLE LAMPS and FLOOR LAMPS

TABLES

Cocktail Table

60" x 18"
(153cm x 45.5cm)

Square Tables
(Night table, end table, occasional table, etc.)

18"
(45.5cm)

20"
(51cm)

24"
(61cm)

28"
(71cm)

30"
(76cm)

36"
(91.5cm)

Coffee Table

44" x 22"
(112cm x 56cm)

Round Tables

12"
(30.5cm)

18"
(45.5cm)

24"
(61cm)

32"
(81.5cm)

36"
(91.5cm)

❁

COLOR SECTION

Photography Credits

Luxurious Living Rooms

Fabric: Swavelle/Mill Creek Fabrics

Elegant Entertaining

Fabric: Cyrus Clark
Trims: Conso
Blinds: Hunter Douglas

Beautiful Bedrooms

Fabric: Lanscot-Arlen Fabrics, Inc.

Kids'/Teens' Bedrooms

Fabric: Spectrix

Lullaby Land

Fabric: Fabric Country

Windows: A Different View

Fabric (curtains): Cyrus Clark
Fabric (Roman shade): Gear
Trim (Roman shade): C. M. Offray
  & Son

Pillow Pizzazz

Fabrics: J Yang
         Lanscot-Arlen Fabrics, Inc.
         Kaleidoscope Fabrics
Trim: Hollywood Trims

At the Table

Fabric: Cyrus Clark
Trim: C. M. Offray & Son

Project Information

The color section of this book was designed to inspire you and get your creative juices flowing. These rooms are full of ideas for using fabric, all of which are based on the projects and techniques in this book.

The following information will help you duplicate anything that catches your decorating fancy. For easy cross-reference, the italicized projects and techniques are listed in the INDEX at the back of this book.

Opening Page

The *wreath* on the front door is a variation of the wreath in Chapter 10, DECORATIVE ACCESSORIES, page 197, and the "Tip" on page 199. Here are our modifications:

- The *fast flowers* are created on a conventional sewing machine. For the large flowers, cut 5″ × 45″ (12.5cm × 115cm) fabric rectangles. For the smaller flowers, cut 3″ × 40″ (7.5cm × 102cm) rectangles.

- For the small fast flower *leaves*, cut 4¹/₂″ (11.5cm) squares of fabric. For the fringe flower *leaves*, cut 4″ (10cm) squares.

- The bow was eliminated.

Luxurious Living Rooms

PHOTOGRAPH:

- *Traditional slipcovers* adorn all of the upholstered furniture. The border at the lower edge of the sofa is topstitched in place.

- The border on the *lampshade cover* and the flowers on the *tablecloth* are fused in place.

- The window treatments are a successful pairing of the *one-piece swag and jabot* and the *basic curtains*. The borders are all topstitched in place.

ILLUSTRATION (*lower left*):

- Both chairs are covered with *traditional slipcovers*.

- The green fabric borders on the cream chair and the throw pillow are applied using the *clean-finish border* technique.

- A *Roman shade* is at the window.

ILLUSTRATION (*upper right*):

- A *wrap-and-tie furniture cover*, edged in a decorative flat braid, gives the sofa a new look.

- *Shirred piping*, done over jumbo cording, embellishes the lower edge of the *tablecloth* and the inner edge of the *flat drapes with ring and pole set*.

- The fabric motif on the lampshade is fused in place with Heat 'n Bond.

- The *bow picture hanger* is on the wall.

- The *basic knife-edge pillow* is trimmed with two colors of intertwined jumbo *rickrack*.

Elegant Entertaining

PHOTOGRAPH:

- The *stapled wall* technique is used to cover the walls with fabric. Covered *piping* conceals the staples at the corners. The fabric border along the edge of the ceiling is fused directly onto the wall with Heat 'n Bond.

- For the traditional *swag and jabot* treatments, the swags are mounted in front of the jabots. The tassel fringe is sewn onto the swags. However, to avoid having stitches show on the lining side, this same trim is fused to the edges of the jabots.

- Borders created from the window treatment fabric embellish the square *tablecloth*.

- Motifs cut from the wall fabric are fused to the chair *cushions*.

GLOSSARY

- The *napkins* are trimmed with borders and appliqués cut from the window fabric.

- Before the *bow picture hanger* was assembled, the bow, knot and tail pieces were topstitched to a wider, deep green grosgrain ribbon. As a result, the hanger stands out against the print wall.

- Stripes from the window fabric are fused to the edges of the *lampshade cover*. Our fabric needed a little help to hold the pleats, so we machine-stitched just next to the inner fold of every pleat.

ILLUSTRATION *(lower left)*:

- The *round tablecloth* is finished with a deep *single ruffle*.

- The *basic valance* and *curtains* are finished with a delicate *edging*.

- The chairs have *drop-in seat covers*.

ILLUSTRATION *(upper right)*:

If you wish, everything in this room can be created at the ironing board, rather than at the sewing machine.

- Use fusible web for a no-sew finish at the edges of the *wrap-and-tie straight-back chair covers* and the *round tablecloth*.

- Construct the *cornice* from a cornice board kit.

- Use *fusibles* and *iron-on drapery tapes* to create no-sew drapes to match the cornice.

- The *pasted wall* technique can be used to cover the walls with fabric.

Beautiful Bedrooms

PHOTOGRAPH:

- The *cut-and-drape window treatment* was planned so that the two inside tails end in the middle of the

window and the two outside tails end at the windowsill.

- The *dust ruffle with gathered corners*, the *flanged duvet cover* and the *flange pillows* are all finished with contrasting *bias binding*.

ILLUSTRATION *(lower left)*:

- Contrasting *piping* and contrasting *bias binding* accent the *pillow shams* and the *flounced bedspread*.

- The window treatment is a combination of *pouf valance* and *lined drapes*.

- The *plain bolster pillow* on the bed coordinates with the *round tablecloth*.

ILLUSTRATION *(lower right)*:

- For the bed, see the *basic duvet cover* and the *gathered dust ruffle*.

- The *basic knife-edge pillow* was the starting point for the pillow shams and throw pillows.

- The unlined *ruffled curtains* hang at the windows. To make each tieback, cut two rectangles equal to the desired width and length, plus ½" (1.3cm) all around. Make two ruffles, following the instructions for the *ruffled tieback*. With right sides together, pin one ruffle to each long edge of one rectangle. Pin the second rectangle on top of the first, right sides together. Stitch ½" (1.3cm) from the raw edge, leaving an opening for turning. Turn right side out; press. Slipstitch the opening closed.

- The *bow picture hanger* completes the room setting.

Kids'/Teens' Bedrooms

PHOTOGRAPH:

- The *tufted comforter*, with *machine quilting* and a fabric ruffle,

and the *gathered dust ruffle* cover the daybed.

- For the window treatment, see the *pouf valance with eyelet underlay*.

- The *pillow shams* are trimmed with the *clean-finish border* technique. All pillows are variations of the *basic knife-edge pillow*. For the heart pillow, follow the instructions for *custom shapes*.

- For the table, see the *round tablecloth* and the *swagged overskirt*.

ILLUSTRATION *(upper left)*:

- For the bedcovering, see the *studio couch with bolster pillows*. To make the band trim, cut a stripe from the fabric. Fuse or topstitch it in place along the lower edge.

- The *Roman shade* is trimmed with bands of ribbon and custom-made *tassels*.

- For the alphabet pillows, follow the instructions for *custom shapes*.

- For the table, see the *round tablecloth*.

ILLUSTRATION *(lower left)*:

- For the bed, see the *basic duvet cover*. Contrasting *piping* is used to trim the duvet cover, as well as the *basic knife-edge pillows* and the *plain bolster pillow*. For the *dust ruffle*, see the *dust ruffle with pleated corners*.

- *Lined drapes* are complemented by a *roller shade* made from the same fabric as the duvet cover.

Lullaby Land

PHOTOGRAPH:

- For the *crib quilt*, *dust ruffle*, *bumper guards* and *pillow*, see "Nursery Niceties" in Chapter 7, SLEEPING BEAUTY.

- For the window treatment, see the *pouf valance with eyelet underlay* and the *basic unlined curtains*.

ILLUSTRATION:

- For the *crib quilt, dust ruffle* and *bumper guards*, see "Nursery Niceties" in Chapter 7, SLEEPING BEAUTY.
- For the heart pillow, follow the instructions for *custom shapes*.
- For the window treatment, see the *basic unlined curtains* and the *easy twist valance*.

Windows: A Different View

PHOTOGRAPH (*left*):

See the *Roman shade*. This version is an inside mount. Ribbon trim is stitched or fused at the edges of the shade.

PHOTOGRAPH (*right*):

- For the undercurtains, see the *basic unlined curtains*. Finish the lower edge with the *clean-finish border*.
- For the drapes, make *lined drapes* using *shirring tape*.

ILLUSTRATION (*upper left*):

See the *Roman shade*. This version is an outside mount. Add a border on the wall cut from matching fabric or using a coordinating wallpaper border.

ILLUSTRATION (*lower left*):

See the *cut-and-drape window treatments*.

ILLUSTRATION (*far right*):

See the *basic valance* and the *basic unlined curtains*.

Pillow Pizzazz

PHOTOGRAPH (*left*):

See the *basic knife-edge pillow*. For the bolster in the foreground, see the *firecracker bolster*.

PHOTOGRAPH (*right*):

See the *basic knife-edge pillow*, the *basic flange pillow*, the *plain bolster*, the *Turkish corner pillow* and the *shirred pillow*. For the last, use a solid fabric, rather than a sheer, for the overlay. For the *plain bolster*, use caterpillar fringe instead of piping. For the shell, follow the instructions for *custom shapes*.

ILLUSTRATION:

See the *shirred box pillow*, the *envelope pillow* and the *basic knife-edge pillow*. The *Turkish corner pillow* is trimmed with custom-made *tassels*. For the heart, follow the instructions for *custom shapes*. The cat is an *appliqué*.

At the Table

PHOTOGRAPH:

The edge of the *round tablecloth* is trimmed with purchased piping. The *overskirt* is trimmed with ribbon.

ILLUSTRATION (*upper left*):

- The oval *placemat* and matching *napkin* are trimmed with two colors of intertwined jumbo *rickrack*.
- The rectangular *placemat* and matching *napkin* are edged with the *clean-finish border*. The *knife pleats* were created using the Perfect Pleater™.

ILLUSTRATION (*lower right*):

- The *napkin* is finished with a *serger rolled hem*. Add a fabric *appliqué* for interest.
- The *table runner* is *machine-quilted*, finished with *bias binding* and trimmed with custom-made *tassels*.

Index